Introducing Puppetry

Margaret Arney

Copyright © 2017 Margaret Arney

All rights reserved. No part of this book may be used or reproduced by any means, graphic, electronic, or mechanical, including photocopying, recording, taping or by any information storage retrieval system without the written permission of the publisher except in the case of brief quotations embodied in critical articles and reviews.

This is a work of fiction. All of the characters, names, incidents, organizations and dialogue in this novel are either the products of the author's imagination or are used fictitiously.

Serenity Press Publishing books may be ordered through booksellers or by contacting:

Serenity Press Publishing
www.serenitypress.org
serenitypress@hotmail.com

Because of the dynamic nature of the Internet, any web addresses or links contained in this book may have changed since publication and may no longer be valid. The views expressed in this work are solely those of the author and do not necessarily reflect the views of the publisher and the publisher hereby disclaims any responsibility for them.

The intent of the author is only to offer information of a general nature. In the event you use any of the information in this book for yourself, which is your constitutional right, the author and the publisher assume no responsibility for your actions.

ISBN: 978-0-6481030-1-1 (sc)
ISBN: 978-0-6481030-2-8 (e)

Designed in Australia

Printed on sustainable paper

INTRODUCTION

This is the first of two puppetry manuals.

The second one is glove puppetry in the same theatre.

The program is suitable, and great fun, for all ages.

This manual provides a complete detailed program for a teacher or group leader to easily and successfully make puppets with their group and perform a very outstanding/memorable play for an audience.

Puppetry is an inexpensive and hands on way of learning how to act in theatre and, of course, life.

Puppetry is a great motivator and develops character, initiative, confidence and team work.

Some instructions have been extended to encourage adults to do puppetry because they benefit more and enjoy it far more than children.

I hope this manual, with its simple and illustrated text, will encourage you to have a go and experience the fun and excitement of doing puppetry.

The instruction pages of this manual may be copied and handed out to the puppeteers to follow individually.

There are similar modular systems in other countries, or the theatre can be built in wood.

If something is not clear enough, or you want help, I am happy to answer any puppetry questions ~ email marg@gmail.com

ACKNOWLEDGEMENTS

I wish to thank Cliff, my husband, for writing all the verses contained within the manual. They are always a delight.

I greatly appreciate the constant encouragement both in word and deed of my sister Robin, especially when there are so many things that need simple, clear illustrations and explanations.

Once again I wish to thank Colleen Rintoul for her very valuable input on theatre perspective, props and puppets, whilst painting it so wonderfully for a simple puppet theatre.

My thanks to Celine for her thoughtful presentation of the puppets. They are so bright and colourful and show these puppets with attitude.

I am very grateful for the wonderful friends who have always encouraged me, some over many years, and the ladies who come for a laughter-filled afternoon playing with puppets which need photographing.

Thank you again to Karen at "Making Magic Happen" for her skill in publishing this book, her patience and belief that I will get there eventually.

CONTENTS

ADVANTAGES OF PUPPETRY	1
Puppets used in this theatre	3
SECTION 1: THEATRE	4
1. Puppet Theatre design	6
2. Theatre layout	9
3. Purchase of aluminium or substitute	10
4. Tools required	12
5. Assembly instructions	13
6. Strengthening and stabilising the theatre	14
7. Scenery rack	15
8. Blockout covering	16
9. Mounting the curtain track	17
10. Front curtains	18
11. Scenery curtains	19

SECTION 2: PUPPETS

Basic plate puppet ~		23

Head

Human head ~	Hair instructions	24
	Face instructions	25
	Face templates	26
Cat head ~	Face instructions	29
	Face templates	31
Animal head ~	Face instructions and templates.	33
Bird head ~	Face instructions and templates	35
Puppet body ~	Body instructions	36
	Human body instructions	36
	Cat, bird, animal ~ instructions	37
	Hands, paws, hoofs ~ instructions	38
	~ templates	39
	Bird wing	43
	Bird tail	44
	Animal tail	52
Puppet rack		54
Puppet scarves and collar, etc.		55
Puppet hat, caps, etc and templates		56
Scenery ~	Set materials and effects	61
	Some templates	63
	Illustrations	65

NURSERY RHYME SCRIPTS

Human ~ Jack and Jill.	69
Making the puppets and scenery with music to add.	71
Animal ~ Three little kittens and making the puppets	74
Making the rat and scenery with music to add.	77
The farmers wife and three blind mice	82

STORY SCRIPTS

Henny Penny ~ birds and an animal puppet	87
Making - Henny Penny	88
Cocky Locky	89
Ducky Lucky	91
Goosey Poosey	91
Turkey Lurkey	92
Foxy Loxy	94
Making the scenery, music to add and photos of final result.	95

The Little Red Hen ~ bird and animal puppets	101
Making - Little Red Hen	103
Chickens	104
Duck	104
Cat	104
Dog	105
Pig	106
Making the scenery, music to add and photos showing final result.	109
Cows in the Clover ~ human, bird and animal puppets	113
Making - Farmer	116
Boy	116
Cow	117
Horse	118
Cat	120
Dog	120
Rooster	121
Bee	125
Making the scenery, music to add and photos of final result.	126
Acting, choreography, performance.	130
My Grandfather's Clock music	132

Appendix Cost of theatre (In Australia)

There are three stages of difficulty outlined in this manual ~

The Nursery Rhymes are designed for the first adult or very young children's puppets.

Henny Penny and The Little Red Hen for the next year or puppetry activity.

The Cows in the Clover for the third puppetry activity.

A suggestion ~

Make the first puppetry activity with the simple instructions given in this manual.

The next puppetry activity can be embellished with more detail.

The third activity lends itself to characterisation.

There are other similar rhymes and stories which would fit into each of these stages.

If there are enough puppeteers it is very advantageous to have 2 groups do the same play but in totally different ways. Then they can watch a different performance of the same story and have an audience experience. This always proves to be very worthwhile.

If some do not want to act their puppets, find them other parts to do, eg. scenery changing, music, announcements, etc. Usually, once they have seen the first performance, they want to be fully involved.

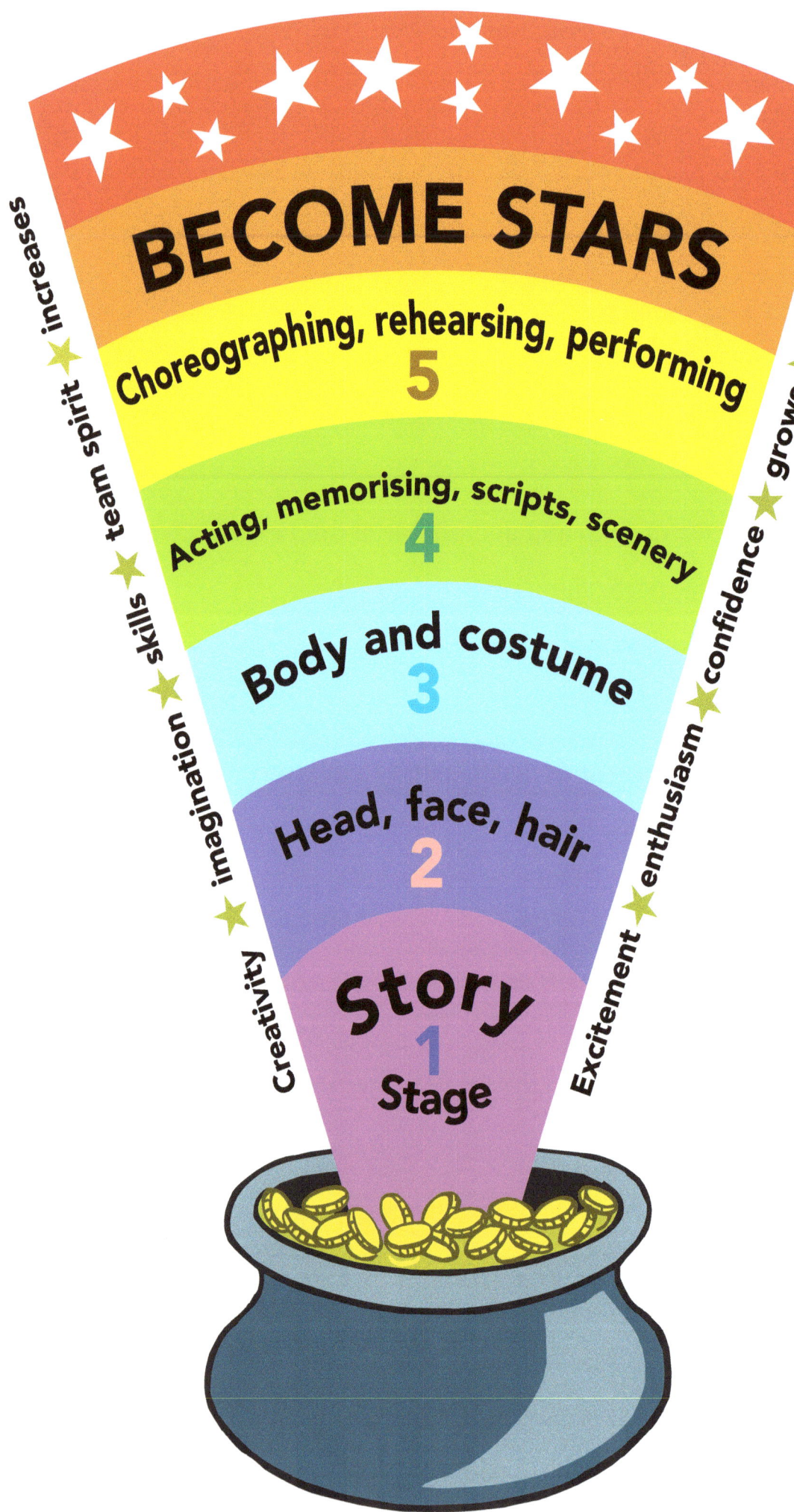

Advantages of introducing puppetry

There are many famous drama, ballet, opera, film, stage schools in the world that teach acting, dancing, singing, set design, lighting, sound, etc.

People attend these famous schools to learn how to develop their gifts and achieve the best results so they can have wonderful opportunites in film and stage careers.

As with any new skill, puppetry needs to be taught step by step so that the children/adults learn how to build a character and make it come alive in a performance.

A well known story provides the basics or skeleton that you can flesh out, dress up and bring alive.

The simplest story can be made highly entertaining. Younger children think older children are awesome and clever when they watch their performance.

This manual shows how to make
* simple basic PUPPET CHARACTERS
* SETS with PERSPECTIVE
* and PROVIDES STORIES to use in their puppetry.

Start simple, have fun, enjoy success and then build on that.

You will learn how to speak clearly, act confidently, use your imagination and work together to achieve something that is very worthwhile and memorable.

It is beneficial to have two groups doing the same play,
You can see others perform what you are trying to perform.
It demonstrates how differently a play can be developed with characters, scenery and story line variations.

Some puppets that suit this theatre.

Cardboard plate puppets
These suit the larger top proscenium.

Shadow puppets   Glove puppets

These suit either size proscenium thus allowing for different sizes of puppets.

Marionette puppets if the extra theatre parts included in the marionette manual are added.

Theatre

Three mice and the Grandfather clock

Three mice began to sing
"The pendulum is a swing
Hey, hey just watch it rock.
Hickory dickory dock."

And so the three climb on
Singing their mousy song
Did you ever see such a thing
As three mice on a pendulum swing.

To get the ticks in step with their song,
They hurry the pendulum along,
With the pendulum in step with their tune,
Midnight will come too soon.

And so the three pass the time,
Still swinging when the clock starts to chime,
Frightened of being found,
They somersault back to the ground.
BUT
Hickory dickory dock
One mouse ran up the clock
The clock struck one
The mouse ran down
Hickory dickory dock.

                                      by Clifford Arney

Theatre design
Material purchase
Theatre layout and tools required
Assembling and strengthening
Scenery rack
Blockout covering, front and scenery curtains

Puppet theatre design

1. **Simple** ~ easy to put together, use and store.
2. **Large** ~ to allow for more children and lots of action.
3. **Light weight** ~ easy to handle and can hurt no one if it falls over.
4. **Collapsible** ~ it can be stored or transported very easily.

The theatre turned up the other way has a lower proscenium for shorter children.

 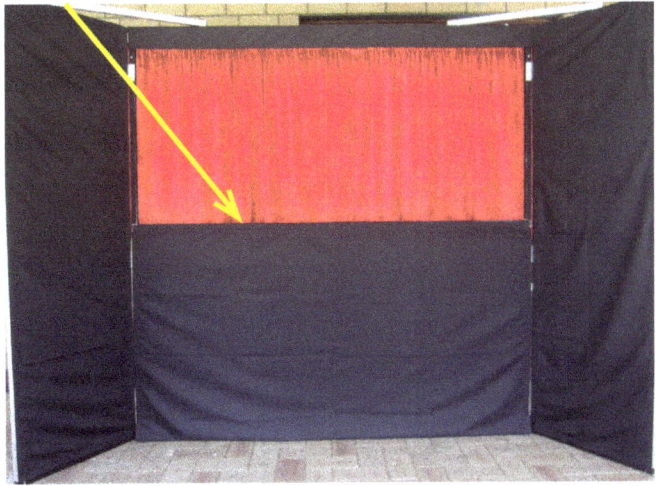

Two curtains that can be drawn apart almost completely off the proscenium.

Puppeteers need to see through the scenery.   Curtain rod mounted behind proscenium.

 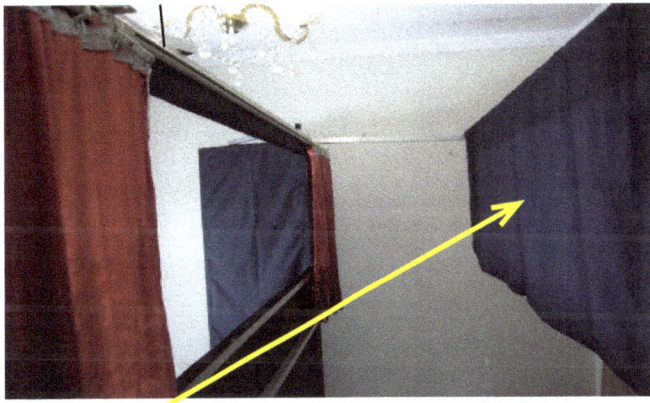

Reading light   Standard light   Block out curtain – to stop any light from behind.

With extra framework behind the larger proscenium at the bottom it is used for marionettes.

Stage lights and curtain mounted behind.   Scenery and leaning rail   Side wings

Follow the design exactly to finish up with the 4 different theatres.

Theatre extension

The theatre can be extended to give more acting space or to suit adults.

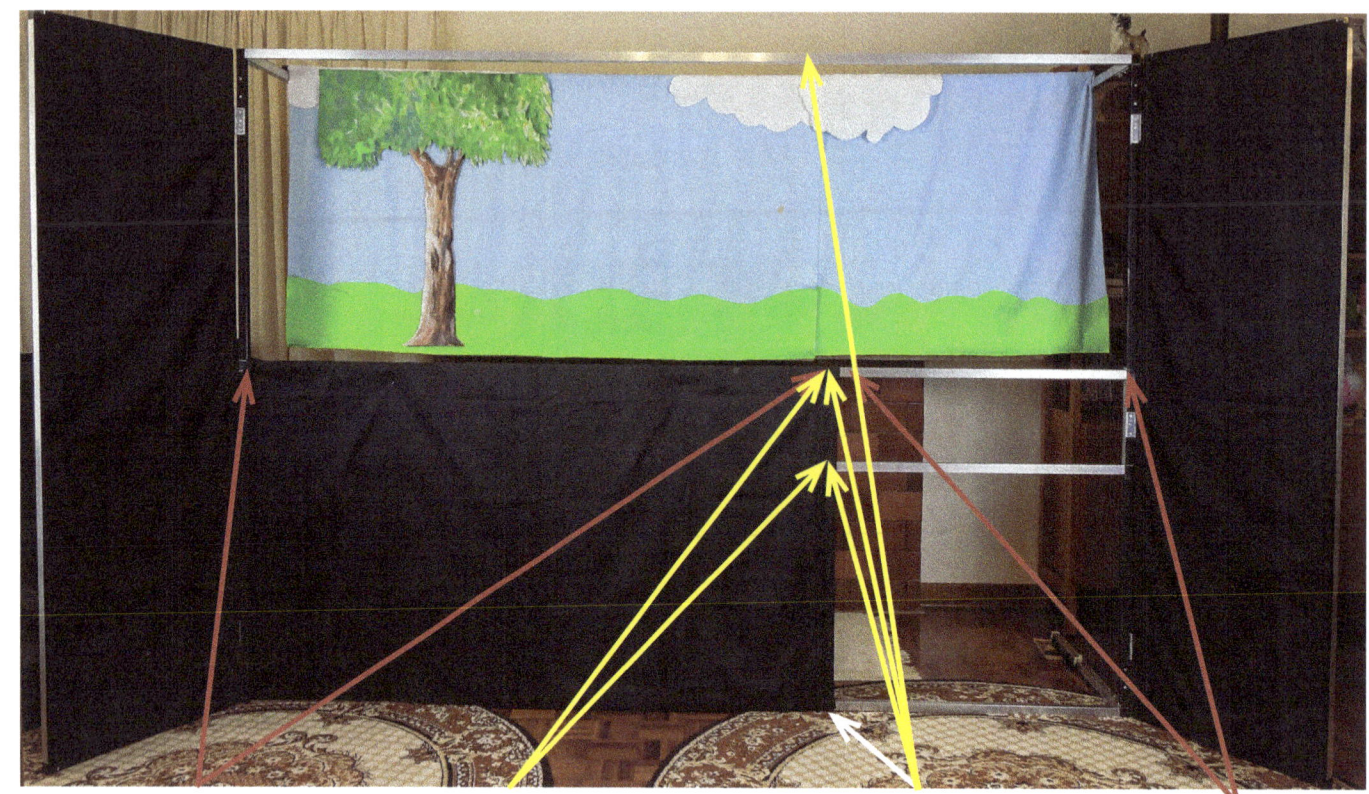

180cm original theatre   24cm (check your measurement between these.)   The 4 x 'T' connectors   90cm extension

One 6.5m length of Qubelok and 4 x 'T' connectors will extend the theatre.
The simplest way to extend the scenery and blockout is to join on 90cm more of each so either theatre can be used. The bottom leg of the 'T' can be cut off or left on 'e' and 'h' facing back, this is the strongest position for the joiner.

The theatre can be placed on a riser to enable adults to use it.

Pop riveted strap on the sides of the riser top rail form a channel for the theatre to sit in. When the theatre is put on top of the riser the back-ground supports must be moved down to the 3-way connectors on the riser.

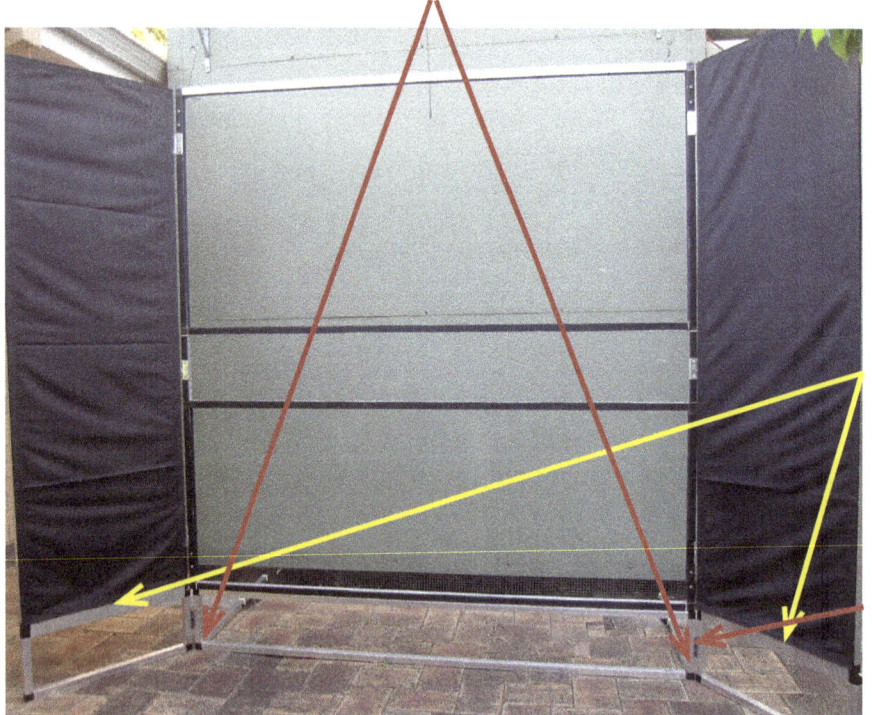

2 x 90cm pieces joined into the riser for larger theatre.

Channel

The height of the riser can be changed by altering the length of the uprights.

The side wing sitting inside the channel.

Bolts can be put through this or straps put around it to hold the theatre in place.

One hinge joins the side wing to the middle section of the riser.

Aluminium needed for extension ~ 4 x 90cm pieces and a 24cm piece (check your length) to go between 'f' and 'g' joining the two 'T's and strengthening the middle section. Need 4 x 'T's.

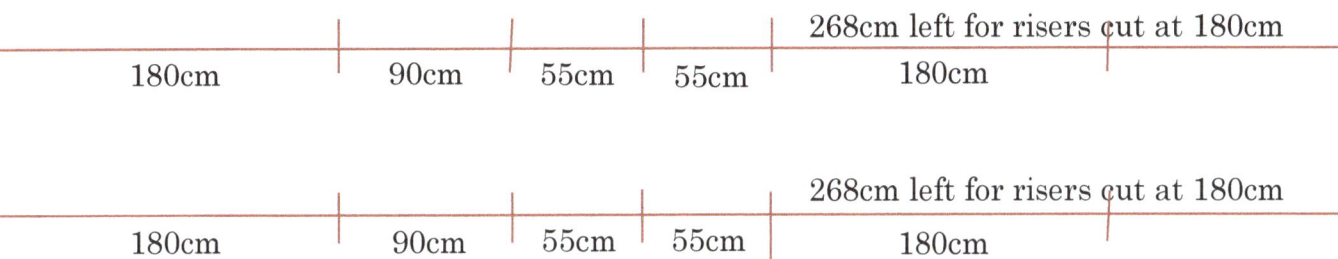

Aluminium needed for riser ~ 2 x 6.5m lengths of qubelok and some 50cm wide strapping.

The leftover pieces will be a bit less than shown because of the fraction lost in all the cutting. Cut them at 180cm for storage and use them for sets of different length risers.

Connectors needed for the riser are - 10 right angles, 2 x 'Ts" and 2 x 3-ways.

The versatility of this theatre is more than doubled when using the extension and the riser.

Theatre transportation

As mentioned on page 9, if the theatre is too big to transport, separate it as shown below.

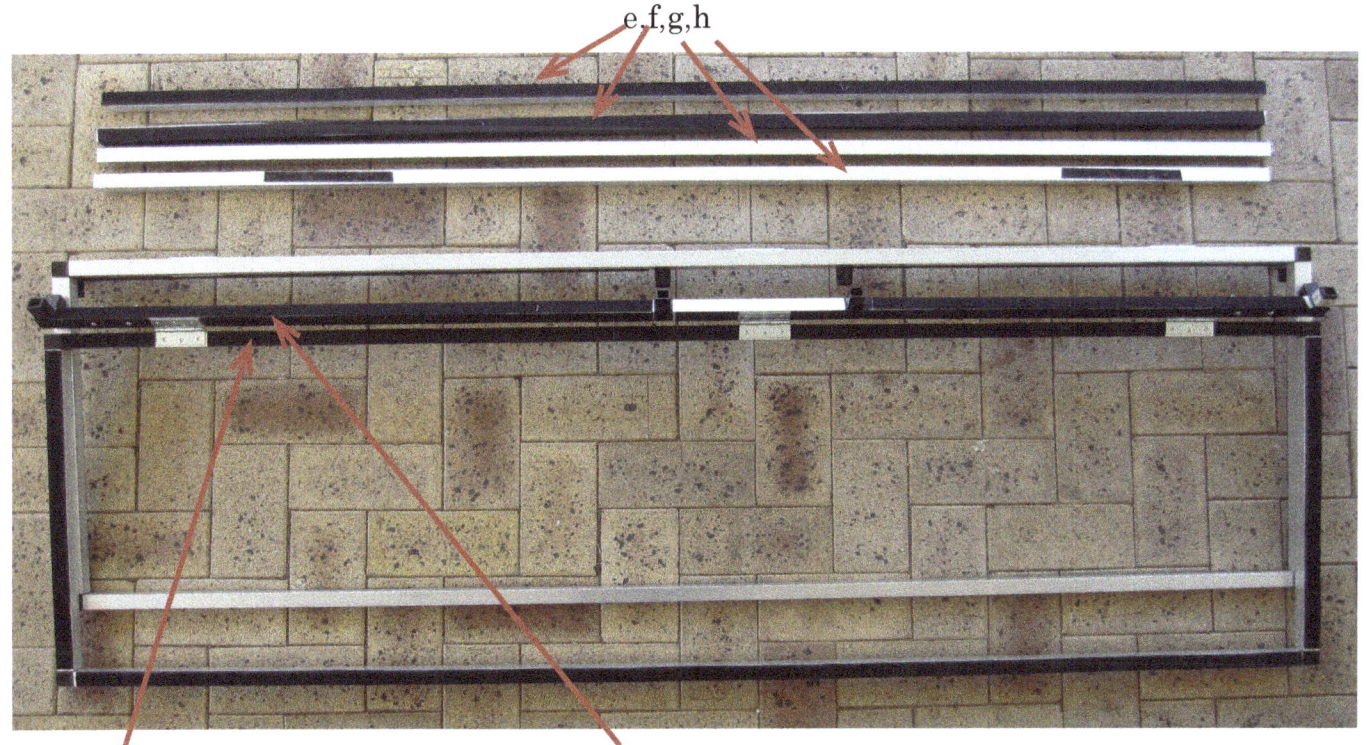

The side wings stay joined to their middle uprights.

REMEMBER to file the connector arms down a bit as shown on p 9 so they do not break when separating the joint.

WHEN REJOINED, screw in the corner angle brackets to keep the theatre tightly together.

Theatre layout

If the centre section (180cm x 180cm) is too big for transport, remove 'e, f, g, h' and it is reduced to the side sections as shown on the previous page.

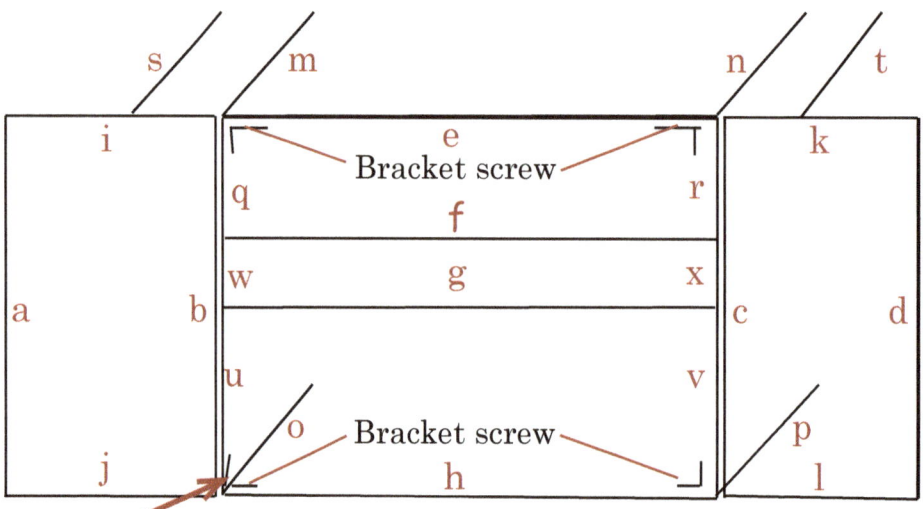

Pieces in alphabetical order

One small bracket in each of the four middle section 3-way corners will keep the theatre firmly together. Use small self tapping screws.

Remove the bracket screws in 'e' and 'h' if separating theatre for travel. Put screw back in when reassembled.

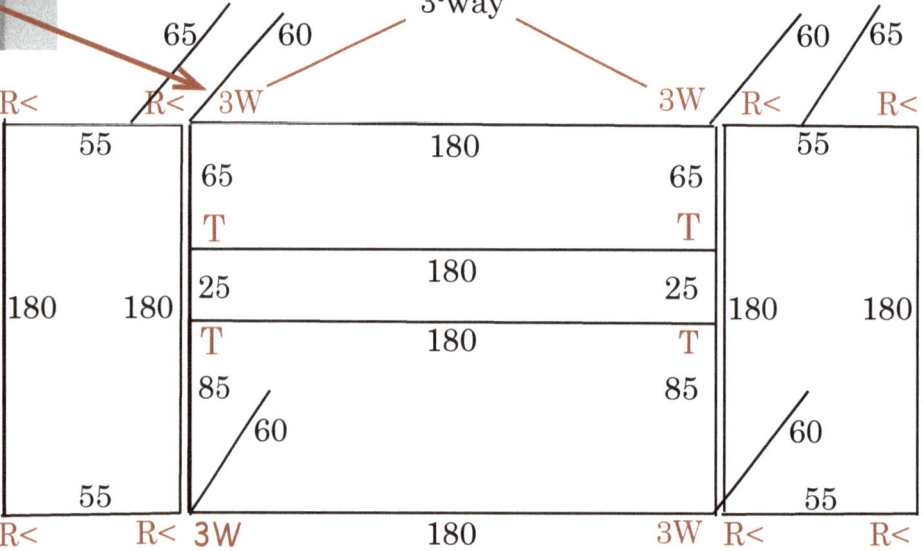

Lengths are in centimetres.
Connectors : Right angle = R< ; Tee = T ; 3-way = 3W
File the ridges off the back leg of the 3W connectors at the 4 corners so the supports come off easily for transportation or to turn theatre upside down. Leave 4 corner brackets on uprights as shown above.

* The top and bottom of the theatre is kept perfectly straight so it can be turned upside down, thus providing two different heights of proscenium. On p 14, step 23 is - put velcro on the top and bottom of the theatre, then the front stay can be used. (p = page in this manual)
The top front stays and back ground supports will keep the theatre upright and safe.
In the marionette manual there are extra parts to go in in place of the ground supports.

Aluminium puppet theatre
Ordering information

This theatre is designed in Qubelok - an aluminium modular framing system available in Australia at Capral. There are similar systems available in other countries, otherwise the alternative is to use wood.

This theatre design is stable, uses 180cm measurements to keep cutting simple and can be turned upside down to provide a different proscenium height.

The aluminium pieces and plastic connectors are called QUBELOK.

The plastic connectors needed are:-

8 x R< (right angles)	4 x 'T's	4 x 3W (way)	4 x end stoppers
300333	300335	300334	300340

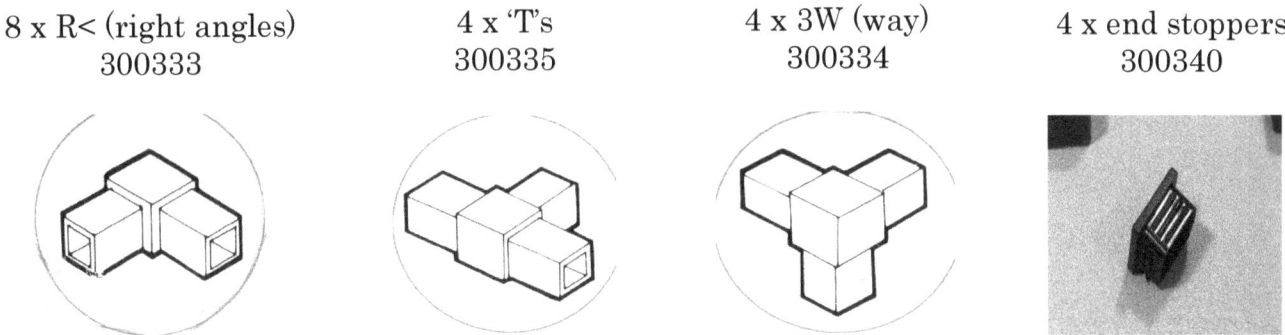

The aluminium and plastic joiners can be ordered from Capral in any Australian capital city. They will cut and package it for you if presented with this cutting layout. (For schools this service might even be free).

They will deliver Australia wide.

I have dealt with Welshpool Capral, Perth, WA. (08) 9356 7811 or email - capral.com.au

MAKE SURE YOU ASK FOR ALL THE OFF CUTS as you will need them. Capral do not cut anything shorter than 50cm.

CAPRAL cutting instructions

The 4 lengths are designed to be cut simultaneously for each of the 180cm, 180cm, 55cm, 60cm and 65cm measurements, thus providing 4 of each that are exactly the same length.

Then cut only 2 together for q and r = 2 x 85cm pieces.

a to d make the four side wing verticals.

e to h the four horizontals in the middle section.

There should be approximately 2 x 37cm and 2 x 118cm pieces left over, KEEP THEM. When making the theatre, cut 2 x 25cm lengths out of the 2 x 37cm pieces and keep ALL the remaining pieces in case you do the marionette theatre conversion.

2 x 6.5m lengths of 16mm piping = 6 x 190cm curtain rods for scenery drops + 2 off cuts.

If making the large theatre add in the Qubelok from p 8.

Also remember the Qubelok for the scenery rack on p15.

CAPRAL cutting layout for puppet theatre

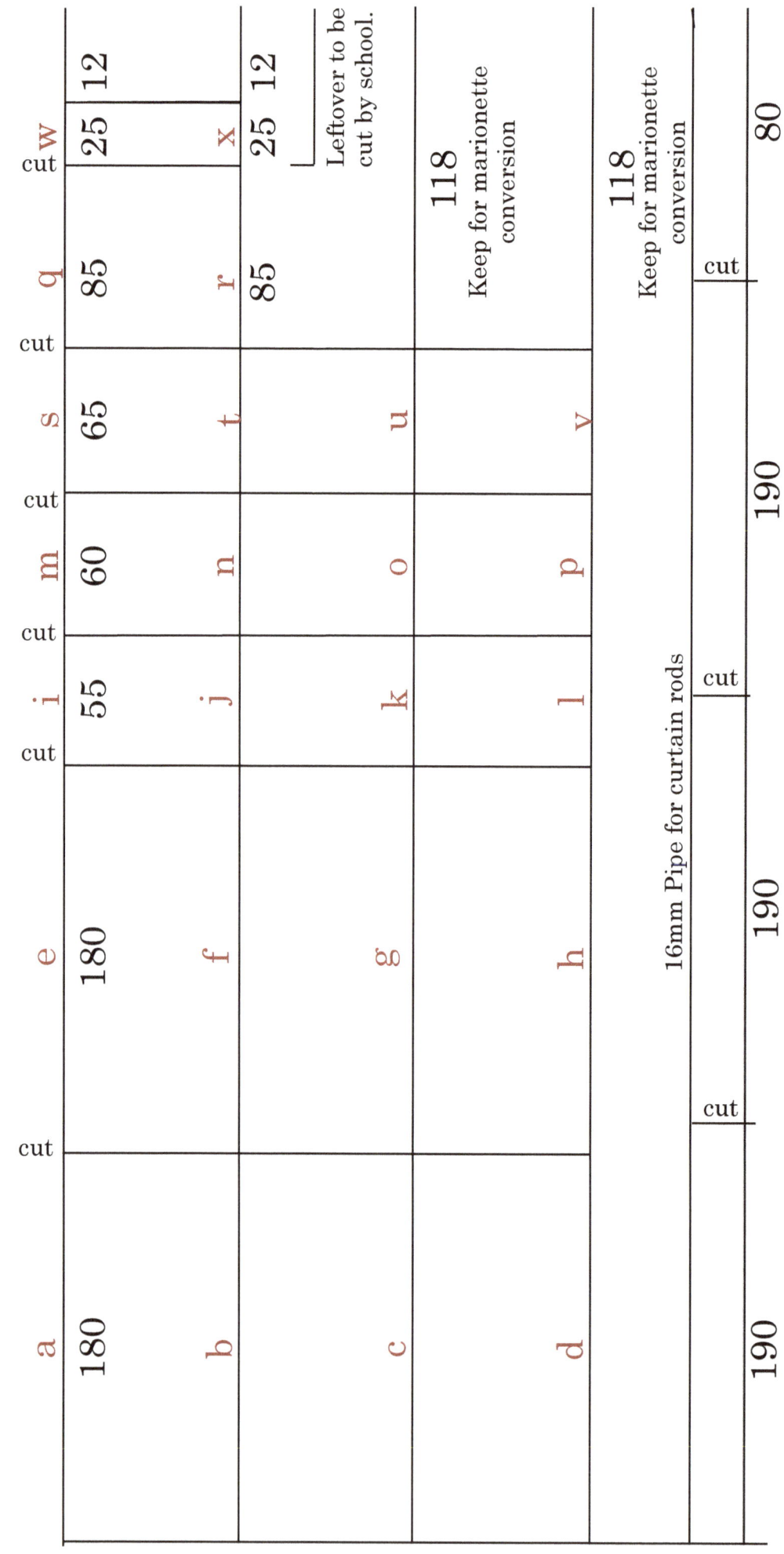

All parts are in alphabetical order to match the theatre layout.
Measurements are in centimetres. Keep all off-cuts/leftover pieces.
If you are going to make the larger theatre add in the Qubelok from p 8.

Tools required.

Metal rasp to file the rough ends smooth

Set square to mark the 'w' and 'x' cuts square

This is a small vice that clamps onto a bench or table, the top swivels.

A full sized or small hacksaw

Be very careful when taking joints apart, the connectors can break and be stuck in the tube. First use a flat screwdriver in the corner to ease it off, then gently wiggle and knock it apart right in the corner.

Hammer to hit the centre punch

Electric drill and 3mm, 4.5mm, 5mm drill bits

Pop rivet gun and 5mm x 6.5mm blind rivets

18 x 5mm x 38mm nuts and bolts

4 x 10 x 10cm brackets or larger 12.5 x 12.5cm

4 x 25mm angle brackets and self tapping screws

A small clamp to hold the bracket while you drill and bolt it in place

5mm lock nuts for the bolts holding the brackets on the uprights

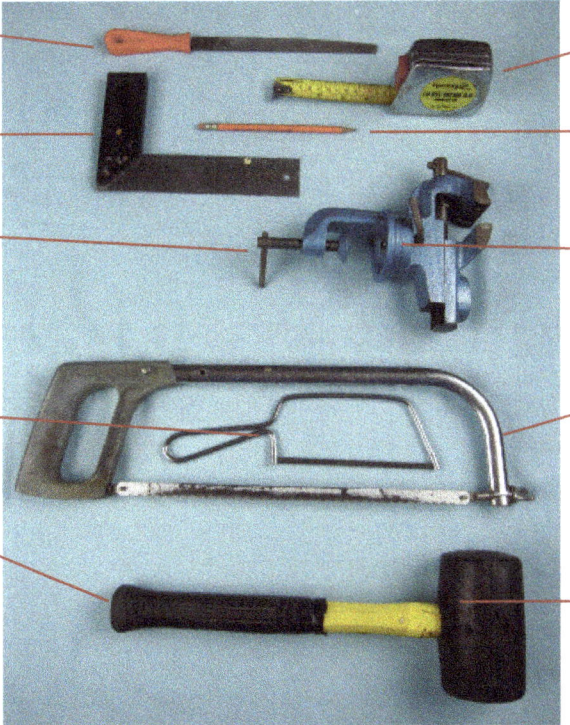

Tape measure

Pencil or marker

Vice to hold Qubelok when doing holes, brackets and hinges

Hacksaw to cut 'w' and 'x' pieces out of leftovers

Rubber mallet to knock the Qubelok together

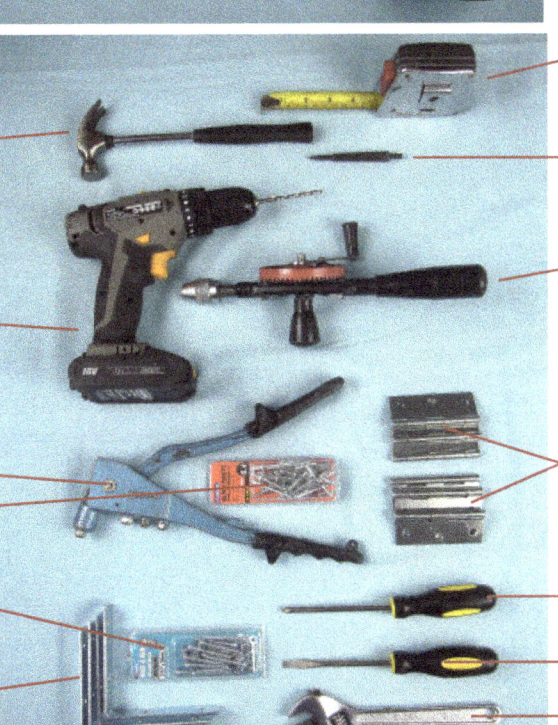

Tape measure

Centre punch to make a centre point for the drill bit

Hand drill if you do not have an electric one

Six 85cm hinges

Philips screwdriver

Flat screwdriver

Shifting spanner

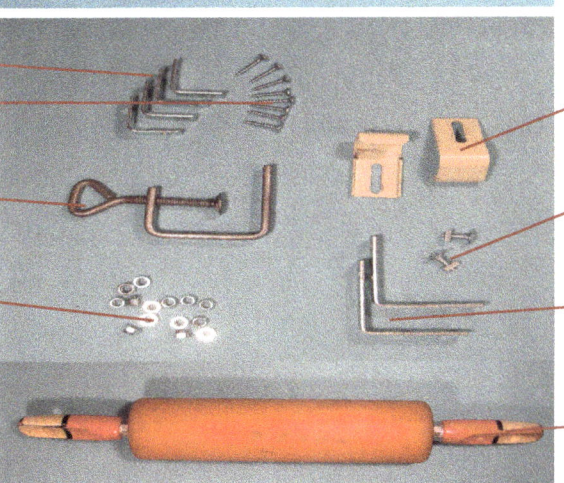

The 2 curtain rod attachments are bolted to the brackets with 2 x 5mm nuts and bolts.

Two 5 x 5cm brackets to hold the curtain track

Rolling pin to roll the adhesive velcro hook

12

Assembling the pieces.

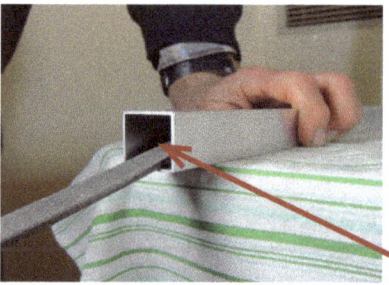
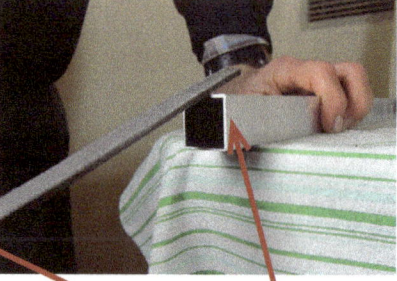

rough edges   1. File all the rough edges inside and outside.   smooth edges

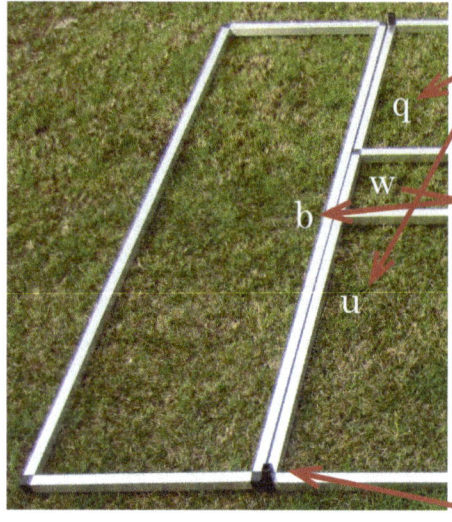

2. Knock 'T"s into q, u, r, v with a rubber mallet.

3. Place next to b and c in their positions.

4. Check length of w and x in case it is not exactly 25cm. Cut out of 37cm leftover pieces and knock into place.

5. Put a small corner bracket in each of the 4 main corners using screws.

Keep the leftovers.

Knocking together with a mallet

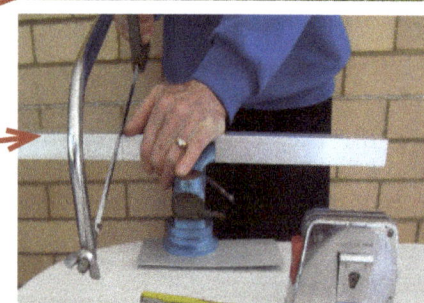

6   7   8   9

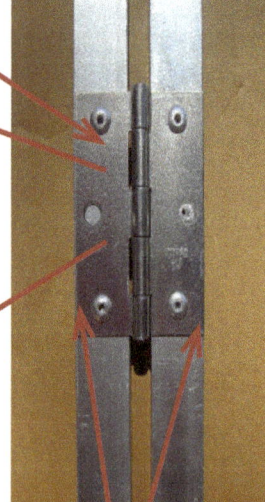
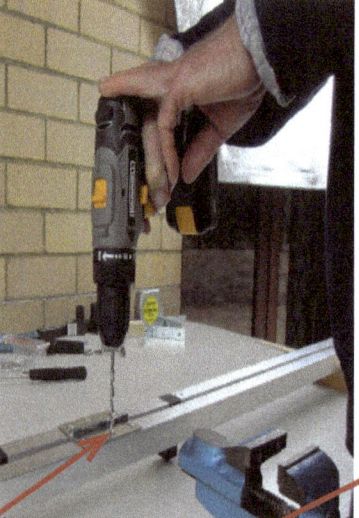
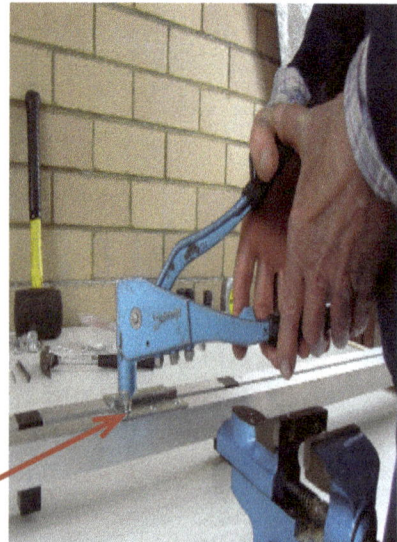

6. Join centre to side with   85mm hinges   at top, bottom and on 'w' and 'x'.
7. Line hinges up with outer edges leaving   gap in between the uprights for the material.
8. Drill holes for rivets.
9. Use 5mm x 6.5mm blind rivets.

Strengthening & stabilising the theatre

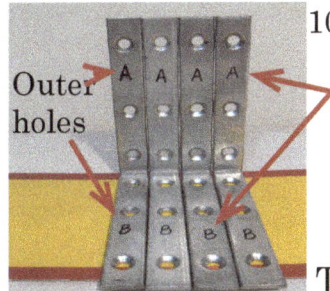

10. The holes on the bracket arm are usually spaced slightly differently, so line them up together with the same arm up and mark those arms with an 'A' and the arm lying down 'B'.

Always bolt this arm 'A' to the theatre front and the other arm will automatically be on the addition so the bolt holes will always line up.

The brackets are essential to strengthen connectors and joints.

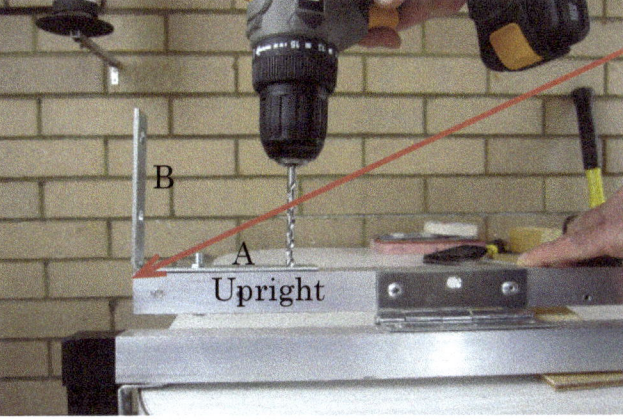

11. Hold the 'A' arm of a 10 x 10 x 2mm or larger bracket level with the top end of 'q+w+u' upright. Centre punch the two outer holes.
12. Drill a 5mm hole right through the tube.
13. Use 5mm x 38mm bolt to hold it in place.
14. Put another bracket 'A' arm on the bottom end of 'q+w+u' using the same steps.
15. Repeat top and bottom on upright 'r+x+v'.

16. Take a bracket off, and join its 'B' arm to the end of curtain support rod 'm' or 'n'.
17. Repeat this for the other curtain support rod.
18. Repeat for bottom theatre supports 'o' and 'p'.

19. Join in e,f,g,h between the middle uprights using 3W at the 4 corners with 3rd leg protruding at the back. Join side wings together with R< connectors.
20. Put adhesive velcro hook on all the front surfaces and go over it with a roller.
21. Put adhesive velcro hook on the top of the curtain support rods.

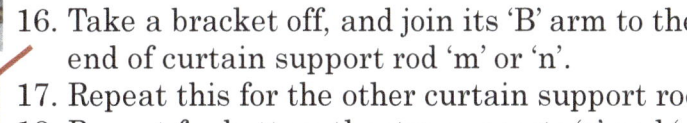

22. Stick 10cm of velcro loop on the ends of the front two stay pieces 's' and 't'.
23. Stick velcro hook on top of 'e' and bottom of 'h', also side wing tops 'i', 'k', and bottoms 'j', 'l' where the stays will sit.
    The stays stop the theatre falling forwards.
24. Join curtain and bottom supports back to the uprights and bolt with lock nuts.

Be sure to file the ridges off the 3W connectors as shown on p 9 so these stays and supports come off easily and the connectors do not get broken.

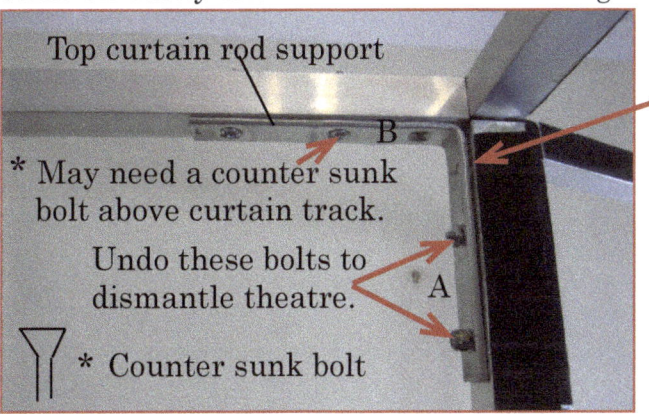

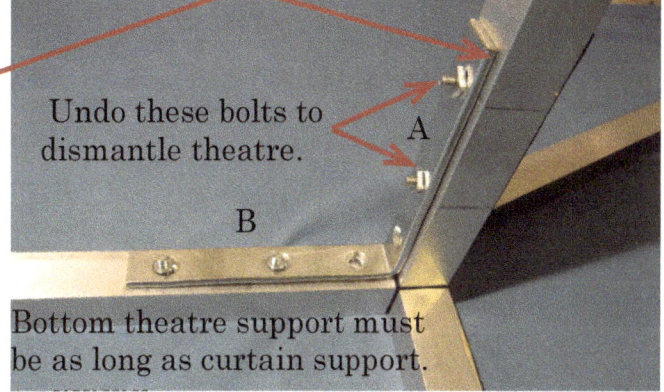

Scenery rack for small theatre

Here is a cheap simple scenery rack built from two 6.5m lengths of Qubelok Aluminium plus eight 3W connectors.

Cutting instructions. Capral will cut these.

1. With the two lengths together cut them in half.

325cm	325cm

2. Then place all 4 pieces together and cut at 180cm, then 90cm and 55cm will remain.

180cm	90cm	55cm

3

4

Qubelok and connectors.

3. File the rough bits off inside and outside of the ends.

4. Knock together as illustrated with a mallet.

5
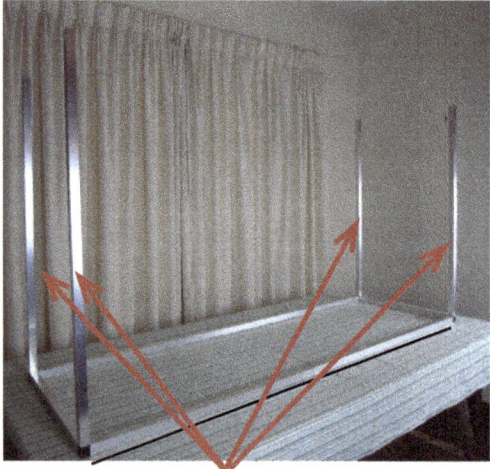
6
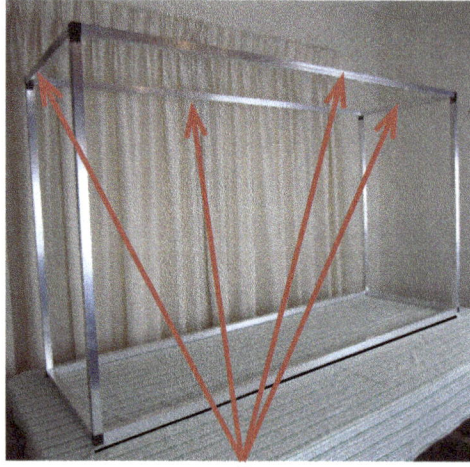
7

5. Knock top and bottom frames together.
6. Knock uprights onto bottom corners.
7. Knock top frame into place on top of these uprights.
8. Stick velcro loop along top two ends of the frame.

8

Scenery in finished rack.

Blockout covering and curtain

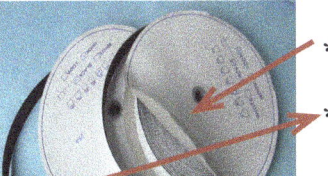

Materials needed:
* One 25m roll of self-adhesive velcro hook
* One 25m roll of sew-on velcro loop
  (Velcro available at www.tapesonline.com.au)
* 6m of 150cm wide black blockout material

Measure your frames when assembled (they will be slightly different to these) then adjust.

Long side		long side		
Side wing 'a'	Short side	Middle 'c'		Scenery Blockout
Side wing 'b'	Short side			
Top 'd'				
2m		2m		2m

Add in more if covering the extension and riser.

Blockout Material

Divide the length of fabric into thirds and cut.
Check your theatre measurements. Add at least 3cm each side (may differ slightly to manual).

1st third ~ side wing frame plus 3cm all round for a single hem so it will = 193 x 67cm.
1. Draw the measurements on the back of the material and cut it out.
2. On opposite sides 1 and 2 of the side wing 'a' and 'b', turn a single 2.5cm wide hem (the same width as the velcro) and machine the loop onto it. Do the same on sides 3 and 4.
3. Take the leftover 'd'. Turn a double hem on the two short sides and then on one long side.
4. On the last long side turn a single hem and stitch loop on to it.
   This piece goes on the top rail to hide the curtain rod.

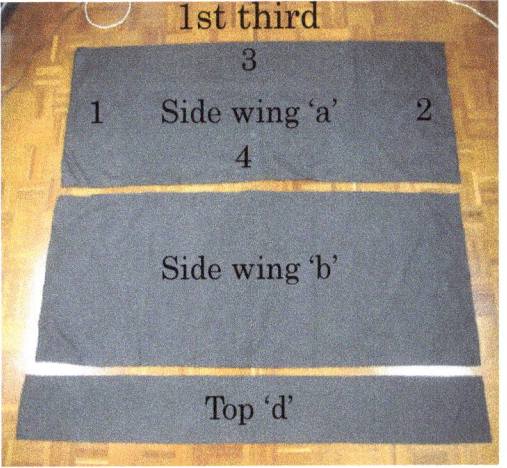

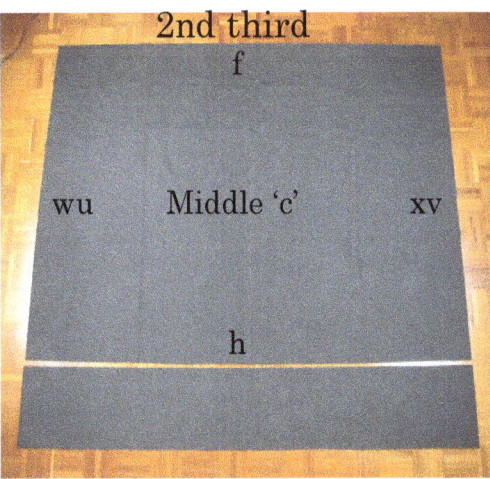

2nd third ~ the middle section p 9 from 'f' down to 'h' and across from 'wu' to 'xv' (include frame) plus 3cm all round for a single hem should be 124cm x 192cm. Cut it out.
1. Turn a single 2.5cm wide hem, the same width as the velcro, along one side and machine the loop onto it. Do this on every side.

3rd third ~ keep for the black blockout scenery curtain.

* Velcro frames, if not done yet, as instructed on p 14, step 20. Lie the theatre flat on its back on the ground and support the frame to apply velcro to the front surfaces.

Blockout curtain

1. Cut the third piece of blockout material 200cm x 120cm.
2. Sew a double 5cm hem on both short sides 'd' and 'b', then long sides 'a' and 'c'.

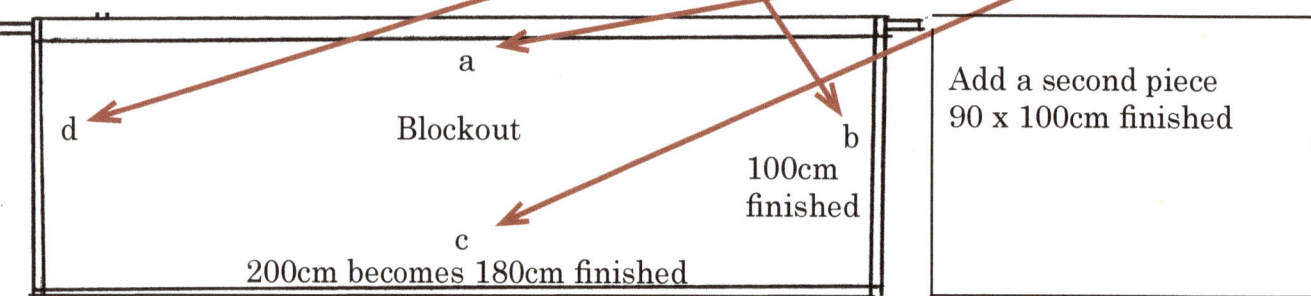

Mounting the curtain track

Purchase an adjustable 2.4m track for the small theatre, so the curtains can be opened back to the sides, or a 3.5m track that will do for both the small and the large theatre.

1. Mount two 5cm x 5cm brackets on the frame above the proscenium, hanging down 10cm in from each side using a 5mm x 38mm nut and bolt.

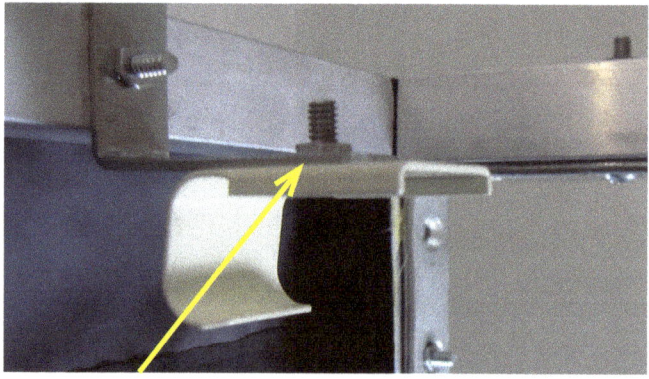

2. Bolt the curtain mounting bracket to the end bracket hole and space it out from the frame to allow curtain to gather.

3. Clip track into bracket.

Use this track system because trackgliders will catch on any screws put in the back of the track.

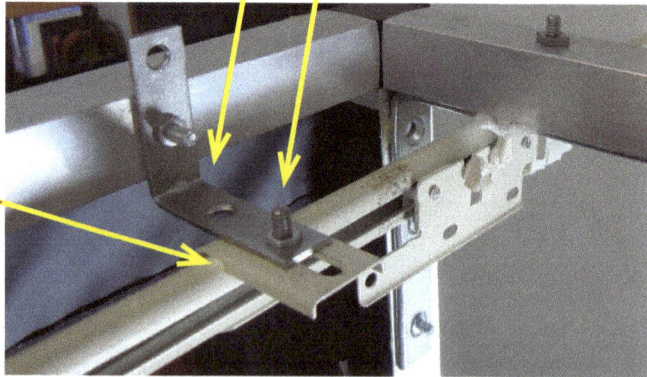

4. Take the blockout leftover 'd' and turn a double hem on the two short sides and one long side.

5. On the last long side turn a single hem and stitch loop on to it.
   This strip goes on the top rail to hide the curtain rod.

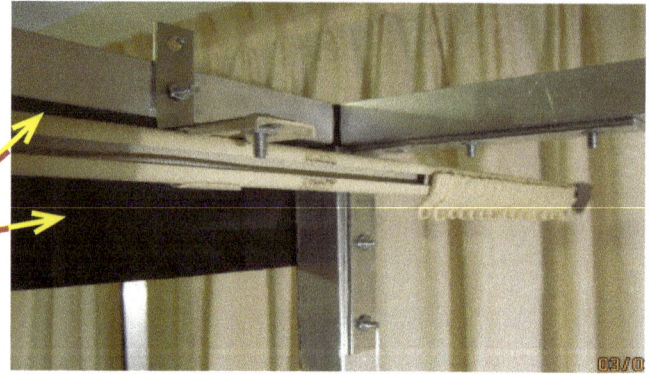

Front curtains

Make bracket holes 10cm in from each side, same as in no.1 on the previous page, in the bottom theatre frame. The curtain can be hung there when the theatre is used upside down.

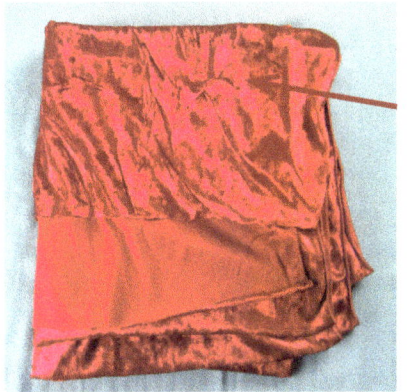

Purchase

200cm x 150cm of fabric for two 100cm x 150cm curtains or a 300cm x 150cm to do the large or small theatre.

300cm gathering tape for small
450cm gathering tape for large
50 or 80 steel curtain hooks

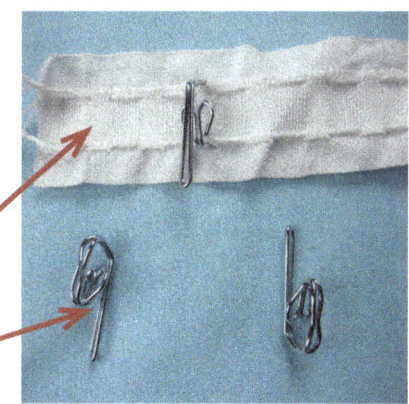

1. Cut material into two (100cm x 150cm) pieces, or add 100cm x half 150cm to each of the above drops for large theatre.

2. Double hem (turn material twice) sides 'b' and 'd' of curtains.

3. Turn a single 3cm hem (width of the gathering tape) along the top 'a' 150/225cm side.
4. Pin the gathering tape to the hem on the wrong side.
5. Machine along both sides of the tape.
6. Space hooks evenly along the tape.

7. Attach them into the track runners.

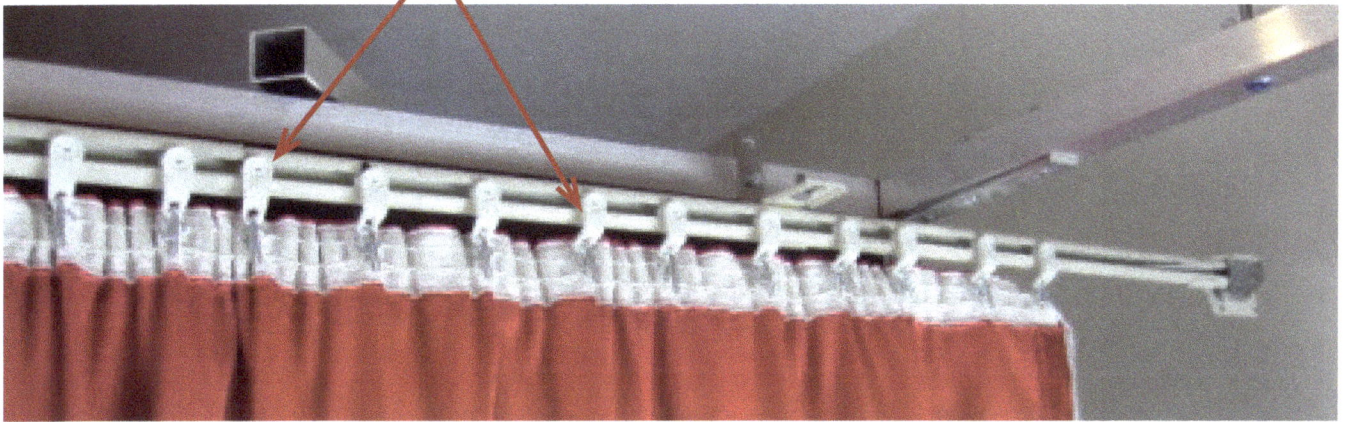

9. Tighten the gather of the tape on each curtain to fit across a little over half the stage.

8. Curtain length needs to be 90cm, so measure it and turn up the bottom side 'c' and hem it. It can then be used when doing glove and marionette plays in this theatre.

18

Scenery curtains

1. Choose a see-through piece of coloured material suitable for an inside or outside scene.
2. Cut it down to 200cm wide x 110cm deep, then it will suit both prosceniums.

3. Sew a double 5cm hem on both short 'd' and 'b' sides.
4. Sew a 6cm hem along the bottom side 'c'.

5. Fold 'a' at 90cm. Machine along at 5cms from the fold with a gathering stitch (which can be easily pulled undone and restitched to suit the shorter proscenium drop) leaving the excess to hang down behind.

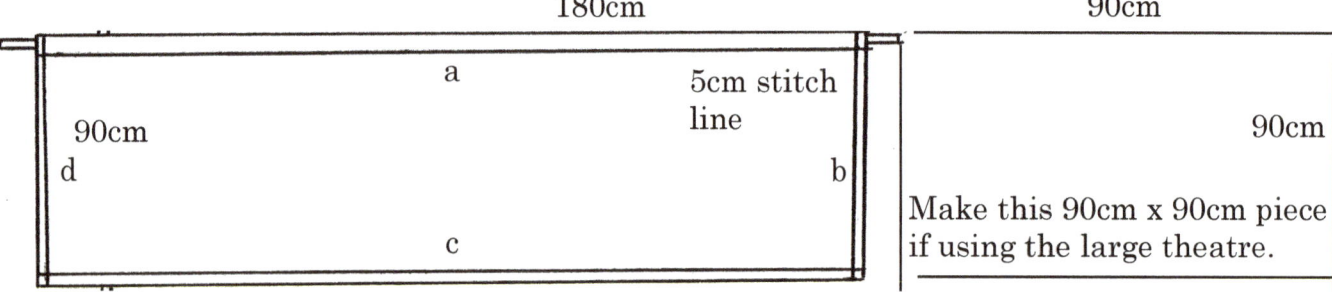

Make this 90cm x 90cm piece if using the large theatre.

6. Stitch or glue green felt along the bottom so you can velcro on scenery trees/shrubs/etc.
7. Hold the puppet in front of it to check the puppets and scenery are the same scale.
8. Keep felt low and don't overload it with objects. Puppeteers need to see their puppets.

Tall objects need threads tied to a piece of hook on its backing to hold it up on a cloud, etc.

* The felt stretches when stitching it on with a machine and the other material doesn't.
All scenery pieces/objects need hook velcro on their back to attach them to the felt.

Locating these curtains

7. Put velcro loop around the ends of 190cm curtain rods.

8. Push a rod through the top hem of each curtain.

9. Locate blockout on the back of the curtain support rod.

10. Scenery curtain approximately 23cm from the front of the rod.

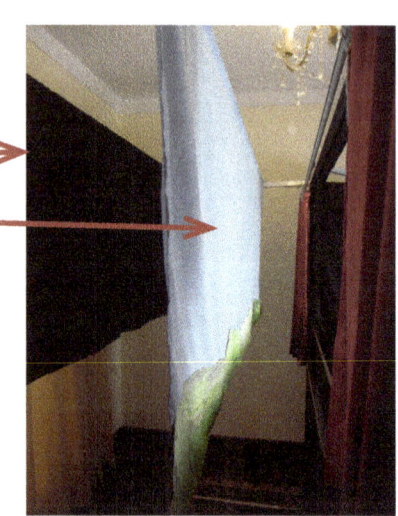

The puppeteers stand in between the black curtain and the scenery curtain so they can watch their puppet through it.

The black curtain blocks any back light so puppeteers are hidden.

Standard lights, or reading lights clamped to the front stays, NEED TO BE FOCUSSED ON THE SCENE so the puppeteers can see their puppets.

Doing Puppetry

Tick, Tock

Tick, tock, tick, tock
Listen to the busy clock.
It tells us all the time of day
And when to act our puppet play.
Chime, chime, chime, chime.
Let's make puppets for a nursery rhyme.
Jack and Jill went up the hill
And we can demonstrate their spill.
The three little kittens had no pie
Our play will let you all know why.
Henny Penny will need to look
Just like a very silly chook.
Little Red Hen's friends didn't help making bread,
They need to look hungry as they didn't get fed.
And we need to make a puppet bumble bee,
Who else could make cows in the clover flee?

Making ~ puppets
~ scenery

Nursery rhymes ~ Jack and Jill
~ The Three Little Kittens
Stories ~ Henny Penny
~ The Little Red Hen
~ The Cows in the Clover

Extras ~ acting your puppet
~ choreographing
~ adding music
~ performance
~ My Grandfather's Clock

Puppetry program

The theatre is best made beforehand and used to illustrate puppetry.

1. Introduce puppets by showing one you bought or made.
2. If possible demonstrate puppetry fun and your invisibility in the theatre.
3. Experiment with the simple plays first and perform them for younger children to enjoy.
4. Gather different versions of the nursery rhymes or stories you have chosen in this manual or elsewhere from your school, home, libraries and the web. Puppet plays benefit from short, action-packed interaction, not l-o-n-g speeches.
5. Sort out the characters and match them with your puppeteers. Two groups for each play.
6. Use the pictures you've collected to design scenery and create your characters.
7. Take your collections of the story and write the script expanding it into a play.
8. Make your characters and scenery. Add in fun things as you go along.

Puppet making

Double plate puppets are simple to make and easy to act in the theatre.
It is going to be a puppet not an art work, so double plates make the head 3D.
Gather the materials needed for the puppets.

Head and Face ~

Cardboard plates
3-4mm cardboard, thinner cardboard, paper, tissue paper and water based glue.
Pens, paints and brushes

Body ~

Strong cardboard, material and glue.

A selection of materials.
May require some trims such as buttons, braids, ribbons,etc. and kebab sticks.

Different sizes of cardboard boxes to cut up for scenery props.
Now it is time to make the puppet.

Basic plate puppet

Packaging places sell paperboard 3·5mm thick and can cut it into 3mm strips, or you can cut it with tin snips or a large guillotine. I go to www.packperth.com.au in WA. 9470 9277

1. Cut two 3 x 45cm strips of strong card.

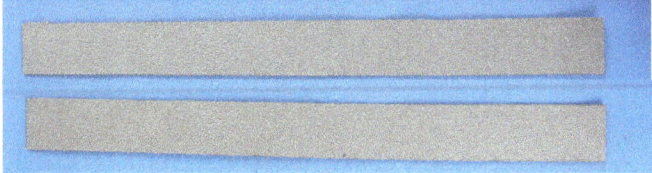

2. Glue them together, it needs to be strong.

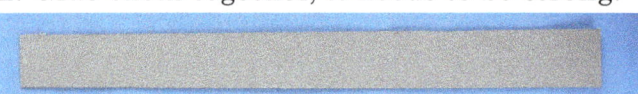

3. You need this card with two 18cm plates.

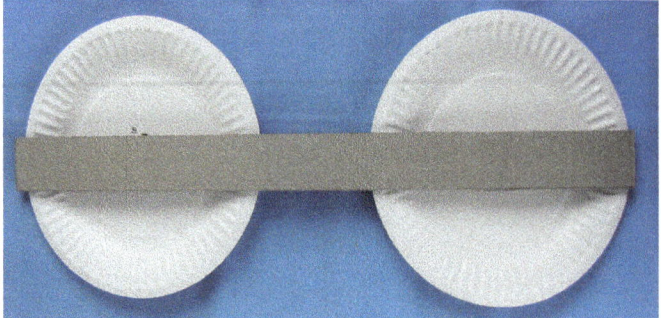

4 - 6 You can stack plates and prick through centre of the pile. Draw the centre line, restack then transfer the edge marks by shuffling the plates. But it's best if the children learn to do it.

4. On the top side of one plate, use a ruler, tape or compass to measure and mark the centre of the plate.

5. Draw a line across the middle of that plate.
6. Mark 1 1/2 cm each side of the centre line on the plate edges.

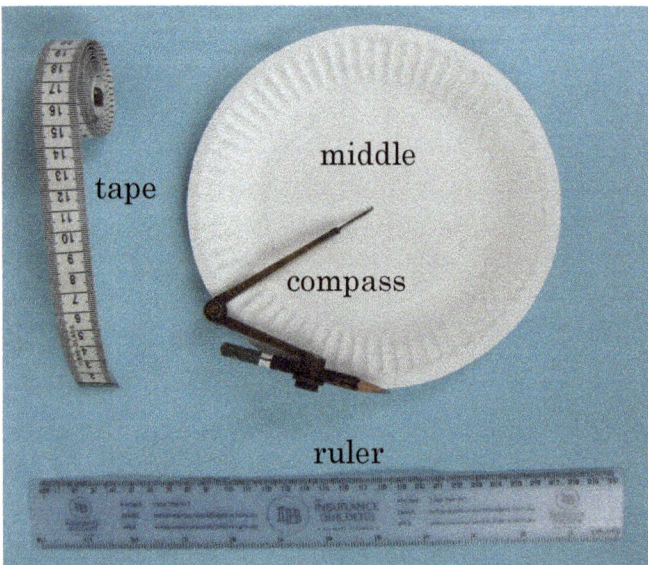

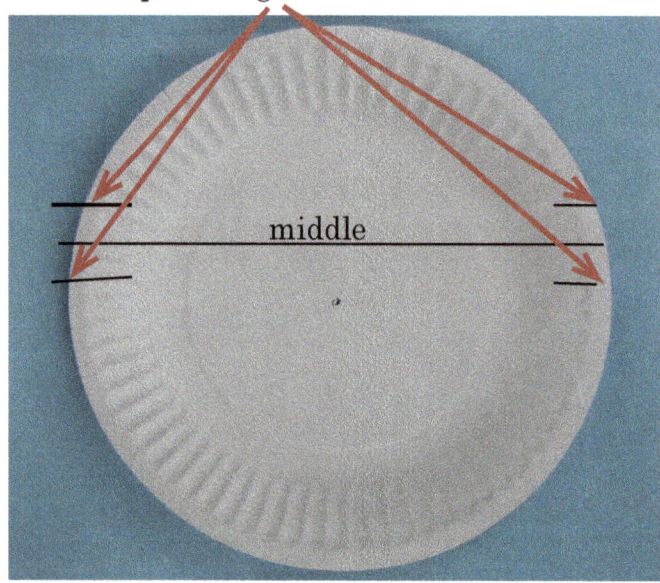

7. Put glue on the edge between the marks.
8. Lie card across the plate on the glue.
9. Clamp in place and allow to dry.

10. Put glue all around the edge of the plate.
11. Then with top sides together clamp the second plate to it and leave it to dry.

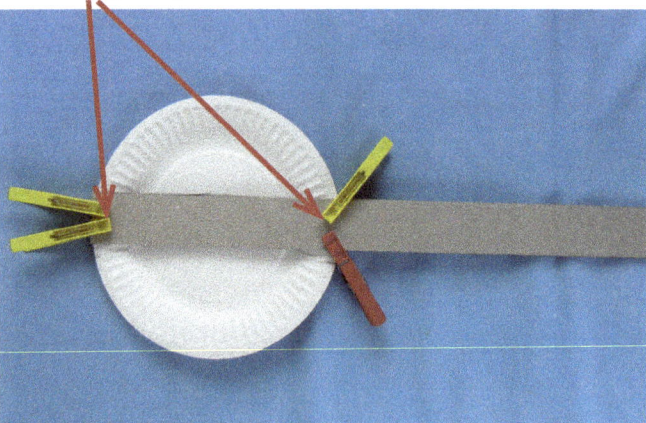

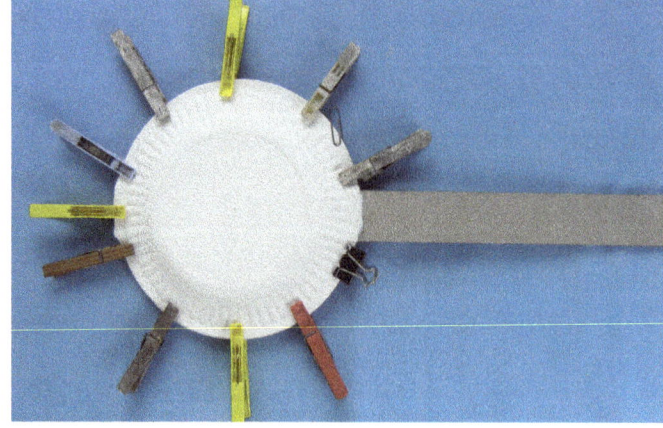

Clamp with paper, metal, or hair clips, pegs, etc. Put weight on the cardboard strips but not on the plates. It will bend them in. A sharp knife through the edge join will unbend the plate.

Human head ~ hair instructions

1. Paint the face side and the neck.

2. Paint the neck and lower back of the head.

3. Draw around a plate on a large piece of paper.

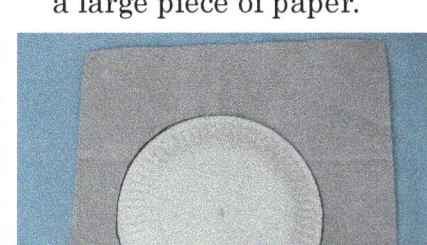

4. Fold circle in half against a window or light.

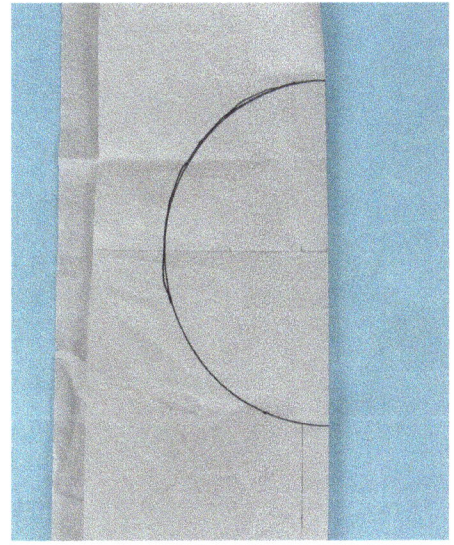

5. Fold again into quarters.
6. Unfold, rule down the fold lines.

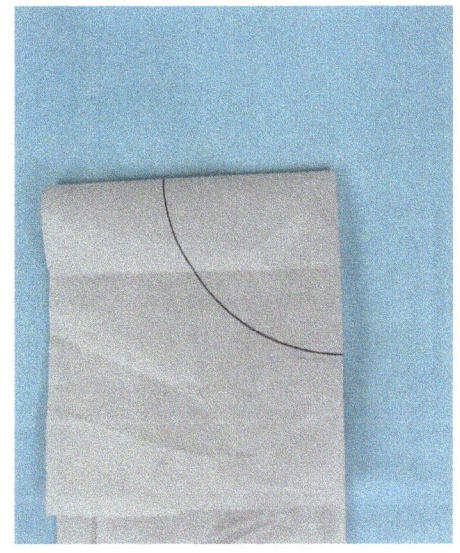

7. Draw eyes on horizontal line leaving 3cm between them. Draw the hair.

The red line is a simple hair style. Black one kicks out half way then grades into the neck.

The front hair coming straight down to the ears or kicking out at the sides.

Where the back hair will be.

Hair cut out of cardboard and glued on top edge only.

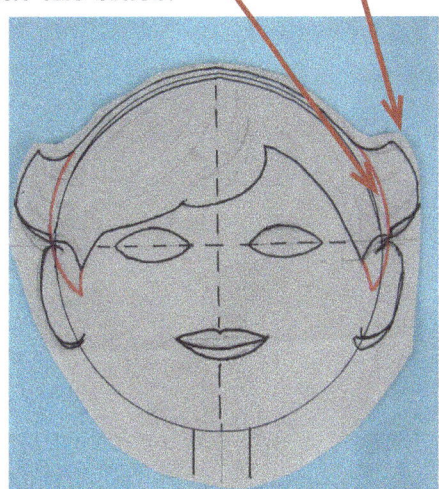
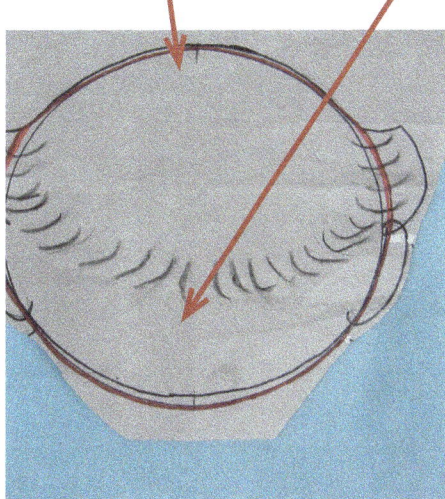
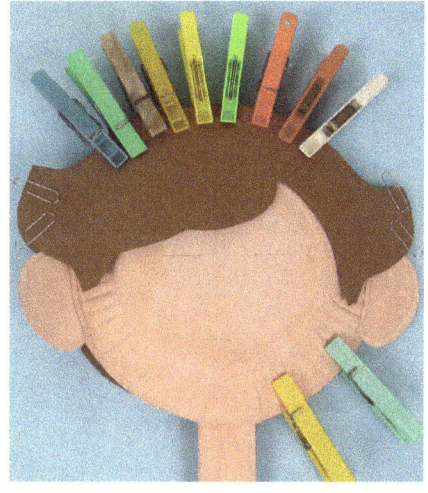

Human head ~ face instructions

1. Select and colour in templates from the previous page or make your own components.
2. Cut out around them then cut them out properly.

3. Eyes go across the centre of the plate with almost room for an eye between them.

4. Mouth goes half way between eyes and plate edge on the inner circle.

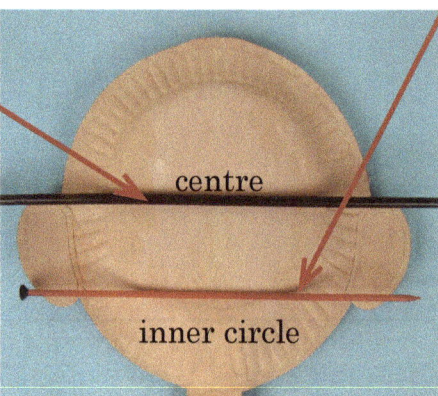

5. Nose goes between eyes and mouth.

6. Ears go near edge of plate between eyes and mouth. Not needed under hair.

7. Eyebrows go above the eyes.

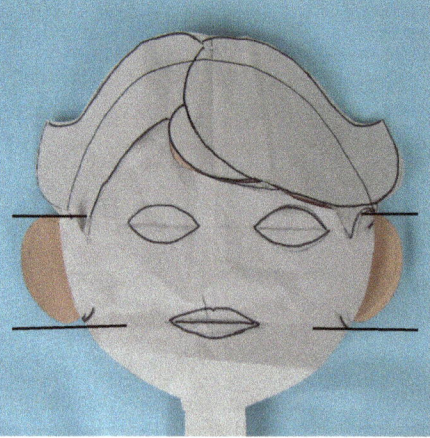

8. When face is finished glue hair together down the sides and trim edge if needed.
9. To give the hair more character it can be streaked with a small, stiff brush and painted in the direction the hair lies.
10. Crayons do not show up on coloured card but they do on white.

| Mother | Jill | Jack |

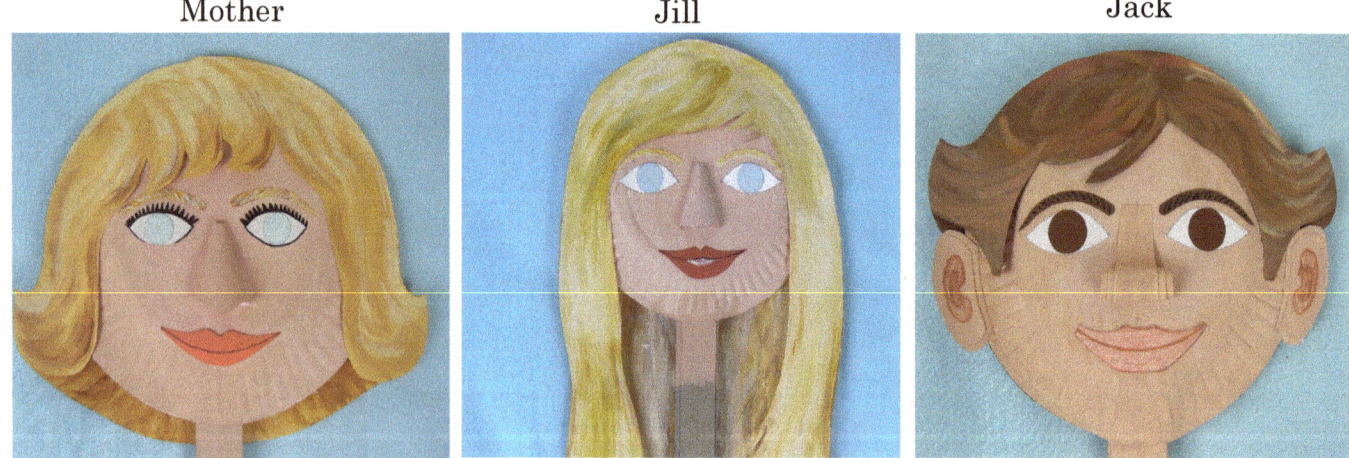

25

Face templates

All templates are very basic and can be upgraded in shape and detail at any time

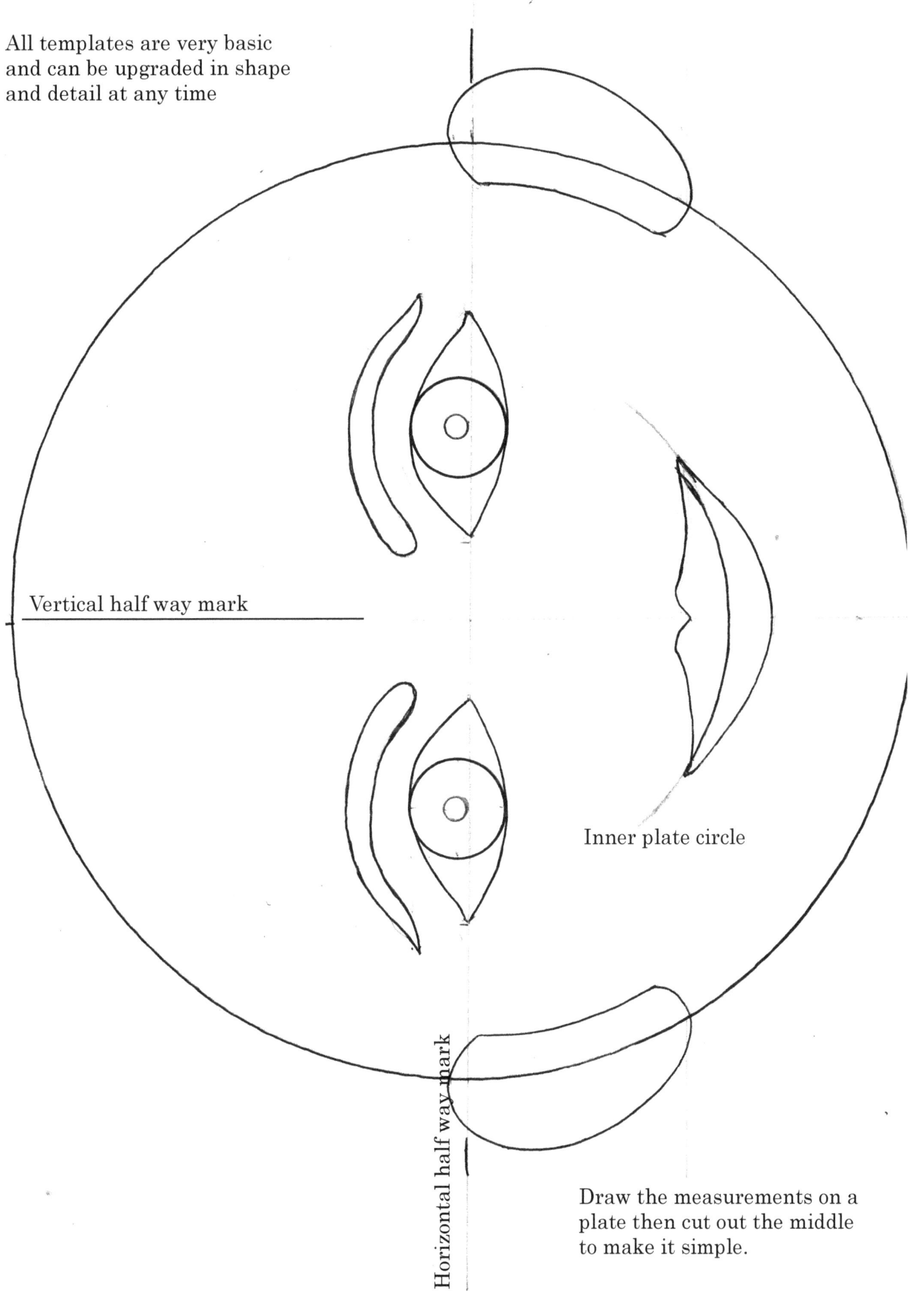

Vertical half way mark

Inner plate circle

Horizontal half way mark

Draw the measurements on a plate then cut out the middle to make it simple.

Woman

Eyebrow

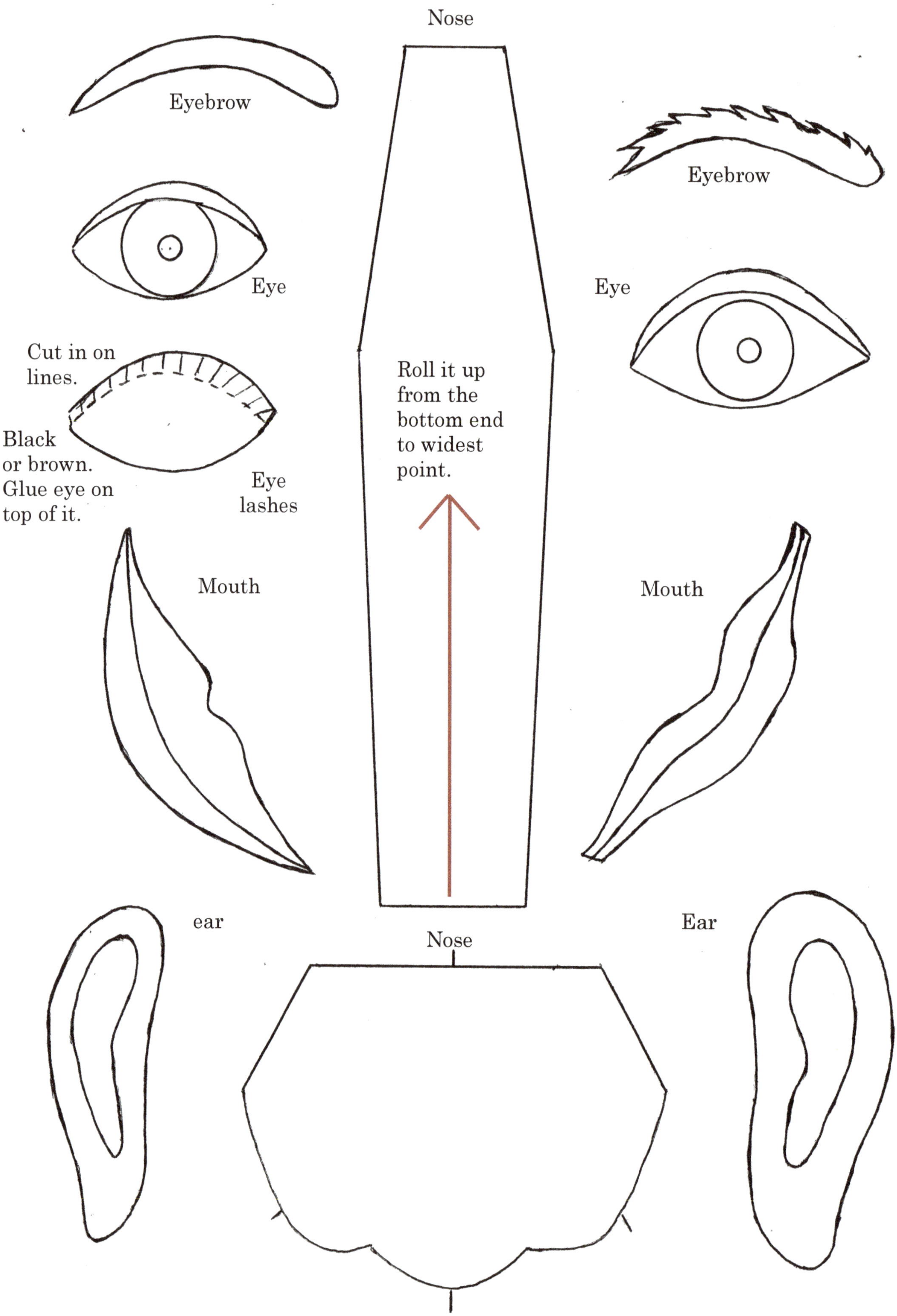

Eye

Cut in on lines.

Black or brown. Glue eye on top of it.

Eye lashes

Mouth

ear

Man

Eyebrow

Eye

Mouth

Ear

Nose

Roll it up from the bottom end to widest point.

Nose

27

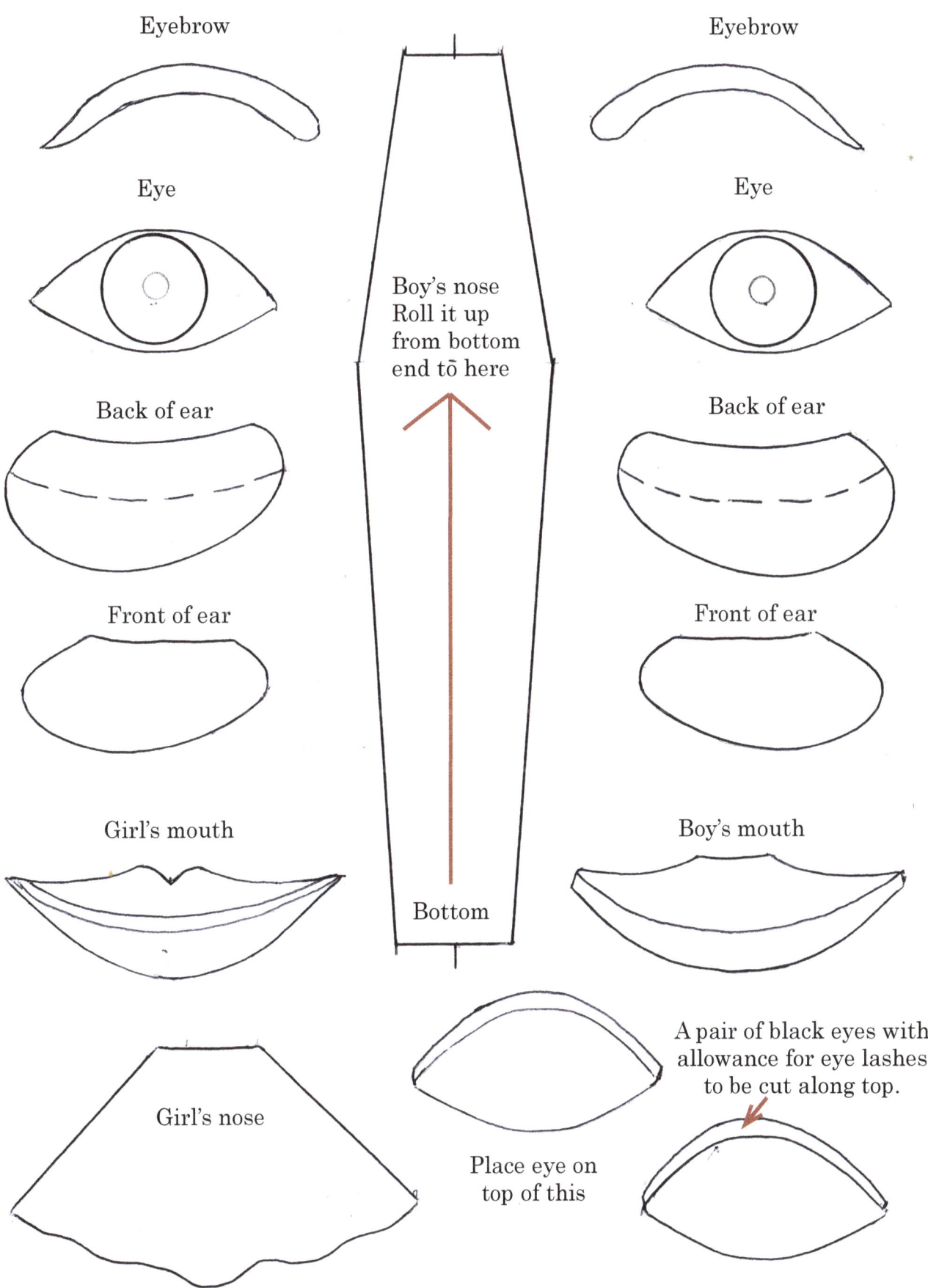

Cat head ~ instructions

Select a 60 x 60cm piece of material for the body of your cat because this will decide its colour and look.

1. Make a basic small plate puppet as shown on p 23.

2. Cut out ear templates and make two inner and outer ears in cardboard.

3. Colour in the eye templates, cut them out or use them to make cardboard ones. If you want a bolder eye make the pupil out of coloured paper or cardboard.

4. Colour in and cut out the nose template or make a papier mache one.

5. Templates and nose assembled.
   N.B. Ears are reversed. These two sides are the same, so ears sit at correct angle.

6. Paint the head, then the back and the front edges of the back piece of the ear to match the rest of the head.

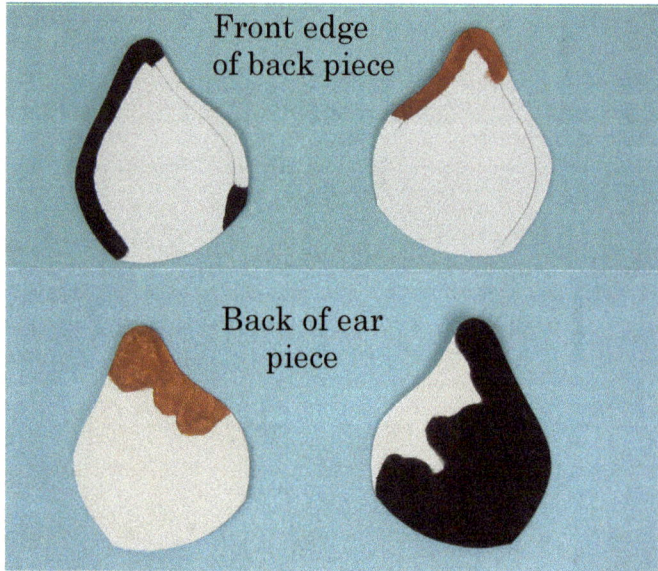

7. Paint the front smaller pieces a plain hairy colour.
   Once again they are OPPOSITES.

8. Glue the 2 pieces together around the sides leaving the bottom 1cm UNGLUED. Bend the ears so they hold their shape.

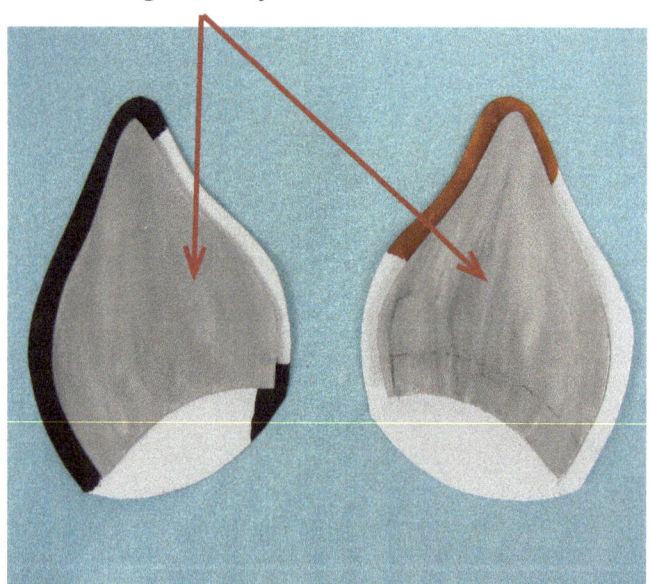

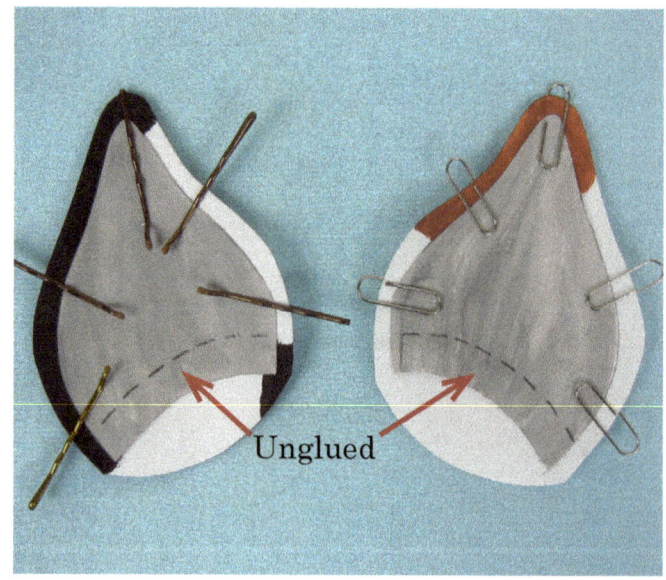

9. Mark the top of the plate at 4cm either side of the centre - where the ear starts.

10. Fit the unglued bottom edge of the ear over the edge of the plate.
Check they are on the right sides, ie. sticking up and not out to the sides.

11. Remove, put glue along front and back edge of plate. Put ear back and clamp until the glue is dry.

12. Place eyes and nose on the face, mark where they sit. Glue in place. Draw and colour in the bottom of the mouth.

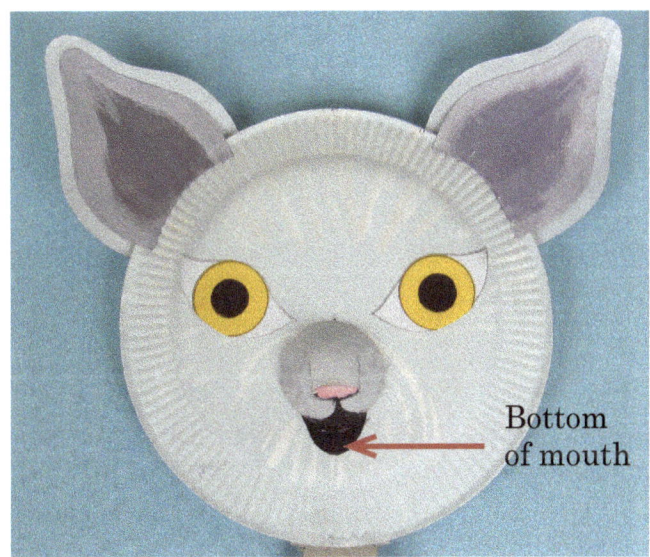

Bottom of mouth

The mother's plate is 23cm, the eyes and the ears are the same size but the nose is bigger so she looks like a cat not a big kitten.

Ears 12cm apart

The back of the kitten's head.

30

Cat head ~ templates

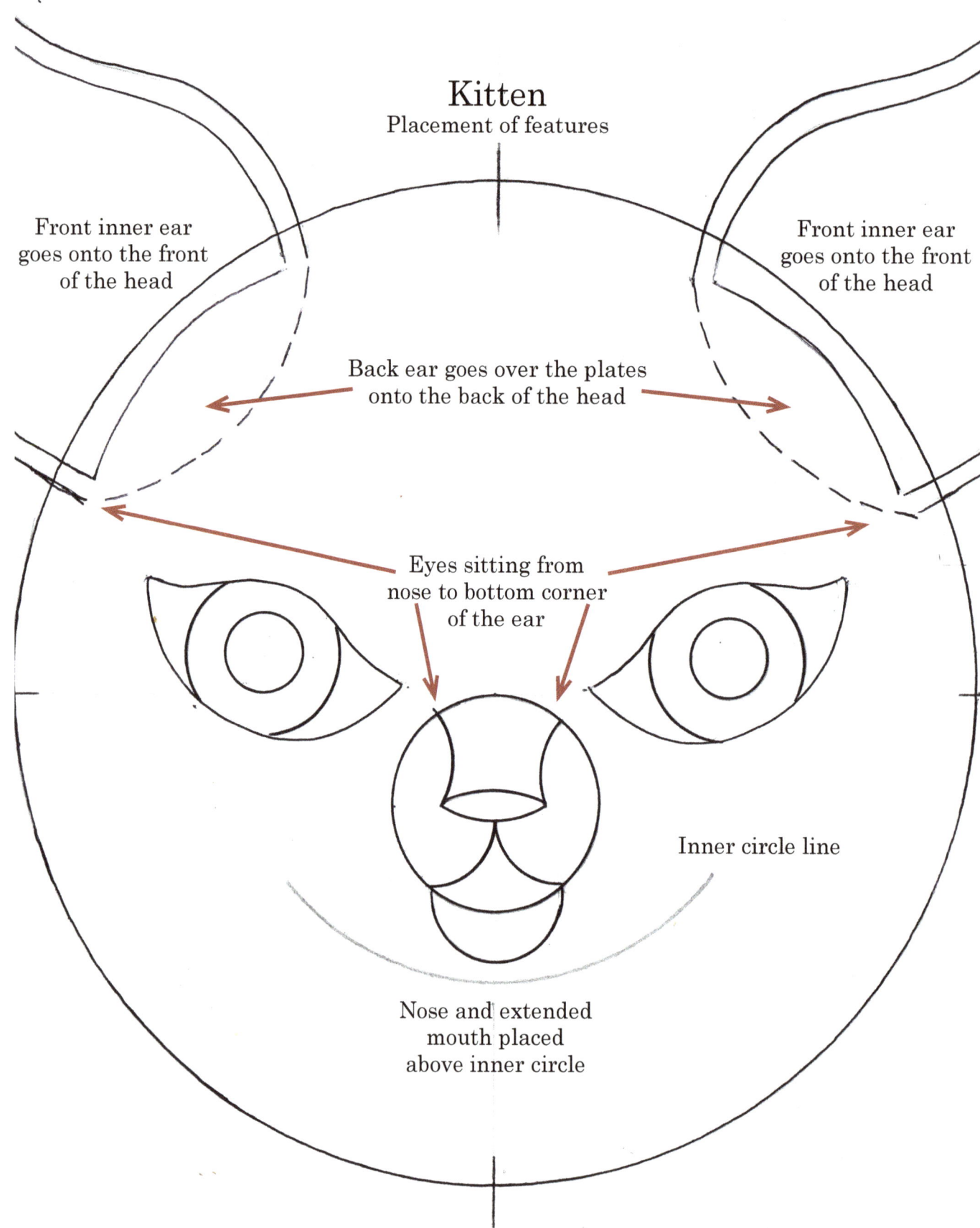

Mother

She is made using a big 23cm plate.
She has a bigger nose which can be drawn or made 3d in papier mache.
The eyes and nose still sit near the inner circle. This puts them further away from the ears so she looks like an adult cat.

Front of ear

Back of ear

Reverse eye and ears for second one

Nose and mouth

Kittens

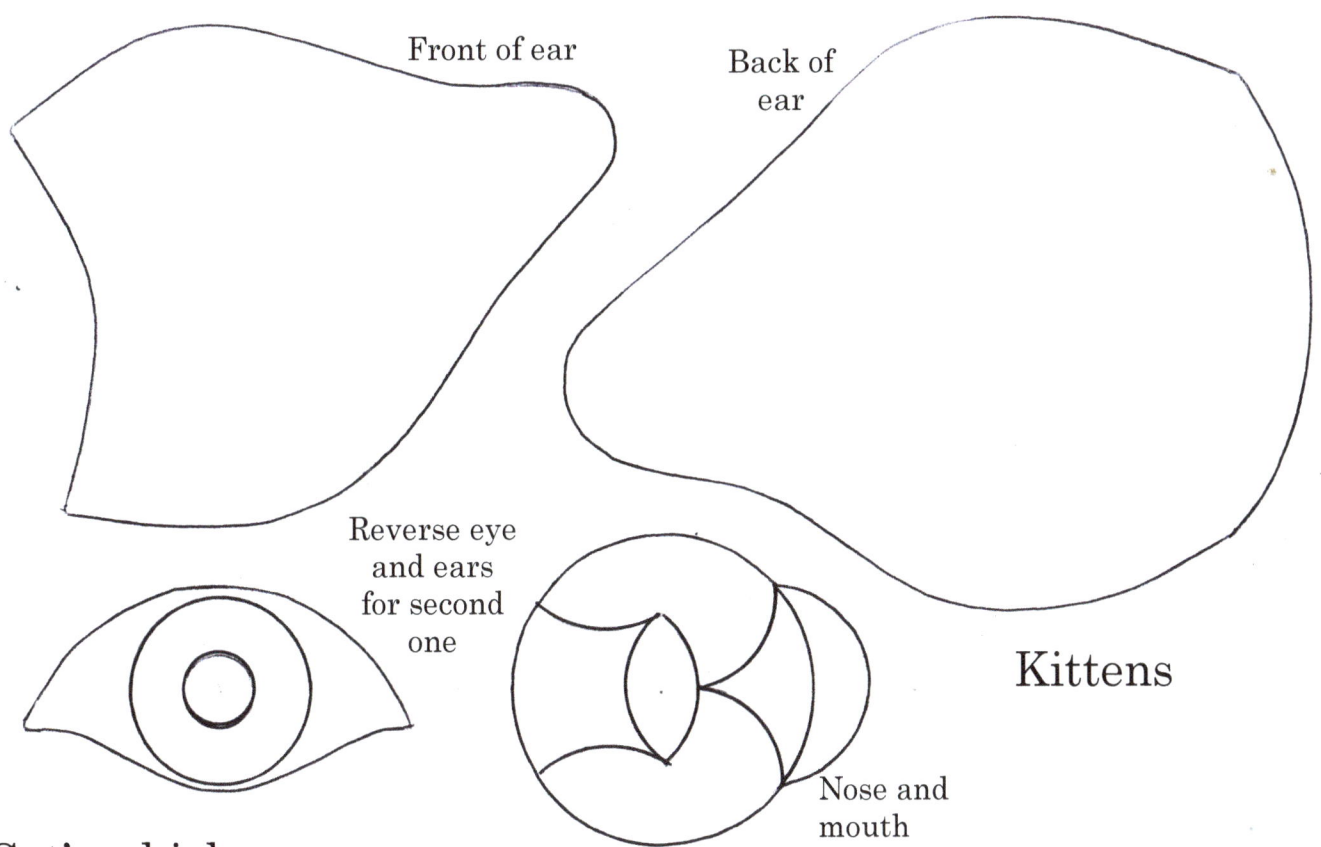

Cat's whiskers

Stick 4 pieces of cardboard together. Allow to dry. Cut in narrow, slightly tapered strips and leave as they curl. Glue the thicker end to the nose. Illustration exaggerates the tapers.

13cm

5cm

Turn the eye and ears over so second one is reversed

Mother cat

Nose and Mouth

Back of ear

Front of ear

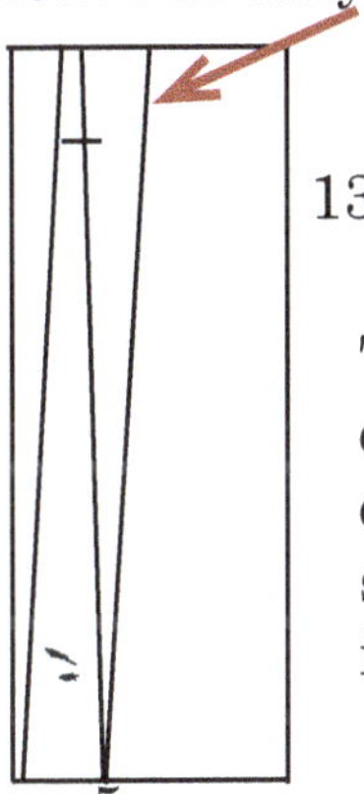

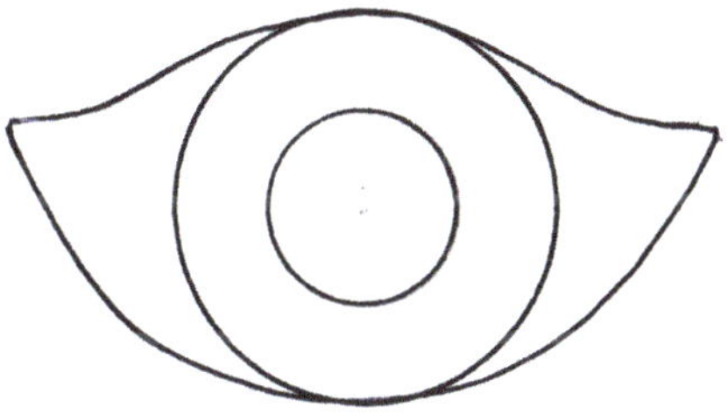

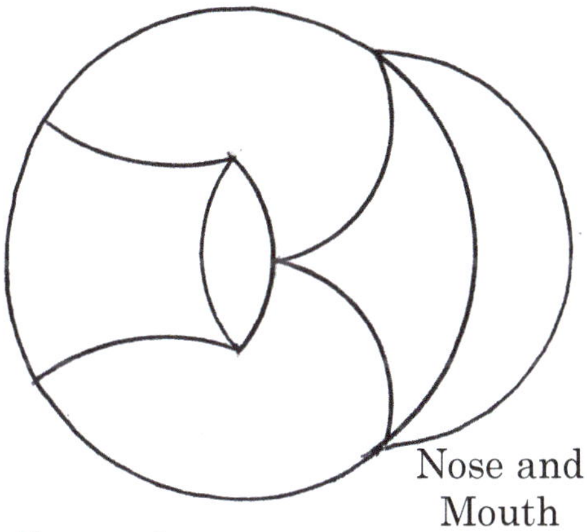

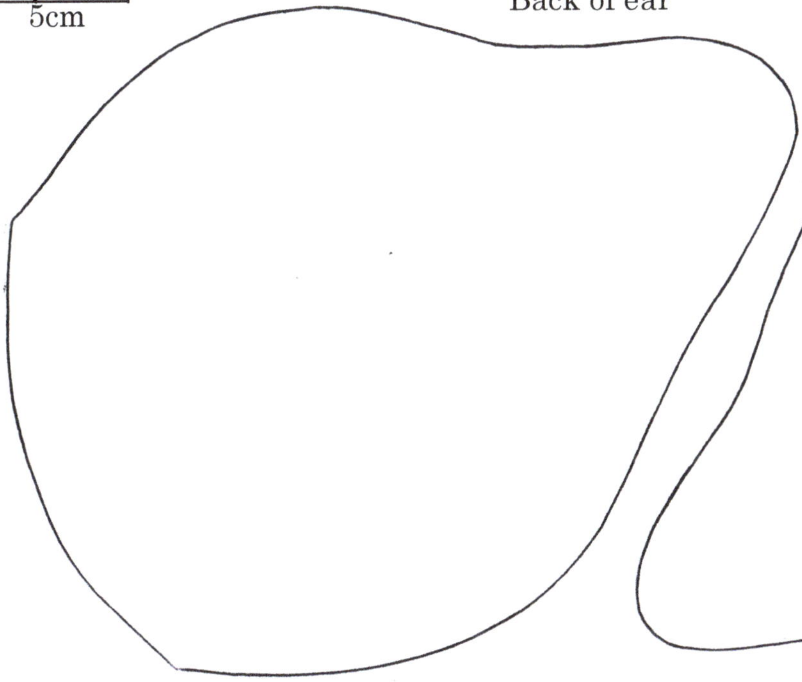

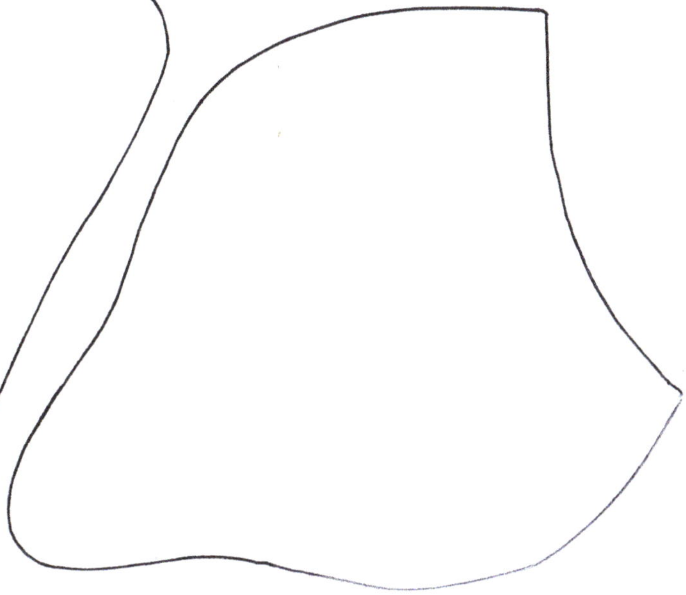

Animal head ~ instructions & templates

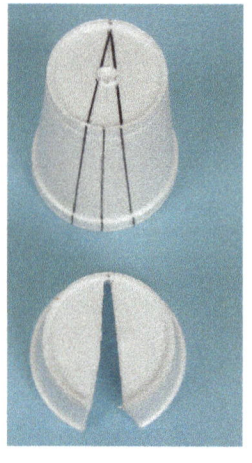  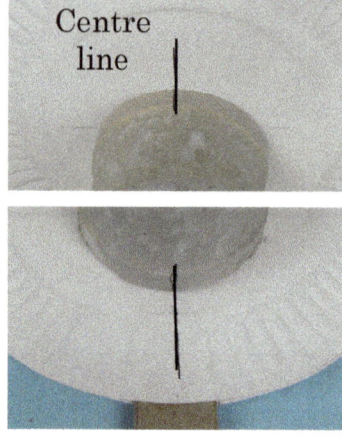 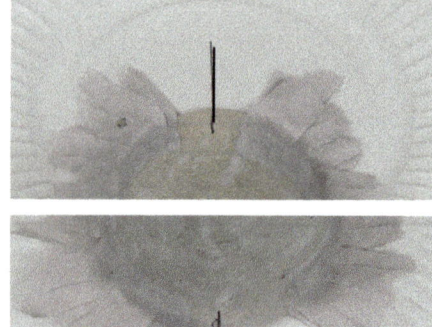

1. Mark across the bottom and down a paper/polystyrene cup then draw a slice as shown.

2. Cut out the slice.

3. Close the slice with tape.

4. Cover cup in gladwrap, glue 5 layers of paper pieces over it.

5. Remove cup when dry.

6. Mark centre top and bottom on back end of snout.

7. Mark centre line on plate above and below where snout will sit.

8. Match up the marks and glue it in place with strips of paper.

   Leave marks visible until snout is firmly in place, then do those two spots.

Note ~ These shapes can be coloured in and cut out or cut out and used as templates to make ones from coloured paper or cardboard.

Cut out two inner and outer ears, turning the template over for the second one so it is reversed.
The second eye is reversed for you.

Eyes

Nose

Back of ear

Front of ear

1. Paint the whole head, the back and the front edges of the back ear piece with the same colour.

2. Paint the front smaller ear pieces a plain hairy colour. Remember they are opposites.

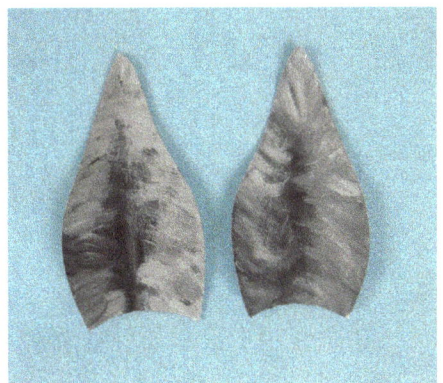

3. Glue front piece to back around the sides leaving the bottom 1cm unglued. Bend ears to shape them.

4. Mark 4cm either side of the centre where the ear starts.

5. Fit ears over the plate edge and check they point up not outwards. Remove ear.

6. Put glue along front and back edge of plate. Replace ear, clamp until dry.

7. Once again use the eye templates or draw your own. Try them in place and then glue them on.

   If you want a bolder eye make the pupil out of coloured paper or cardboard.

8. Again use the nose template and glue it on or paint the black nose end yourself.

9. Draw or paint in the mouth, then the white hair.

Finished puppet

34

1. Colour in 2 beaks, combs, wattles and eyes or use the templates to cut out coloured cardboard ones.
2. Paint both sides of the head and upper neck.
3. Glue outer part of beak and of comb together.
4. Place open side over plate edge. Mark where they go.
5. Glue them on.
6. Glue on wattle and eyes.

Bird head

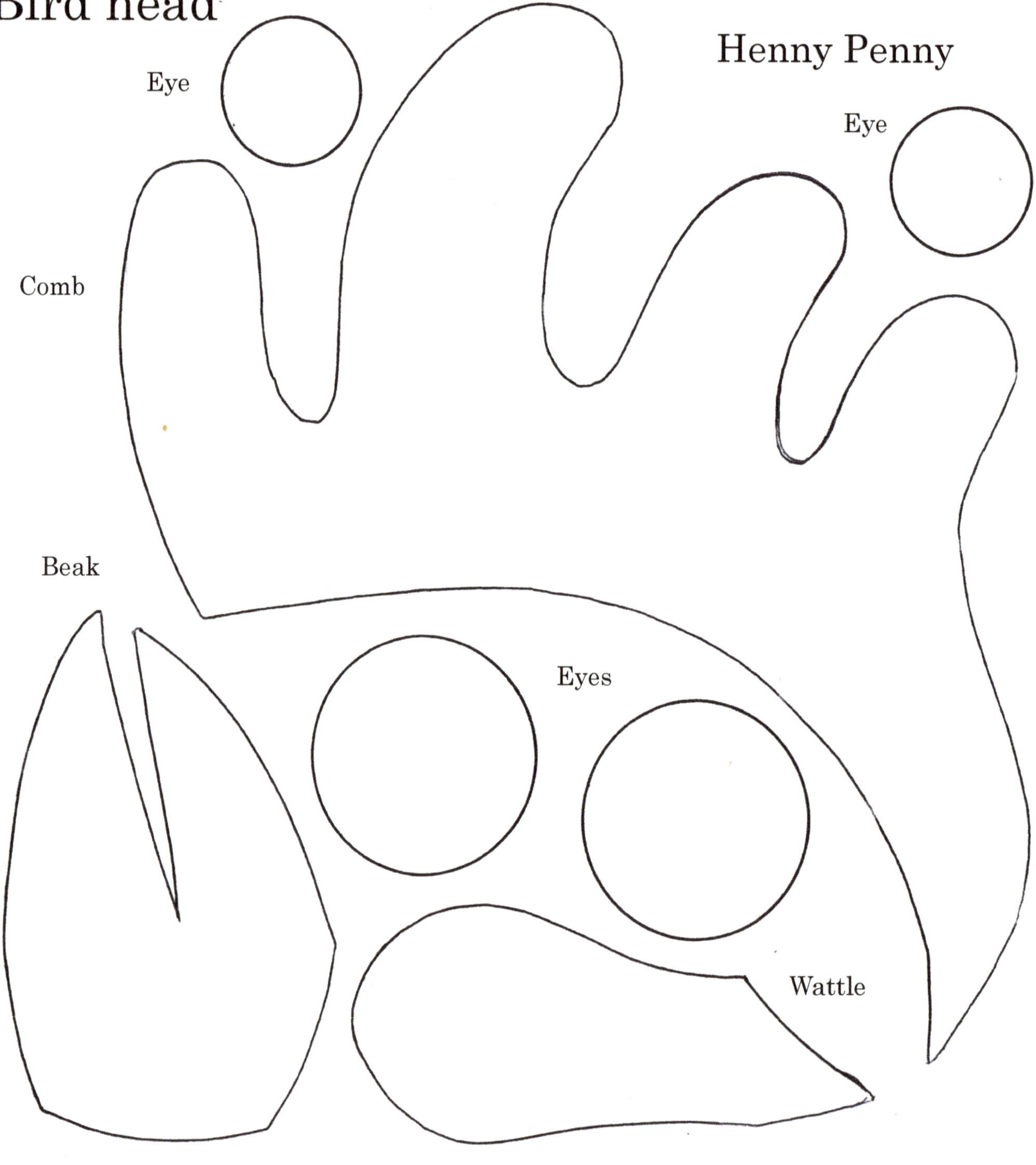

Eye

Comb

Beak

Henny Penny

Eye

Eyes

Wattle

Puppet bodies

Choose a piece of material to make a 50-70cm square. This decides the puppets colouring.

60cm of 115cm polycotton is enough for 2 bodies.	A small 50-70cm square scarf makes a very good body.	A larger square scarf needs a 13cm hem all round.

  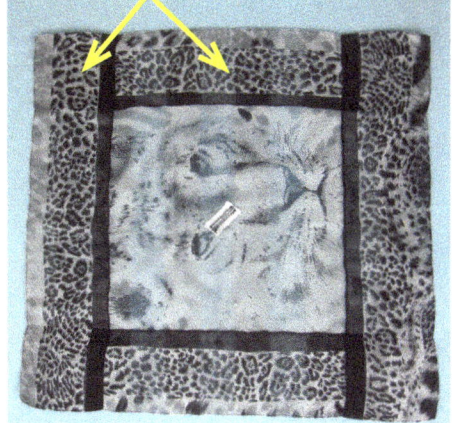

1. Hem all the sides. Measure across diagonally. Draw a 4cm line at centre of that diagonal line.

2. Glue an 8cm x 2cm piece of tape or firm material over the line to reinforce the area.

4. Make a cardboard strip to go across the upright. Put two 1/8" holes in the middle as shown.

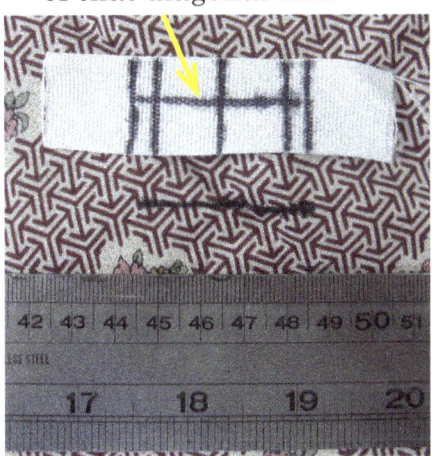

3. When dry, make a 3.5cm cut along that line. The neck goes through the slit.

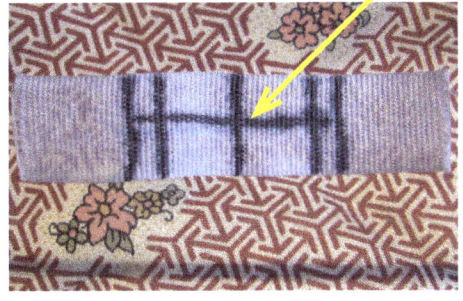

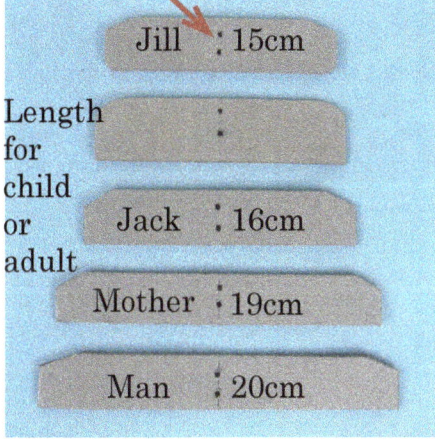

Length for child or adult:
- Jill : 15cm
- Jack : 16cm
- Mother : 19cm
- Man : 20cm

Human

5. Put in place, square to the upright, mark, then make holes through the upright.

6. Slip the material up the upright and position card strip to hold it in place.

7. Fasten together with paper fasteners when everything is in place.

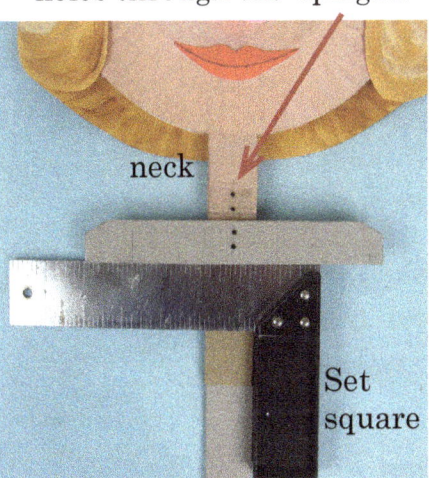

neck

Set square

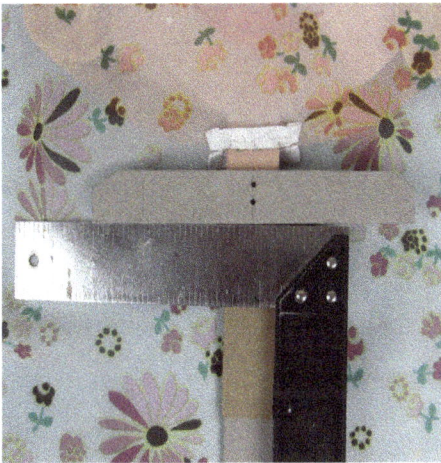

Paper fasteners

36

Cat, birds, animal.

Choose material as mentioned on p 29 and follow steps 1,2,3 to make the body.

4. Make a cardboard strip to go across the upright. Put two 1/8" holes in the middle as shown.

Kitten's chest 12cm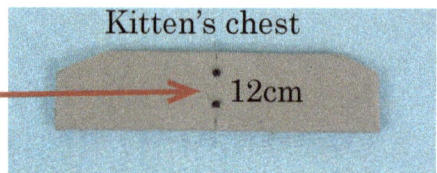

Mother's chest 15cm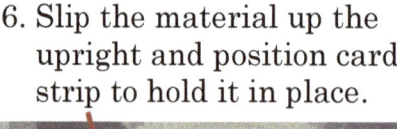

5. Put in place, square to the upright, mark, then make holes through the upright.

6. Slip the material up the upright and position card strip to hold it in place.

7. Fasten together with paper fasteners when everything is in place.

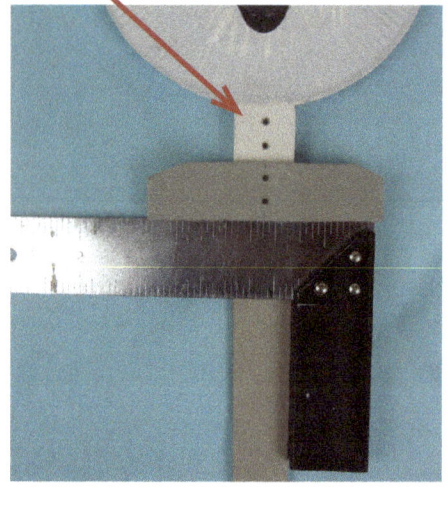 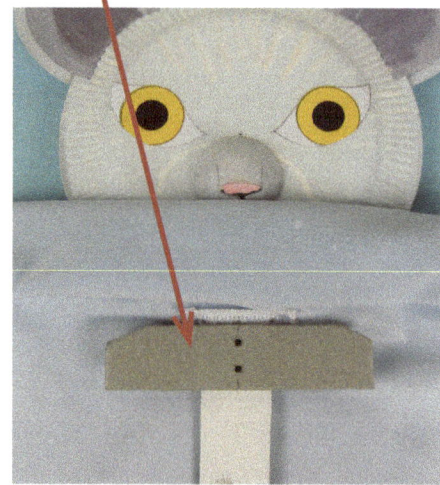 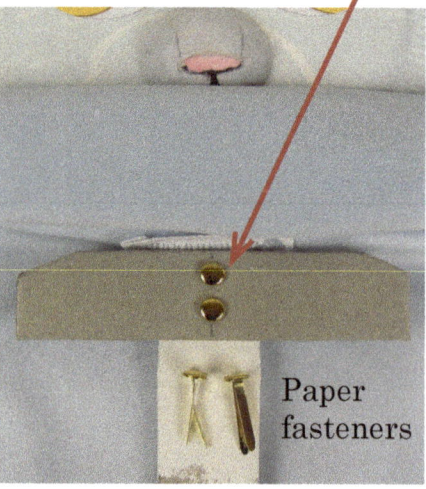

Paper fasteners

4. Make more cardboard strips with holes according to the lengths on each illustration.

Chook
No neck
8cm
Holes in middle
Set square

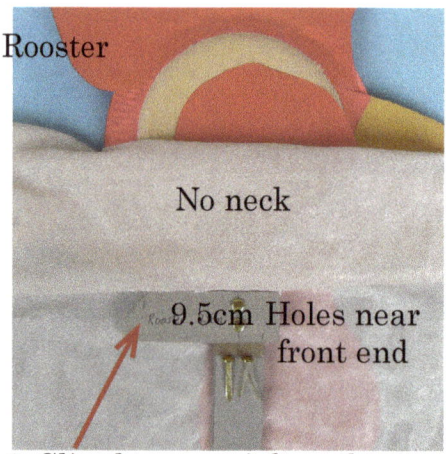

Rooster
No neck
9.5cm Holes near front end

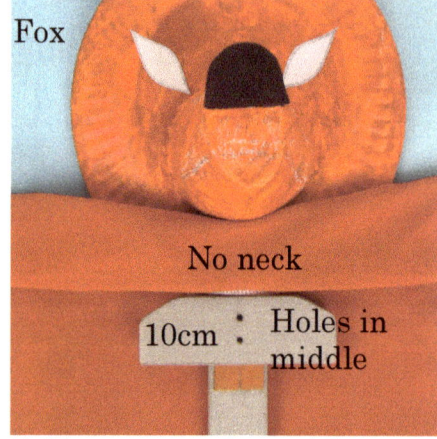

Fox
No neck
10cm Holes in middle

5. Put in place, square to the upright, mark, then make holes through the upright.

6. Slip the material up the upright and position card strip to hold it in place.

7. Fasten together with paper fasteners when everything is in place.

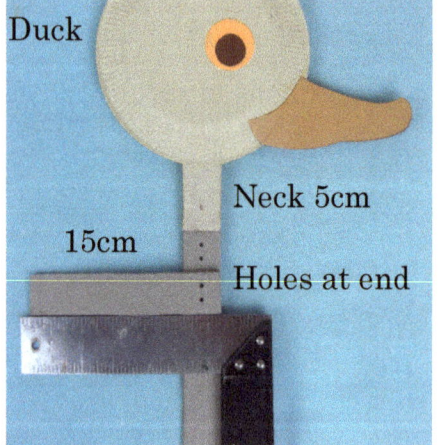

Duck
Neck 5cm
15cm
Holes at end

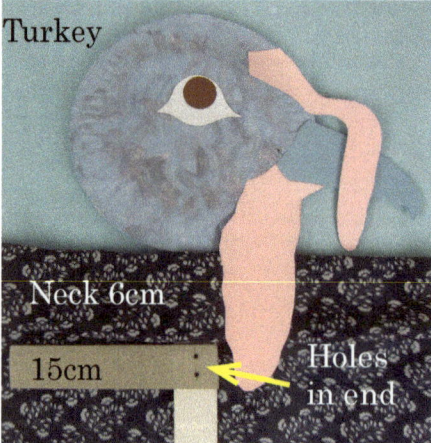

Turkey
Neck 6cm
15cm Holes in end

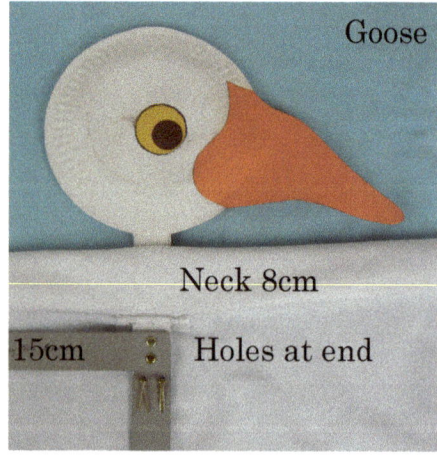

Goose
Neck 8cm
15cm Holes at end

Hands, paws, hoofs.

1. Cut out hands.
2. Paint them.
3. Glue a kebab stick to the back of the hand. (Extend with a second kebab stick if more length is required).
4. Fold back scarf corner.
5. Fold the corner in half.
6. Check the hand fits.
7. Glue scarf along edges.

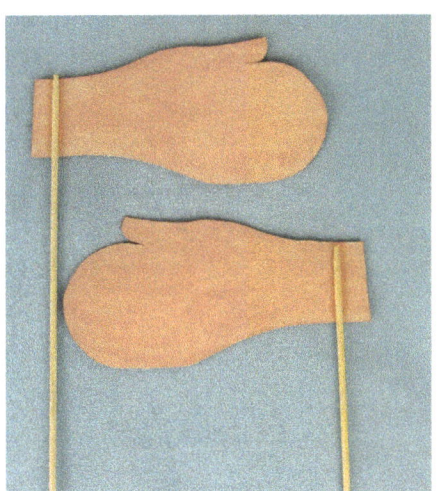   

8. Put glue on the front and back of wrist area, place hand on the scarf with the thumbs up.
9. Fold scarf over it and put slight pressure on it. Leave it to dry.
10. Glue 6cm x 3cm x 1cm rectangle of padding, such as foam, around each kebab as a handle.

* Follow the same steps for paws and hoofs. Remember to do opposites and front and back.

Turn over to get opposites	Top and bottom of cat paw	Top and bottom of fox paw	Top and bottom of dog paw	Kebab joined in
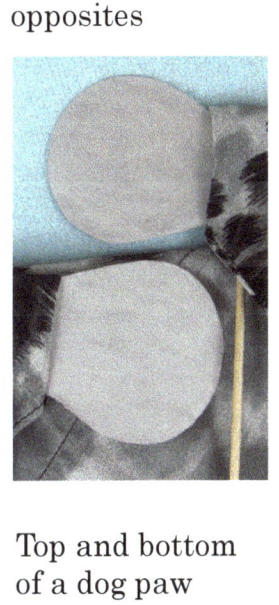	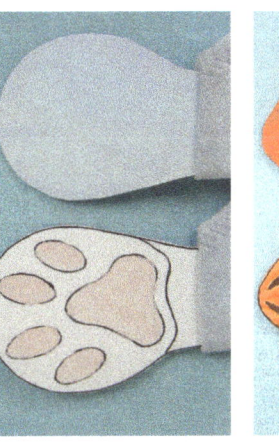		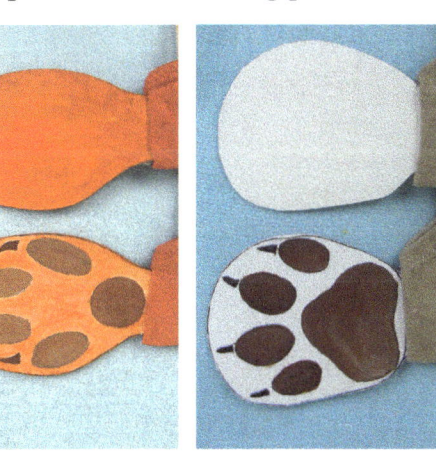	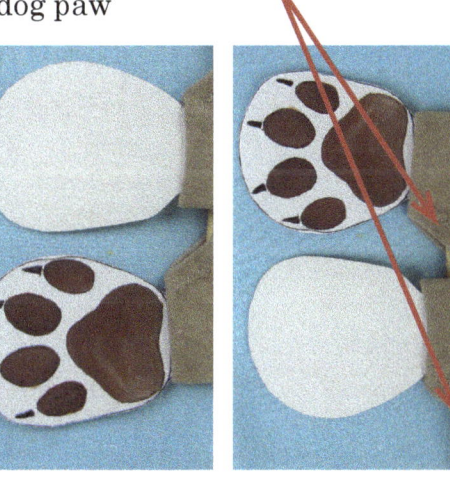
Top and bottom of a dog paw	Pig hoofs	Horse hoofs	Cow hoofs	Kebab joined in
	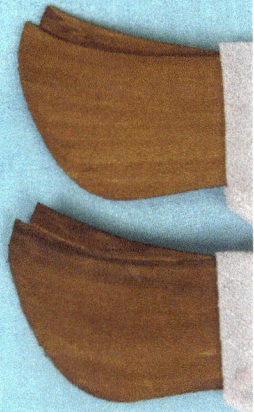	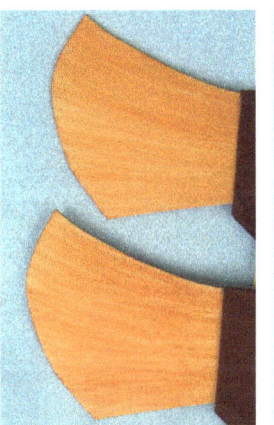		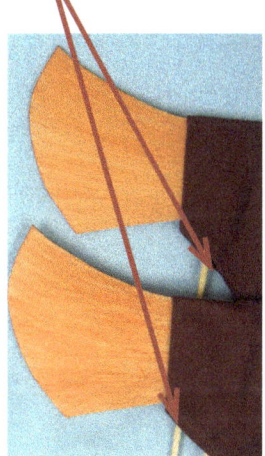

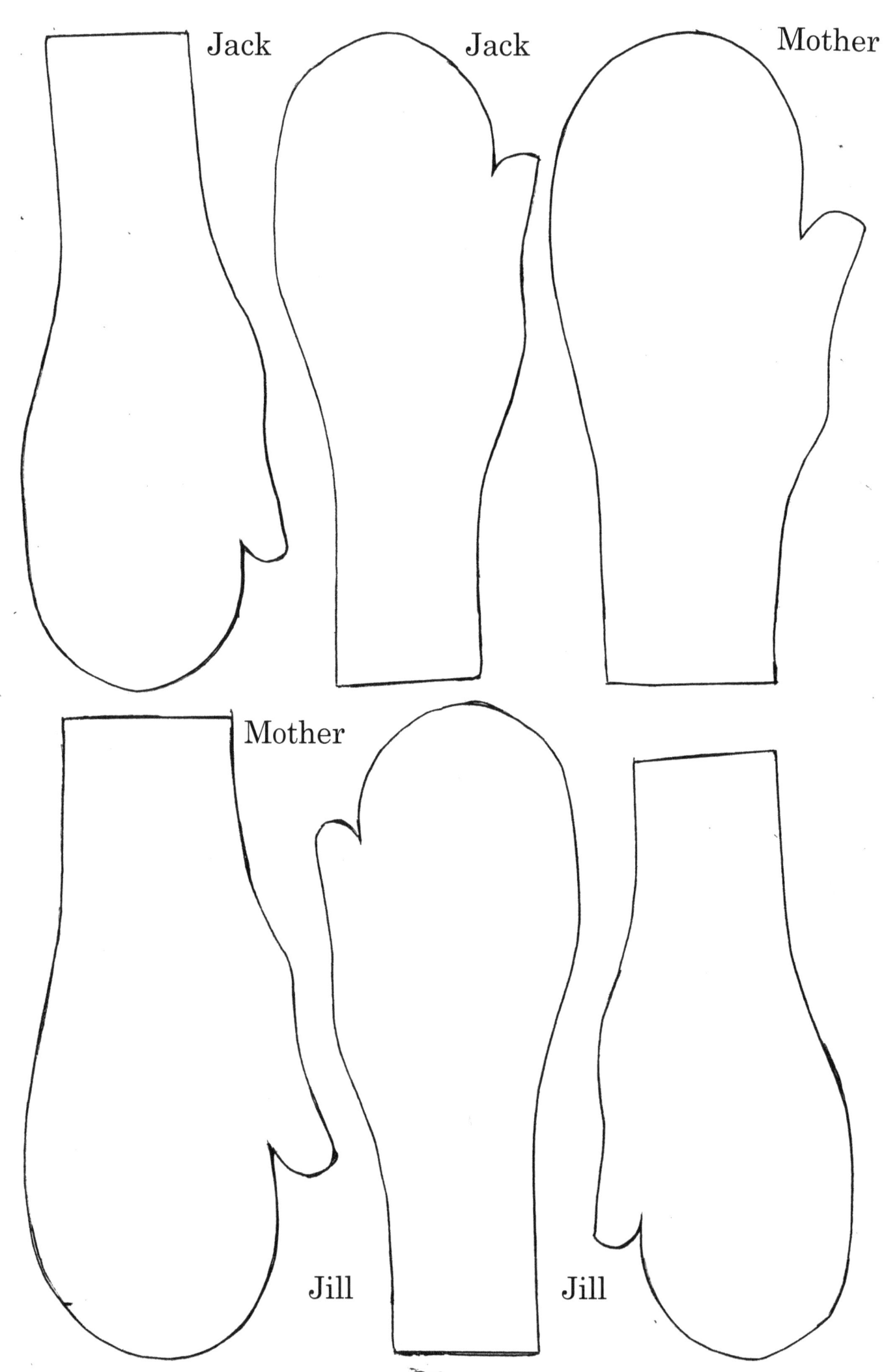

Each pair across is already turned over so is a correct pair.

3 Kittens

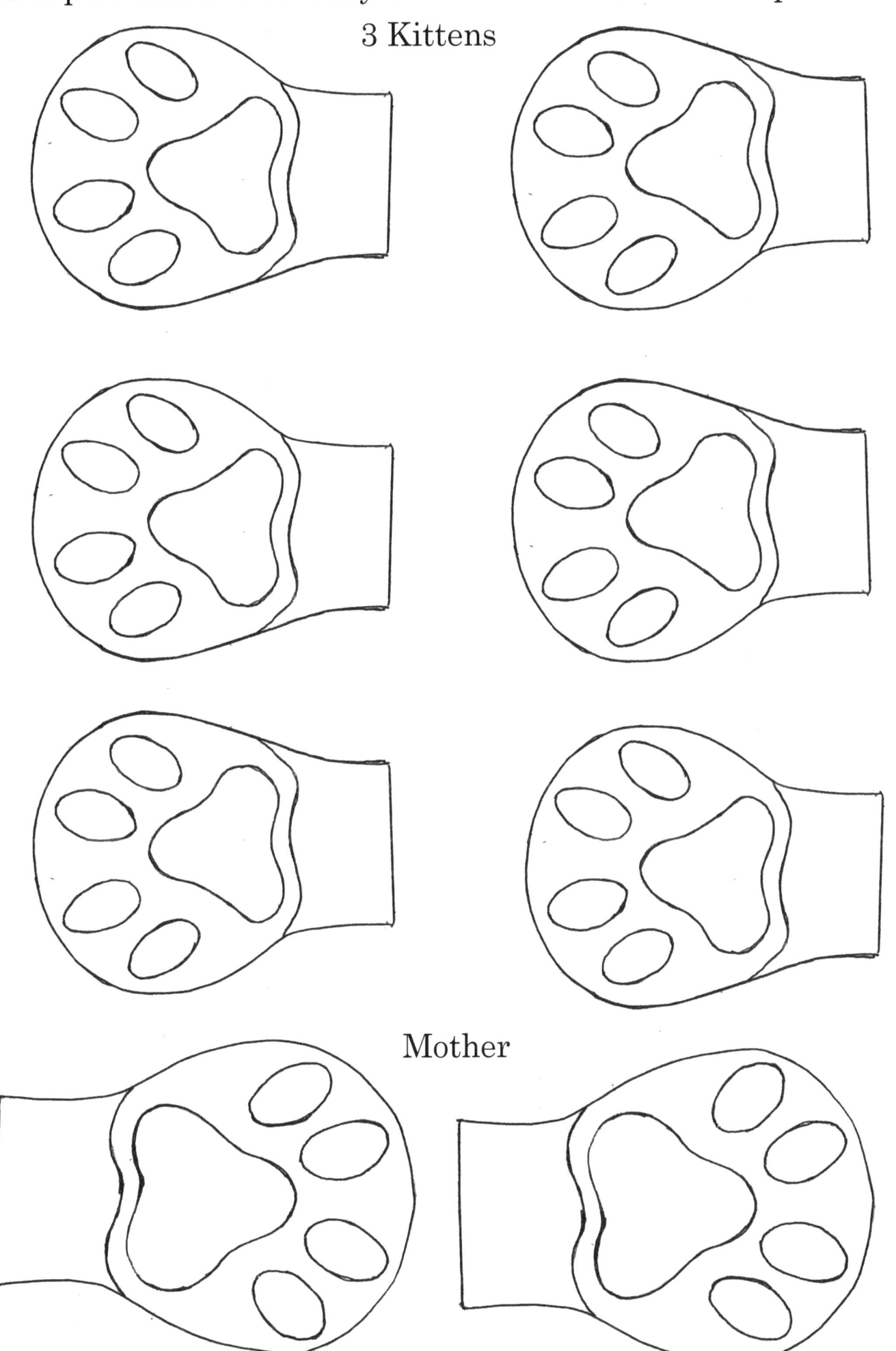

Mother

Each is a correct pair, one is turned over already.

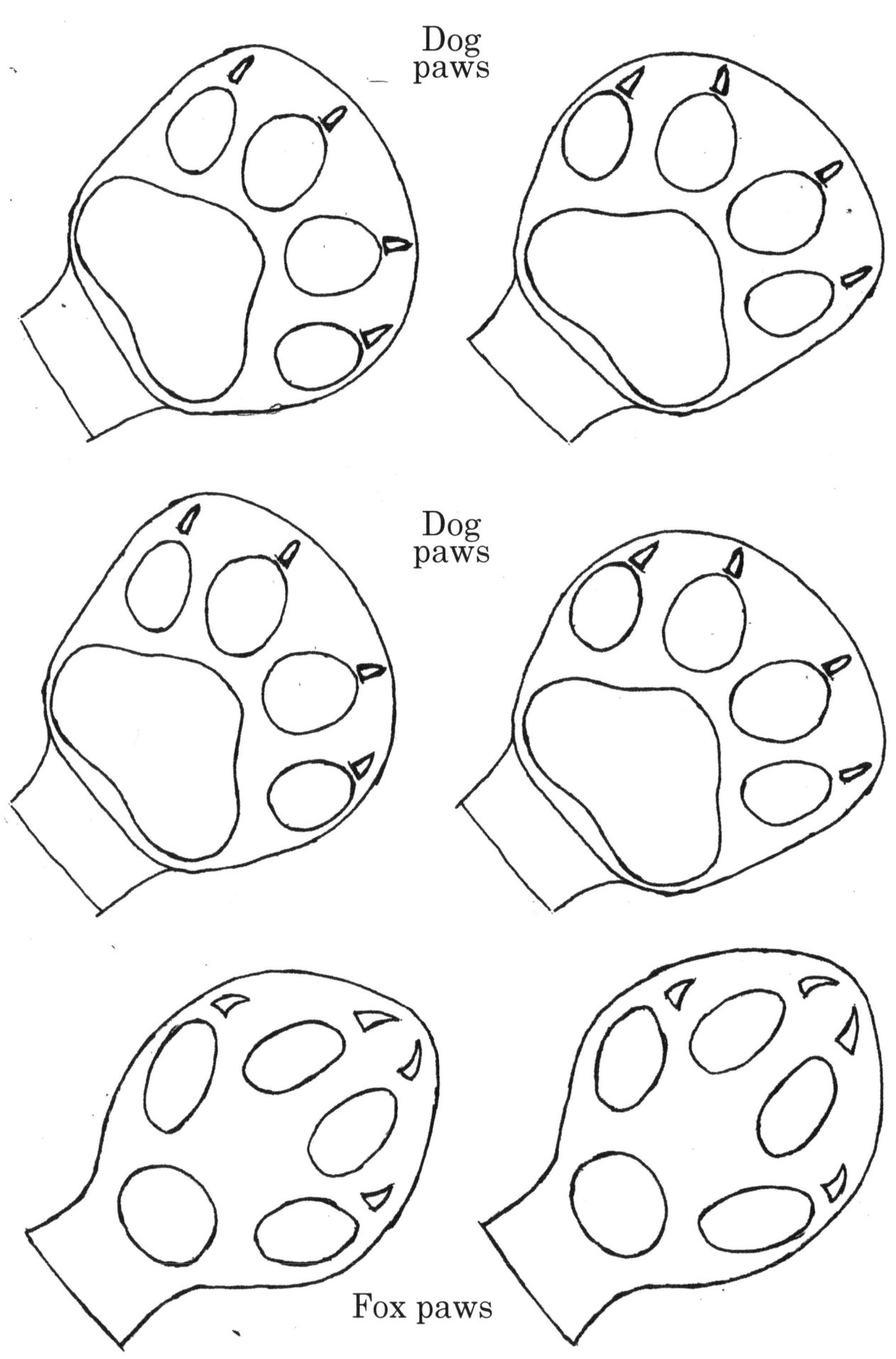

Dog paws

Dog paws

Fox paws

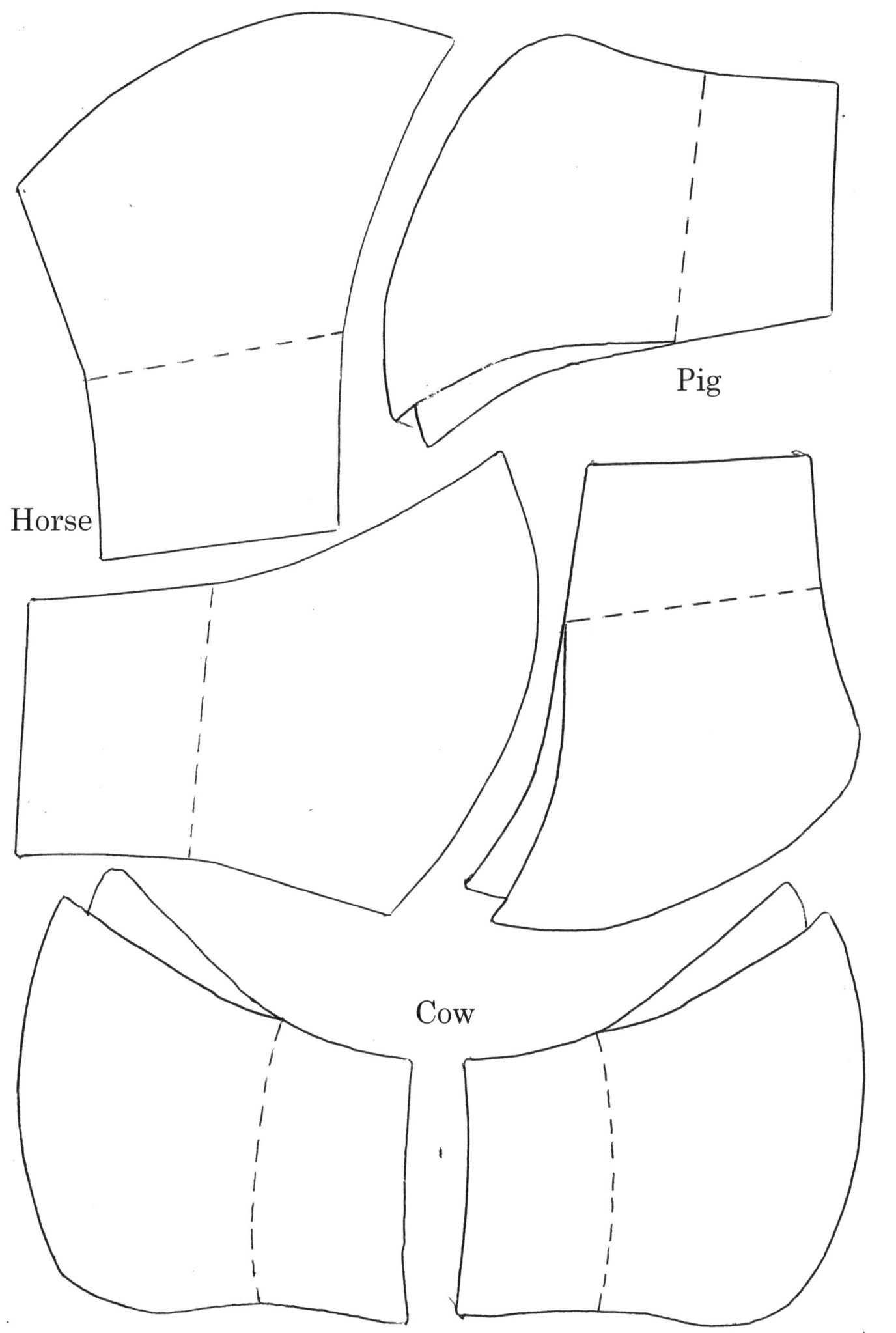

Bird's wing

A wing can be held resting along the bird's back, point at something, hold things and flap in flight, etc.

1. Cut a 7cm x 7cm or bigger cardboard square.
2. Divide it diagonally.

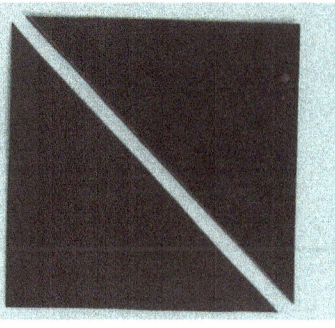

3. Fold triangle in half. Glue in a stick.   4. Put glue on both sides of the triangle. Place it on the bird's wing point.
   5. Fold point over it.

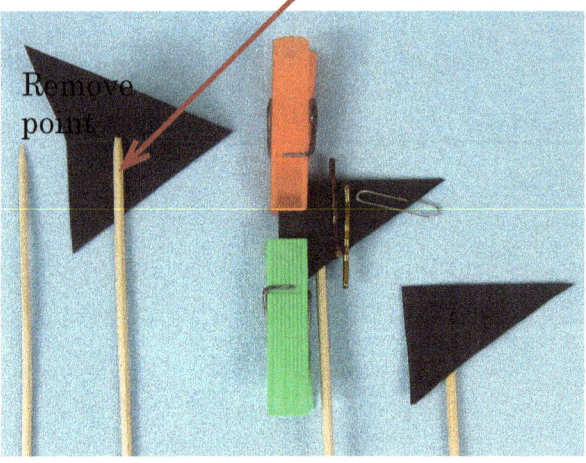

Remove point

Joining kebab sticks together ~ materials needed ~
Glue, tape, scissors, sandpaper, and 2 kebab sticks.

If it is a small overlap, to get maximum kebab length, make it as strong as possible.

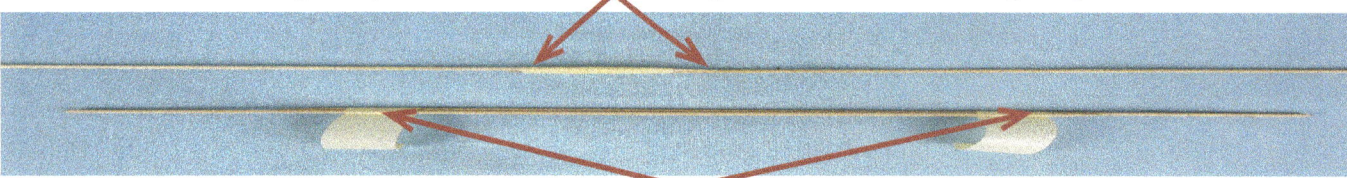

If there is plenty of overlap, bind the join near both ends of the overlap. Pinch the tape round the first stick, then go round the second stick and bind them together with several layers.

Strong joint
Flatten one side of each kebab stick with sandpaper or a file in the overlapping area and glue those flat sides together. Then bind round join with tape.

Glue the two flat surfaces together, clamp and dry.   Place on tape, wrap short end round, pinch tight on sticks and stick tape together.   Wrap long end round, glue, clamp.

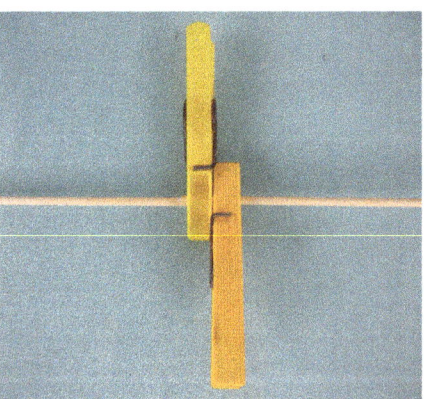
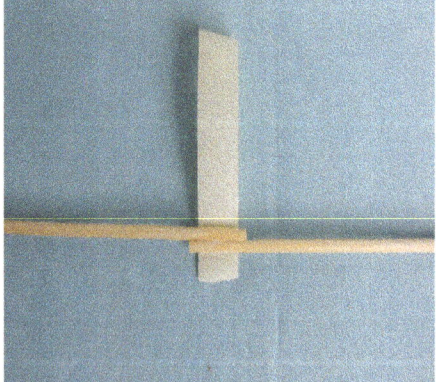
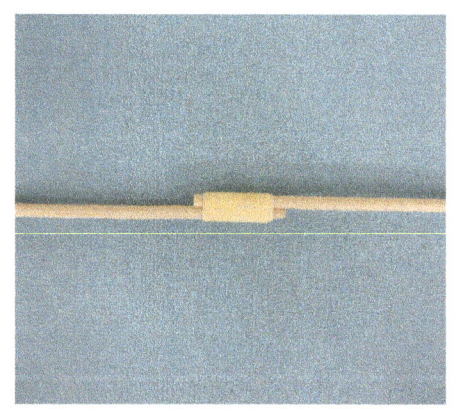

Bird tails

Join a kebab to the tail, fold back the corner of the material and glue like the paws etc.
It can be kept in place poked into a hole in the handle.

Chook ~ bold, slightly fanned tail painted both sides on strong cardboard.

Duck ~ same method as for chook. Make the tail long enough to be seen in the duck dive.

Goose ~ has a small insignificant tail. Card painted on both sides.

Rooster ~ 2 large 23cm paper plates give a good 3D effect. See rooster tail p46.

Turkey ~ could be a simple one and not open in a fan.
For fun this one opens - see the directions on the turkey tail p48 if you want to try it.

The bird's tail kebab can be taken out of its support hole to do actions. They were all glued at about a 45 degree angle.

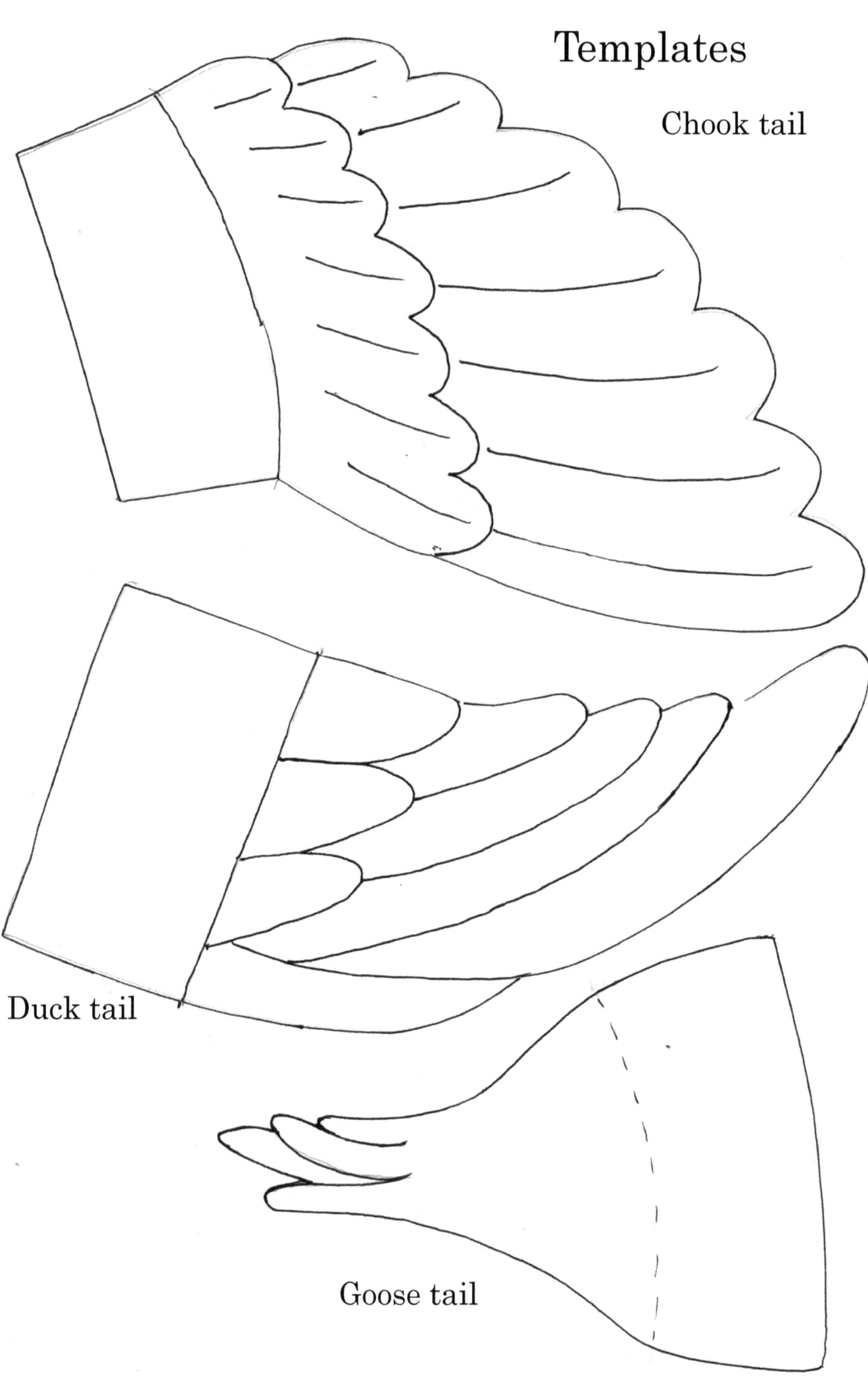

Rooster

1. Draw over template lines with a soft lead pencil then place that side on the plate and draw over the lines again (they are visible through the paper), transferring the lines to the plate.
2. Turn the template over again, draw over the lines again transferring them to second plate.
3. Or draw your own matching feather design on the plates.

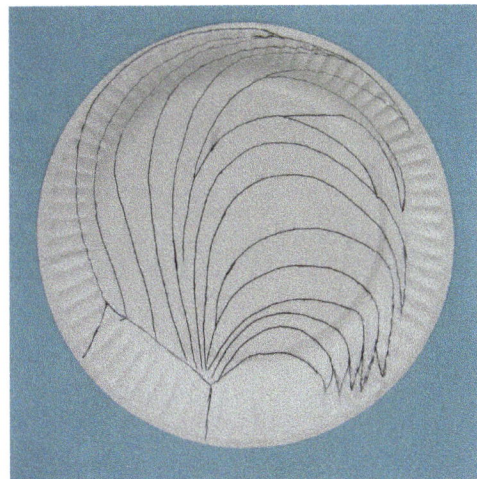

It has to be the reverse on the other plate.

Don't try to fill the plate ripples, they give the tail character.

The other side can be a bit different but needs to be the same shape.

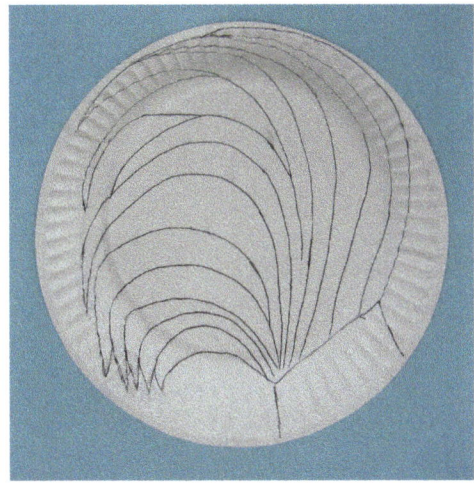

1. Paint feathers on.
2. Cut out edge, join plates.
3. Match feathers.
4. Cut them out.
5. Join them.
6. Join to material

Glue kebab at an angle.

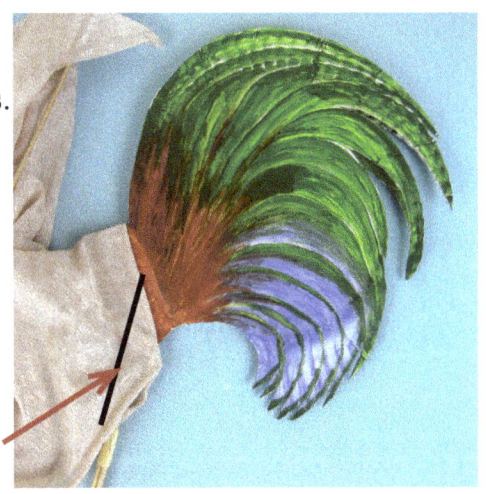

Lengthen wing and tail kebabs.

Make a hole for the tail kebab.

Wing is 2 kebabs in length with a 3cm overlapping joint.

Tail has an 18cm overlapping joint, adjust this to suit your puppet.

Make a hole at an angle in the back of the cylinder with a small skewer. Enlarge with bigger skewer or drill.

Glue a triangular card on the outside to support tail kebab.

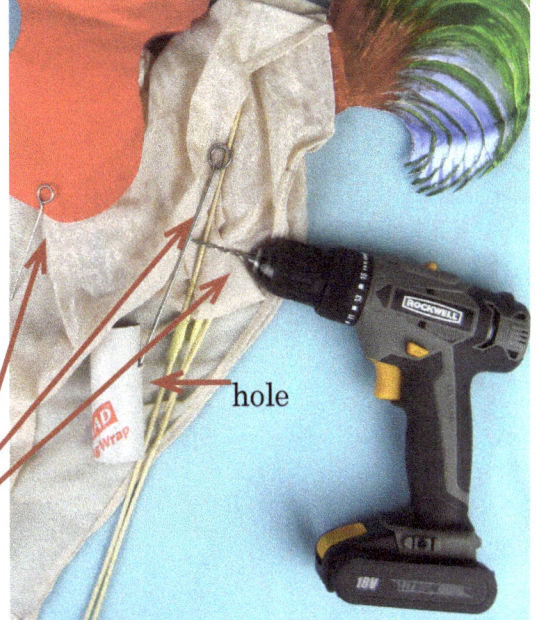

Rooster tail template.

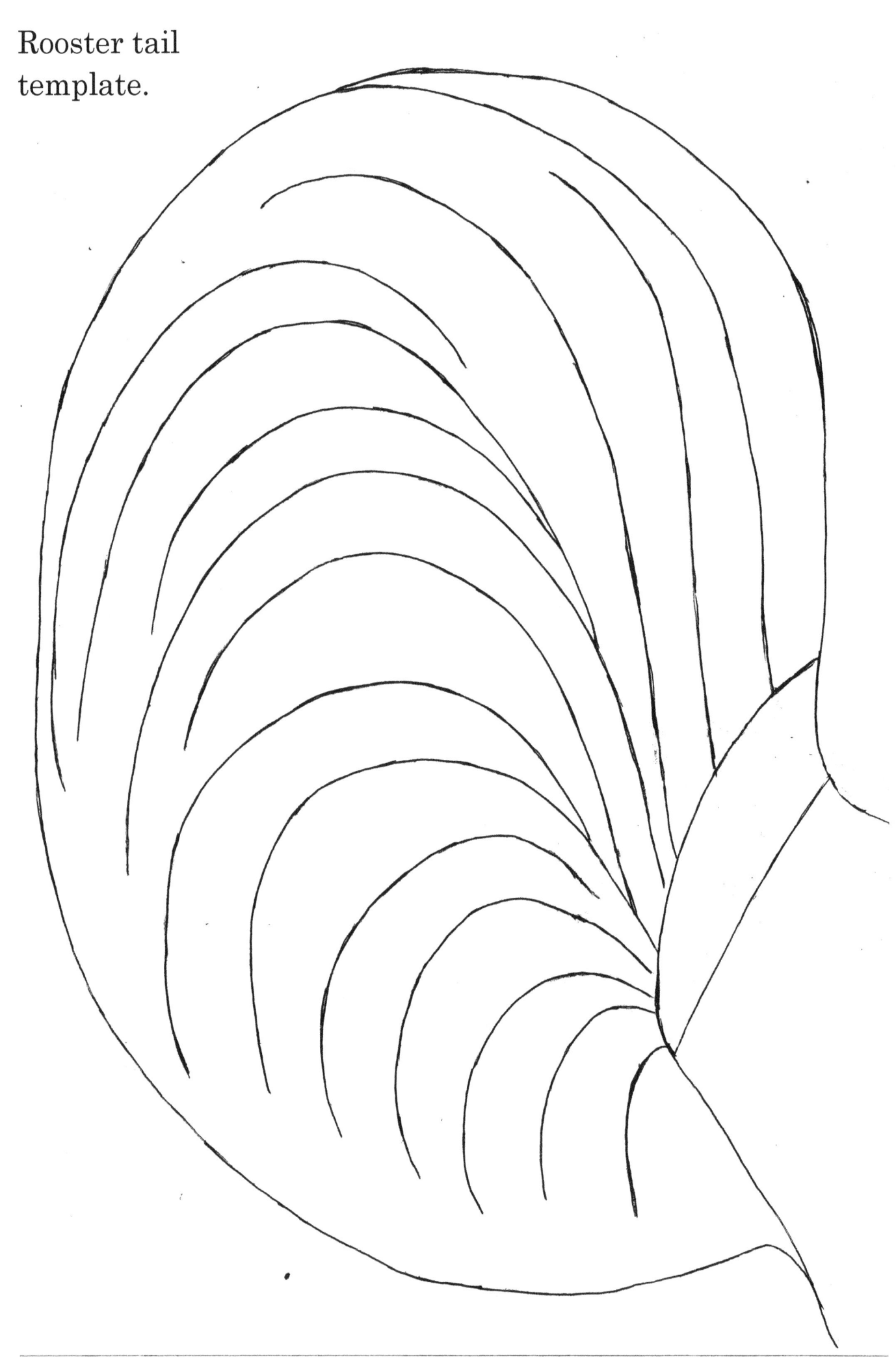

Making the turkey tail.

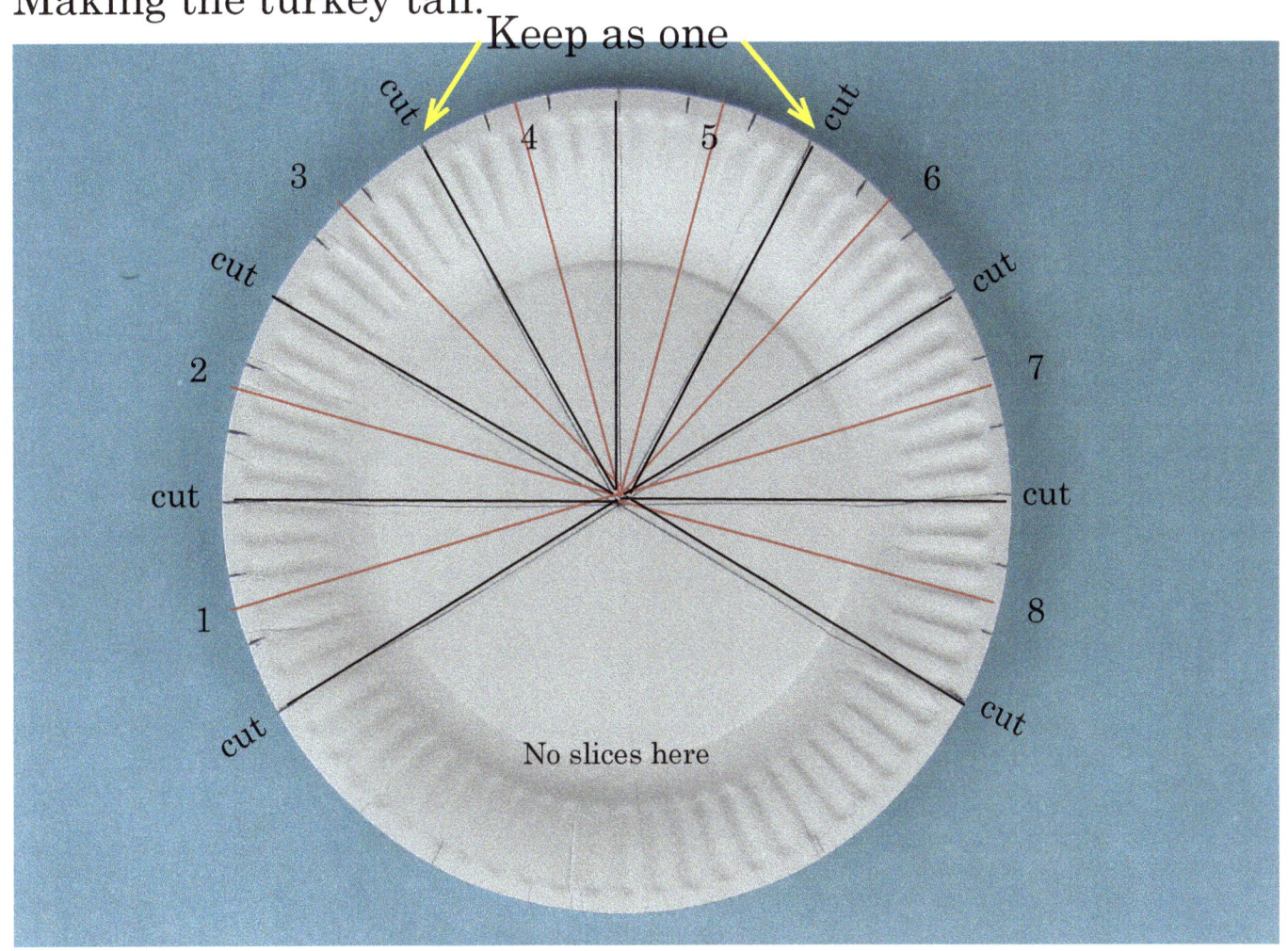

1. Mark a plate into eight 6cm slices (black line) as shown above. (none at the bottom).
2. Mark down the the centre of each slice. (red line)
3. Do not cut the top centre 2 slices - keep them joined together.
4. Cut out the other 6 slices (on the black line).
5. Draw and cut out two 9cm diameter circles in strong white cardboard. Put a hole through the centre of each.

6. On strong white card draw out eight 2cm x 19cm strips.
7. Mark the centre line down each one and a spot 3cm from one end.
8. Cut out the 8 strips (on the black line).
9. Put a small hole through each 3cm mark. (This is to be the centre of the tail)

48

On the underside of the tail glue a strip down the back of each slice. Line up the slice down the centre with the point touching the hole in the following order ~

10. Do no 4 on the centre uncut piece first, then overlap this with a strip on no 5.
11. Glue one strip down the back of each of the remaining 6 slices.

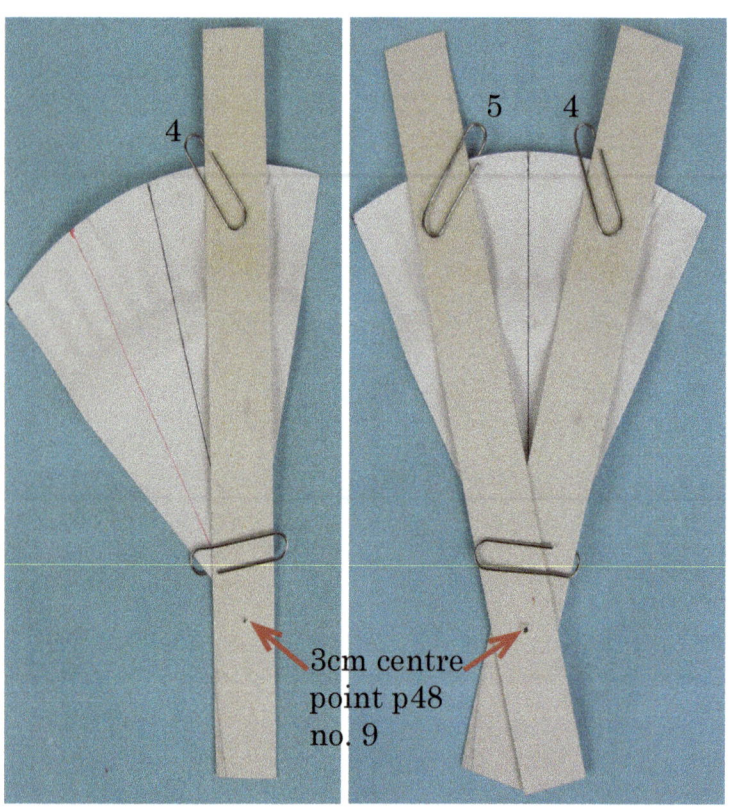

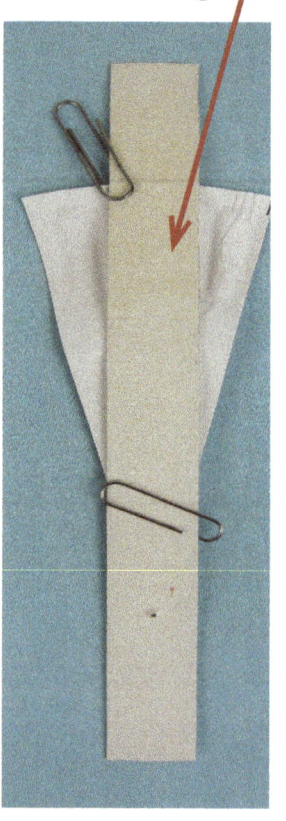

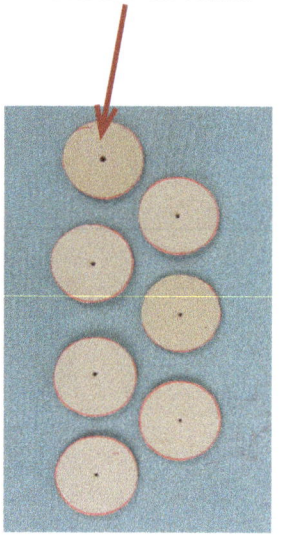

12. Cut 7 x 2cm cardboard washers out of the strip card.

13. Put a hole in the centre of each.

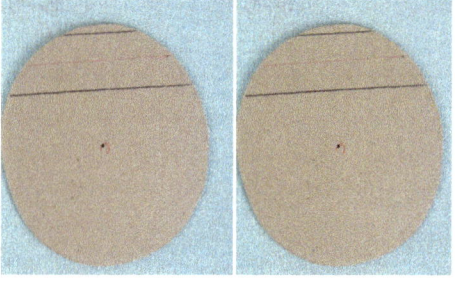

Make this a good strong joint.

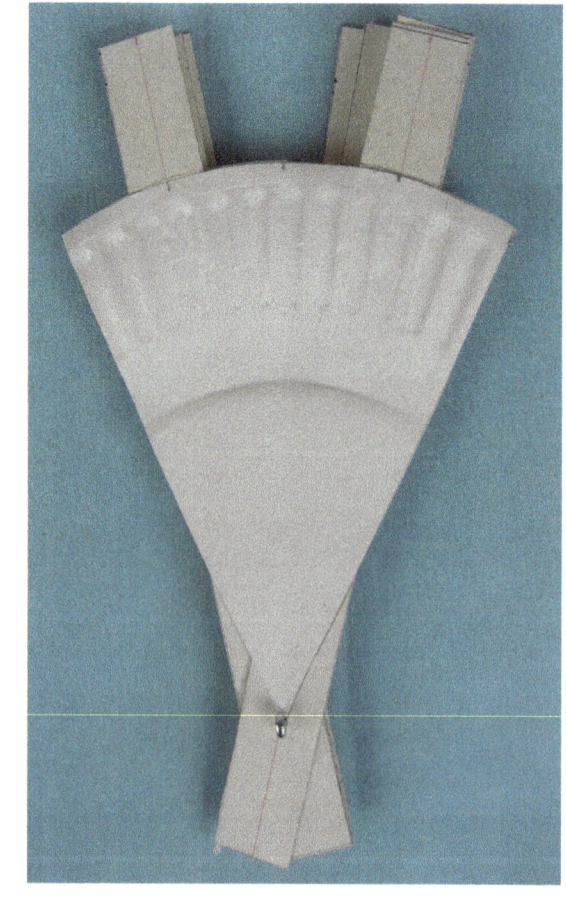

14. Cut 2 x 9cm diameter circles in stronger cardboard (as above).

15. Join each to a white circle cut out at no 5. These are the front and back circles for mounting the tail.

16. Paint, one to suit the front and one to suit the back, on the white side.

17. Enlarge the holes in all the above.

18. Put a wood screw or something through the centre of the 9cm diameter circle. That will be the back of the tail from the right side.

19. Then add a washer, slice, washer, slice, etc. in the following order ~ 1, 8, 2, 7, 3, 6, 4/5. (all slices must be right side up).

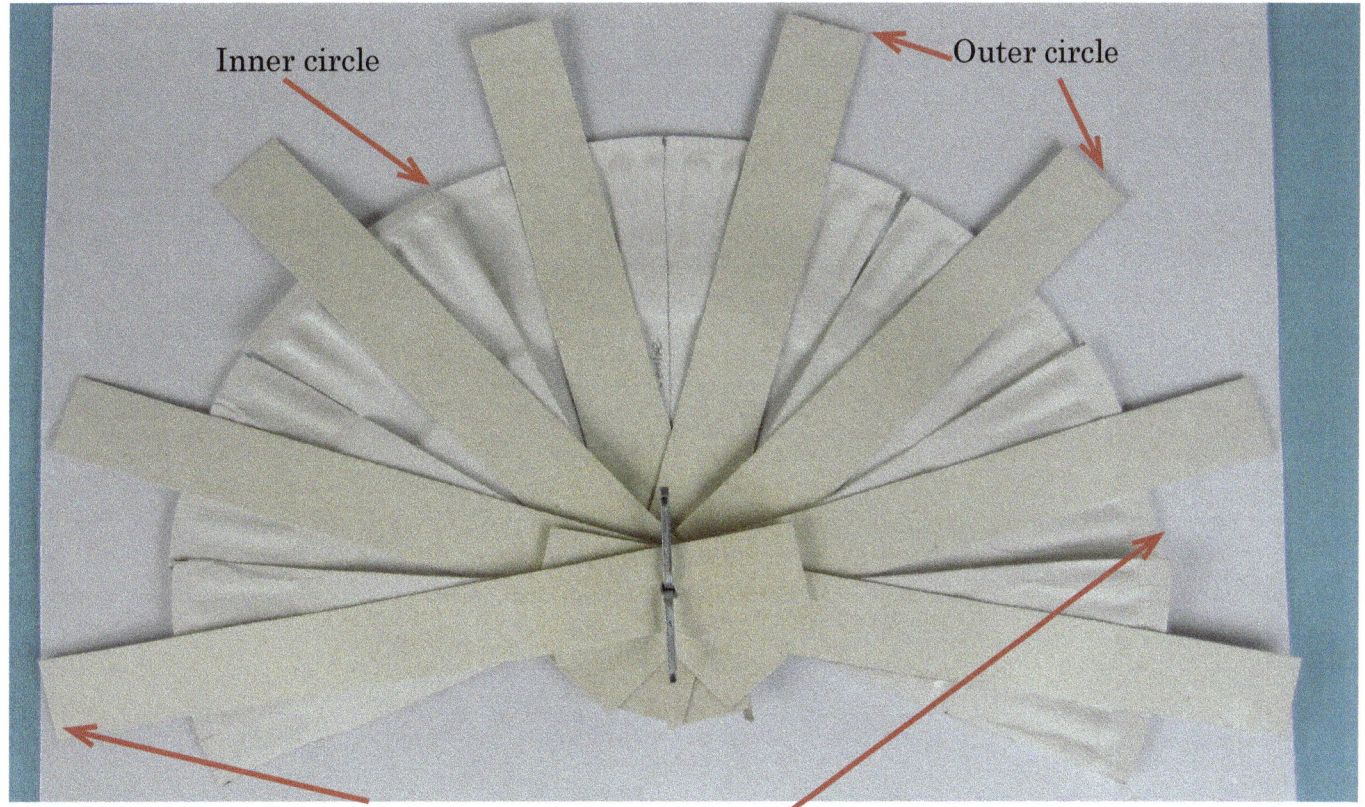

Inner circle   Outer circle

20. Fan them all out on a piece of A4 art paper and draw where the circle goes.
21. Draw another circle 2cm out from this around the ends of the strips.
22. Cut the inside circle out, check it fits your fan tail, then cut the outside circle.

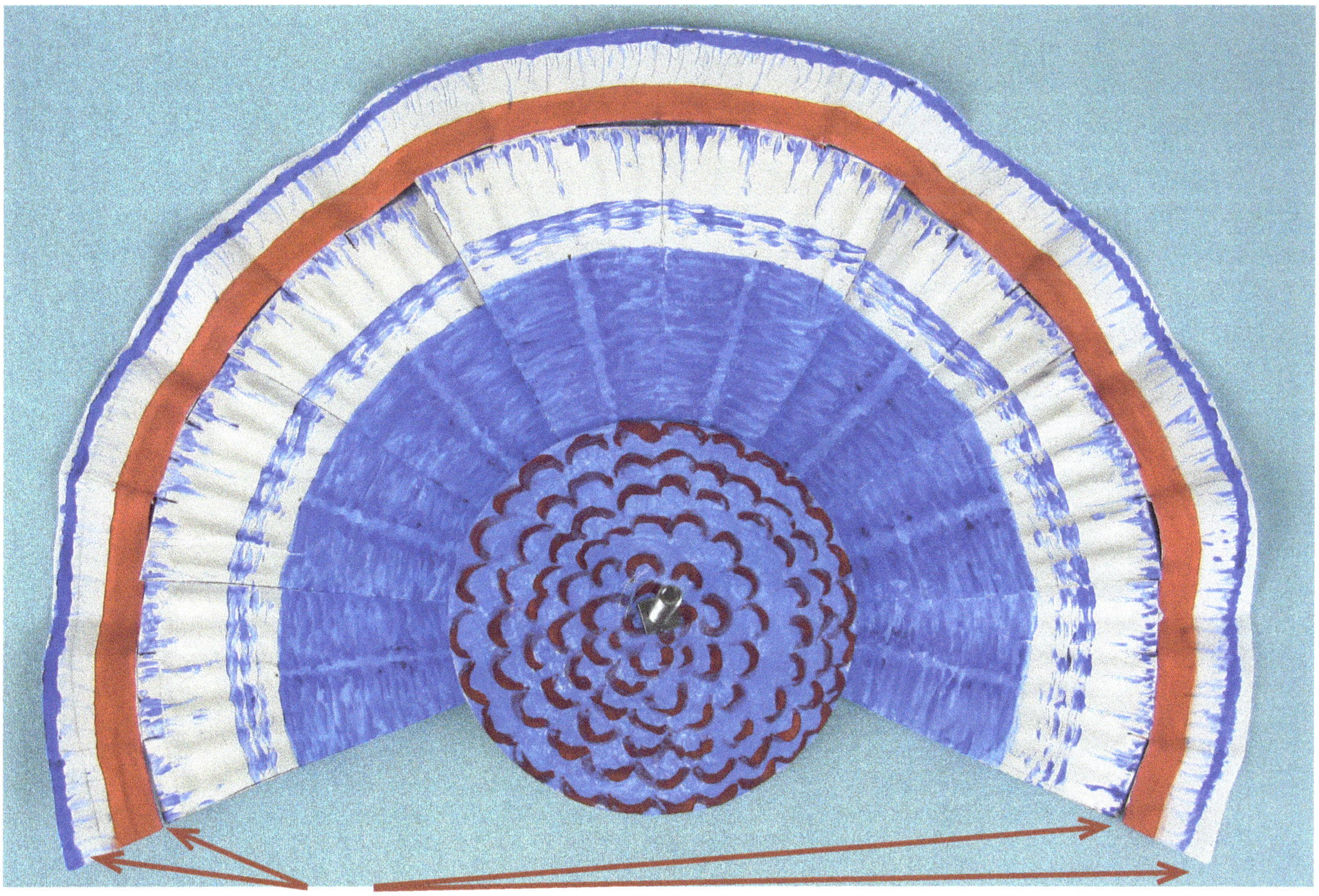

23. Glue it in place (on the right side around the top of the plate) to the strips sticking up.
24. Paint the tail.

Add 12cm lengths of strong cardboard to the 15cm body to match the thickness of the upright. Continue with 15cm strips to go across the upright, make it fit tightly. Extend fitting holes. When finished, cut the end square and straight, to have a good glue surface for the tail joint.

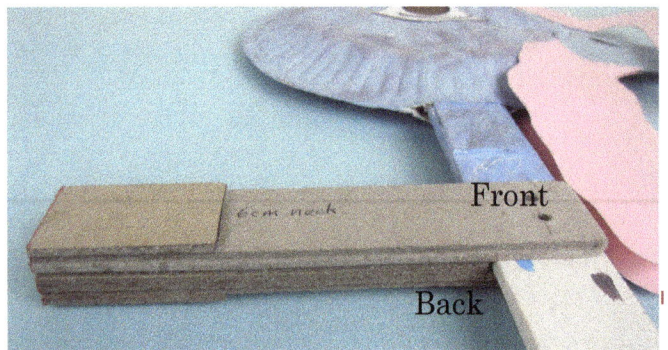

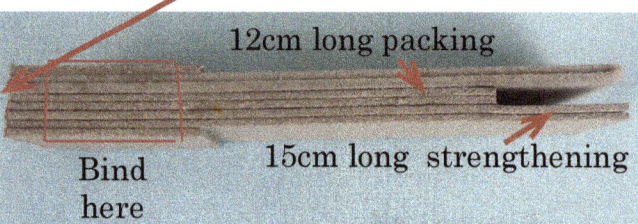

Bind around the end to strengthen it, then drill a small hole in the centre of the end to take a wood screw that will be the tail's axis.

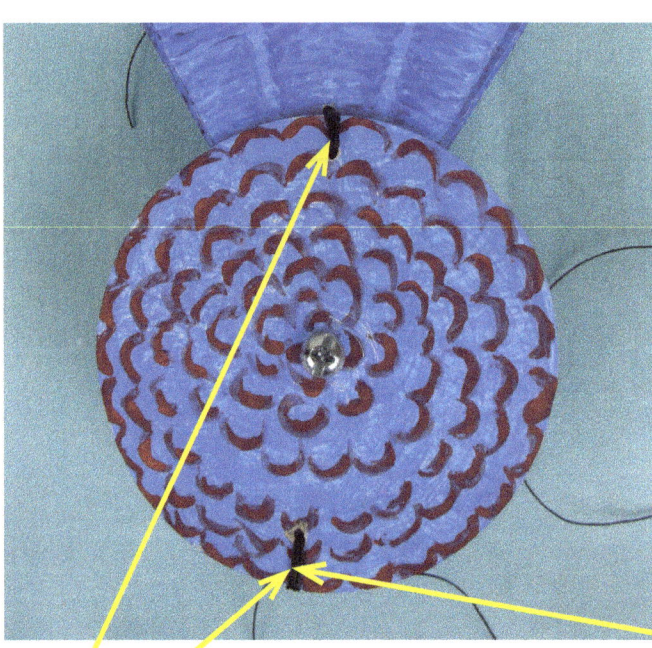

Stitch the 2 circles together top and bottom for strength and to make a barrier at the top so slices can't cross over each other.

Build up a layered cardboard support to hold the 2 circles firmly in place. Tie circles firmly, going inside and outside of this.

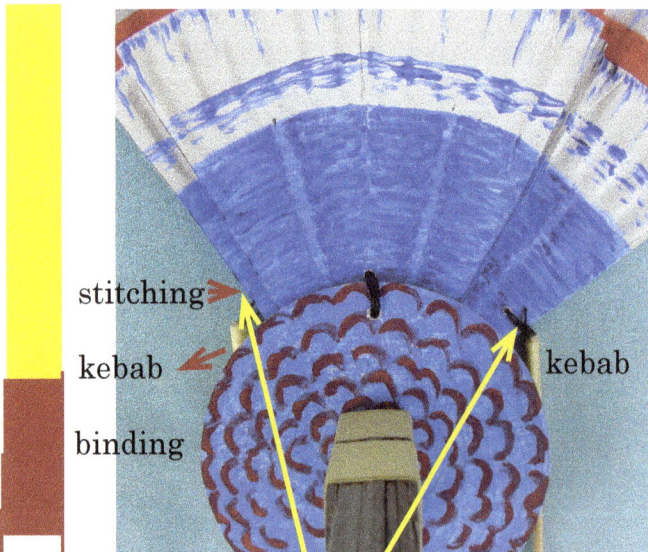

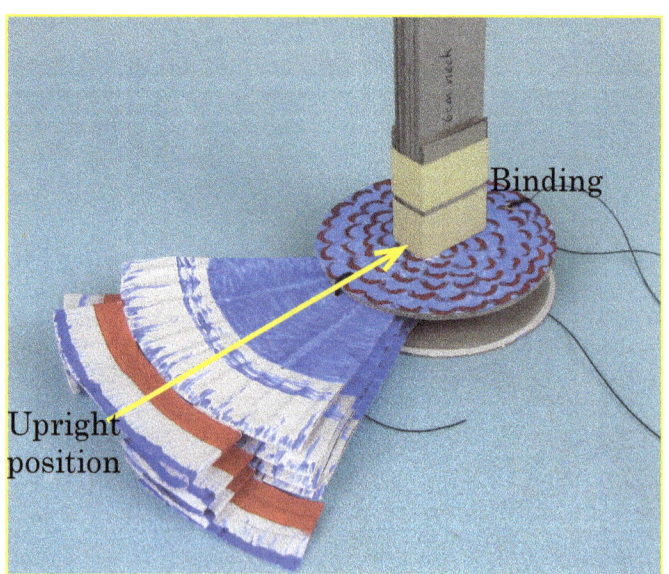

Make a loop of strong thread at the end and bind it to the kebab.
Stitch through it to the edge of bottom slice. Leave a bit of room for the kebab to pivot.
Use the kebabs to gently open and close tail.

Put glue on the body end and a wood screw through the circle centre. Screw into the end hole, keeping tail in upright position.
Tighten gently until glue is dry, then loosen enough for easy movement.

Animal tails

  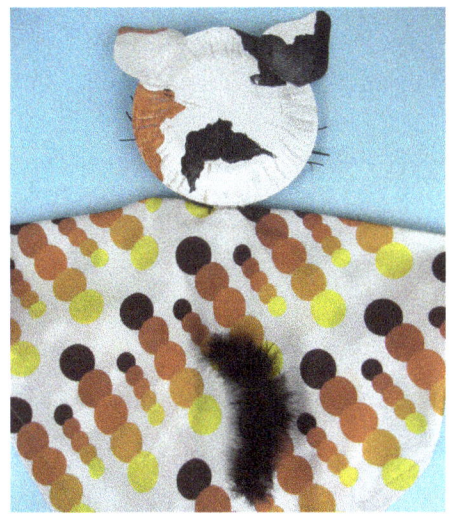

Fox tail is 3 layers of cardboard glued together.

Cow tail is cord and wagging it causes the hoofs to kick up.

Kitten's tail is a small furry feather boa.

Pig tail
1. Glue 4 pieces of card together with the spiral on top.
2. When dry cut the spiral out. It will keep its curl.
3. Cut to the length you want.

Pig tail spiral

Start cutting here.

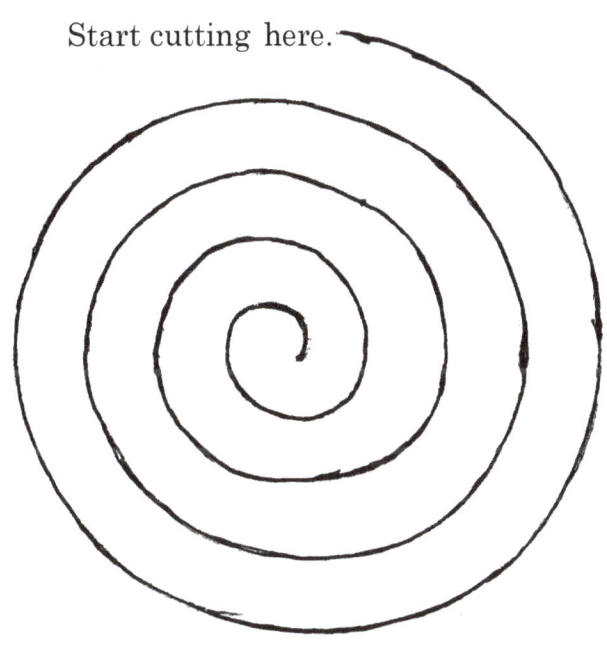

Kebab stick, card triangle, and cut out spiral.

Triangle folded over and glued to kebab and tail.

Clamped until dry. Material glue used for this.

 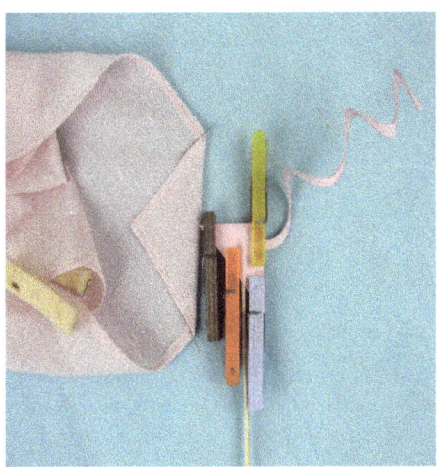 

Fox tail
Three template tails cut out in coloured cardboard joined together so it is stronger and holds its shape. Paint.

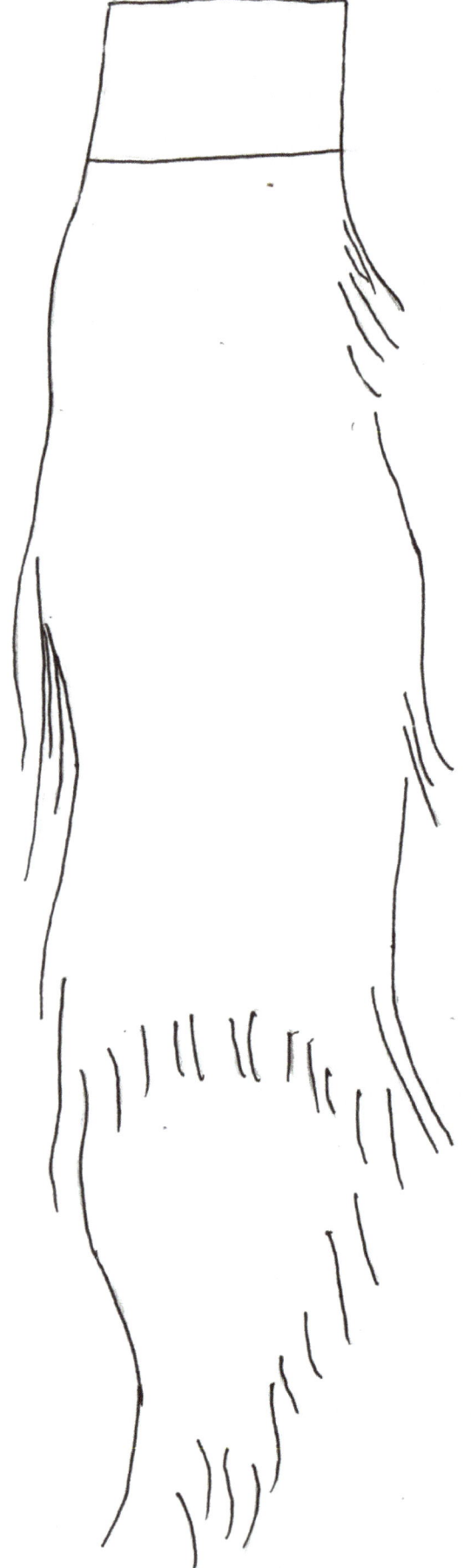

Kitten's tail
A length of brown fluffy boa.
Two 7cm x 4cm triangles cut out of white strong card.
Glue together and pinch tightly round the kebab.
Glue triangle to the inside of the material where the tail is joined on. Glue the tail on the outside.

 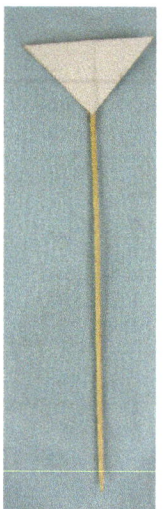 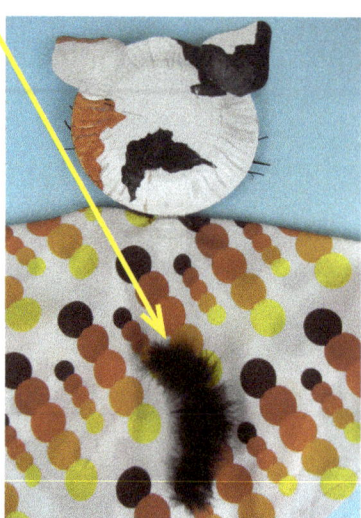

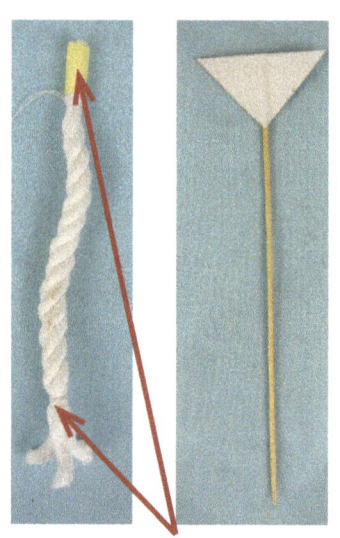 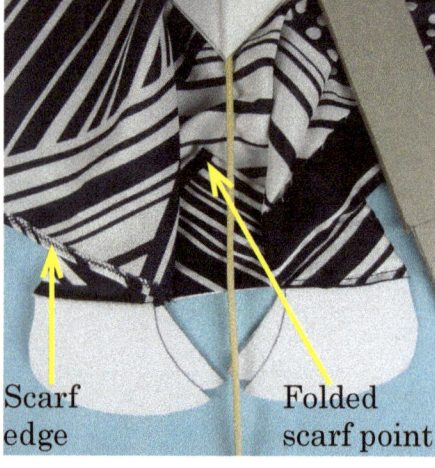

Scarf edge   Folded scarf point

A piece of cord, bound by cotton near the ends.
Frayed for tail end, and taped around to put in through a seam at the other end.

The kebab is mounted on the inside under where the tail is as shown in the picture above.

The material point was folded and glued back.

Each hoof was put at the fold corners. The folded side and the scarf edge were glued to either side of the hoof. They face forward when hanging.

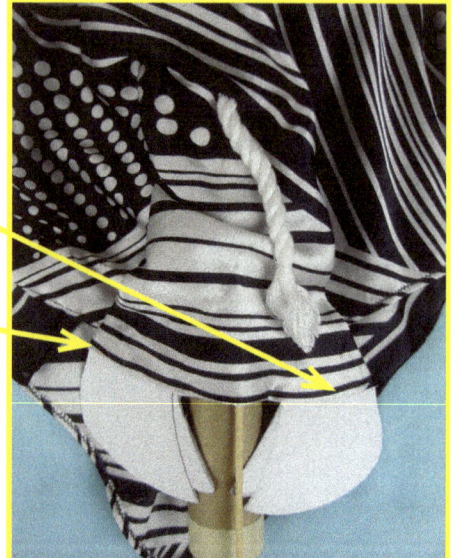

53

Rack for paper plate puppets.

Use strong cardboard cylinders from inside food wrap materials, etc (3cm diameter).

Cut into 3 or 4 pieces and sandpaper ends.

If it is too loose wrap 2 bands of tape around or
glue a sleeve of card inside the holder tube.

Body must fit firmly.

Put it 4.5cm into tube.

Birds go front to back. Animals go side to side.

Make angled holes for tails.

Remove tail out of holes when in holding cylinder.

Inner cylinders standing.
Larger diameter toilet roll cylinders to mount on board as holders, strengthened with black card glued around them.
Same colour indicates the same diameter.
Clamped with pegs and elastic bands.

Keep all the same size cylinders on a rack.
1. Placing circle marked on board.
2. Cylinder standing on spot.
3. 4 nails around it, glued and held down.
4. Taped around nails for added strength.
A toilet roll core slit and glued in tightly around a scottowel core makes a good holder.

Slightly smaller size than the black ones.
1. Green card glued around cylinder.
2. Standing on spot.
3. Nails around cylinder.
4. Inner small handle cylinder standing.
5. Outer holder glued and weighed down.
6. Inner cylinder.
7. Outer green one glued and held down.

Puppets standing in their holders. A tail support triangle will not fit in the holder.

54

Puppet scarves and collars

Doyley colours

Doyleys are excellent for neck lace trims on dresses. They can be white, gold, silver or coloured and in different sizes.

Doyley sizes

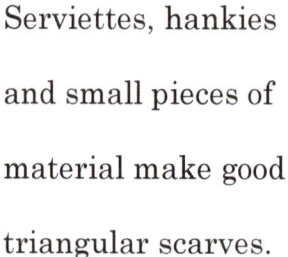
Serviettes

Serviettes, hankies and small pieces of material make good triangular scarves.

A long strip of material will also make a good scarf.

Handkerchieves

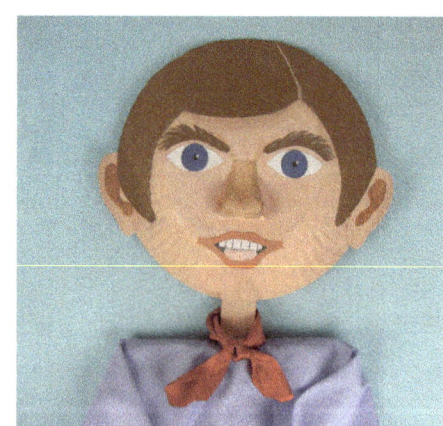

Puppet hats

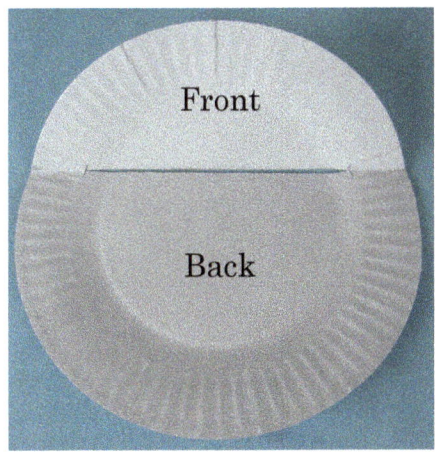

Cut across a large 23cm plate
Most hats 8.5cm, less front,
more over the back.
Can have it across middle.

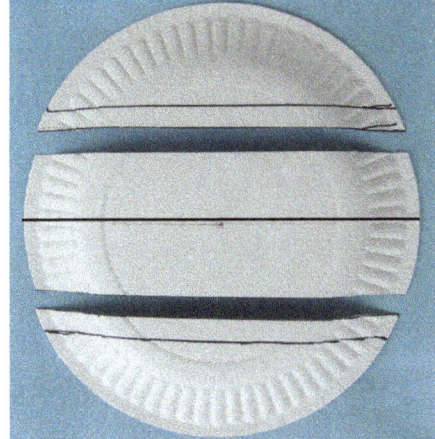

A small 18cm plate
1. Draw a line across centre.
2. Parallel lines above, below.
3. Hat style decides distance.

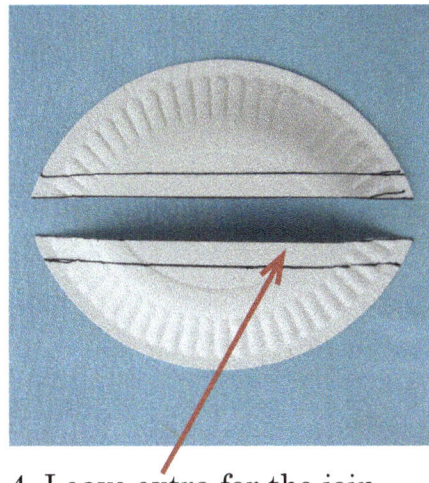

4. Leave extra for the join.
5. Cut flange on crown this
   time like the hat at the
   bottom of this page.

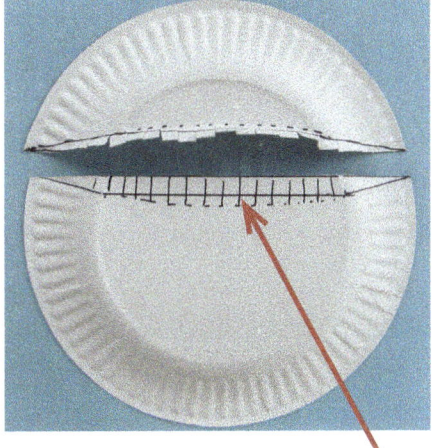

1. Cut right across plate.
2. Small cuts to curved line.
3. Bend up edge.

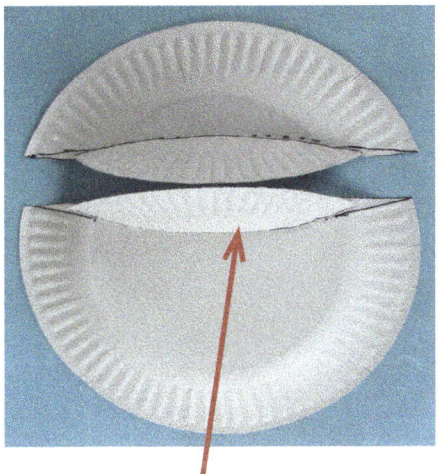

4. Join on to half crowns
   which are not flanged.

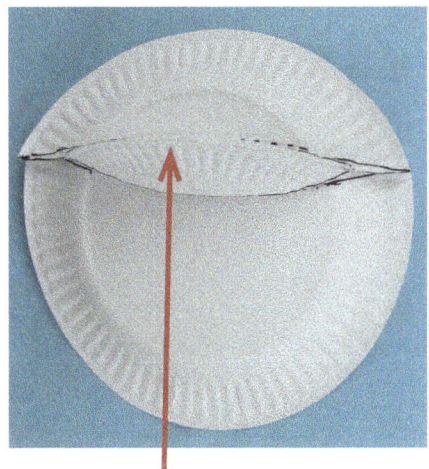

5. Join crowns together
   along top edge.

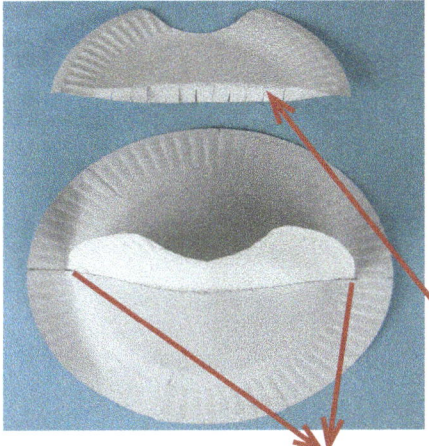

1. This plate is cut in middle,
   not right across the brim.
2. Put crown through plate.

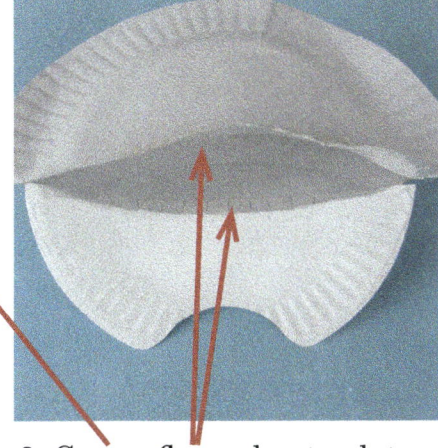

3. Crown flanged onto plate.
4. Join 2nd half onto plate.

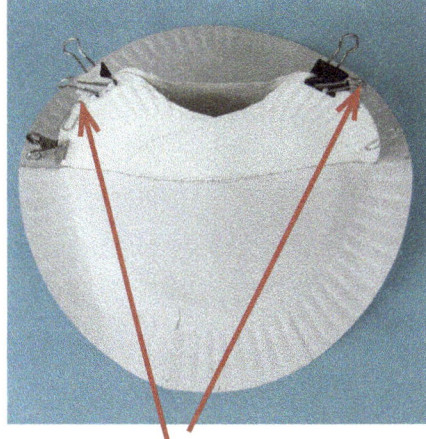

5. Join crowns together.
   This crown was shaped to
   suit a cowboy.

Painting and decorating these hats will add character and flair to the puppets.
They can be worn at appropiate times to make an impact.

Cap, mob cap.

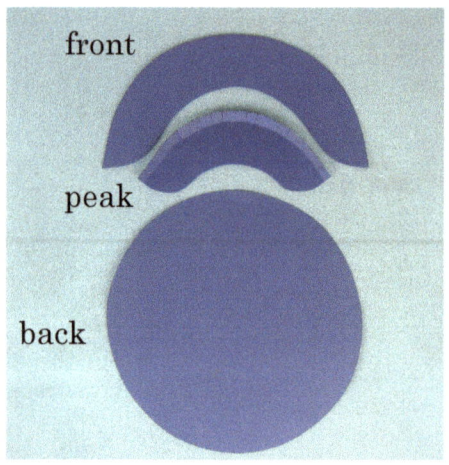
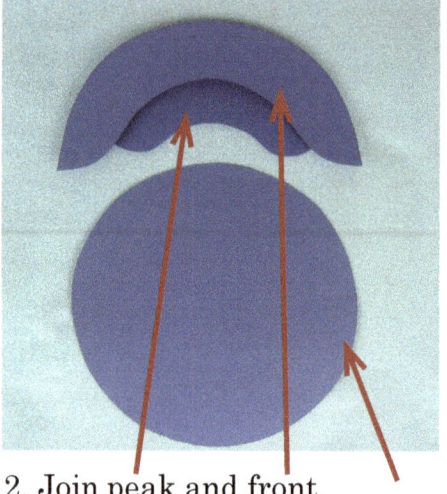

1. Use templates to cut out cap in coloured cardboard.

2. Join peak and front.
3. Join front to back on edge.

Cap should slide over head.

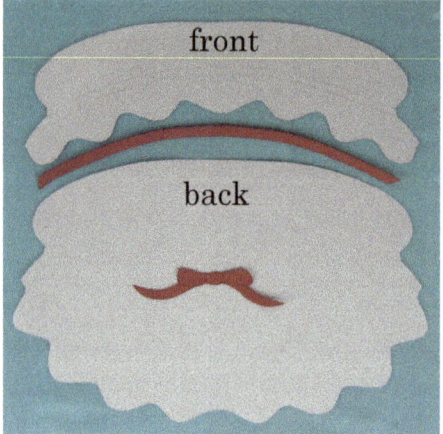
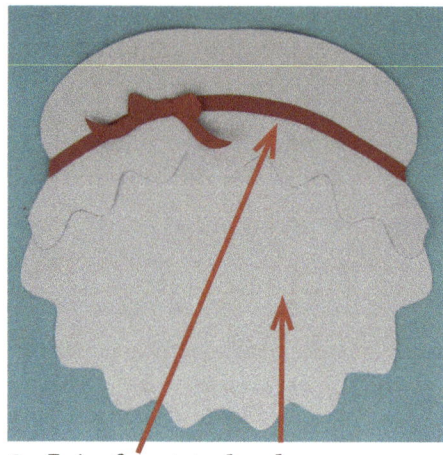

1. Cut out templates, back, front, ribbons and bow.

2. Join front to back.
3. Glue on ribbon and bow

Cap goes over the head. Stipple paint hats.

Farmer's wife's mob cap ~ back.

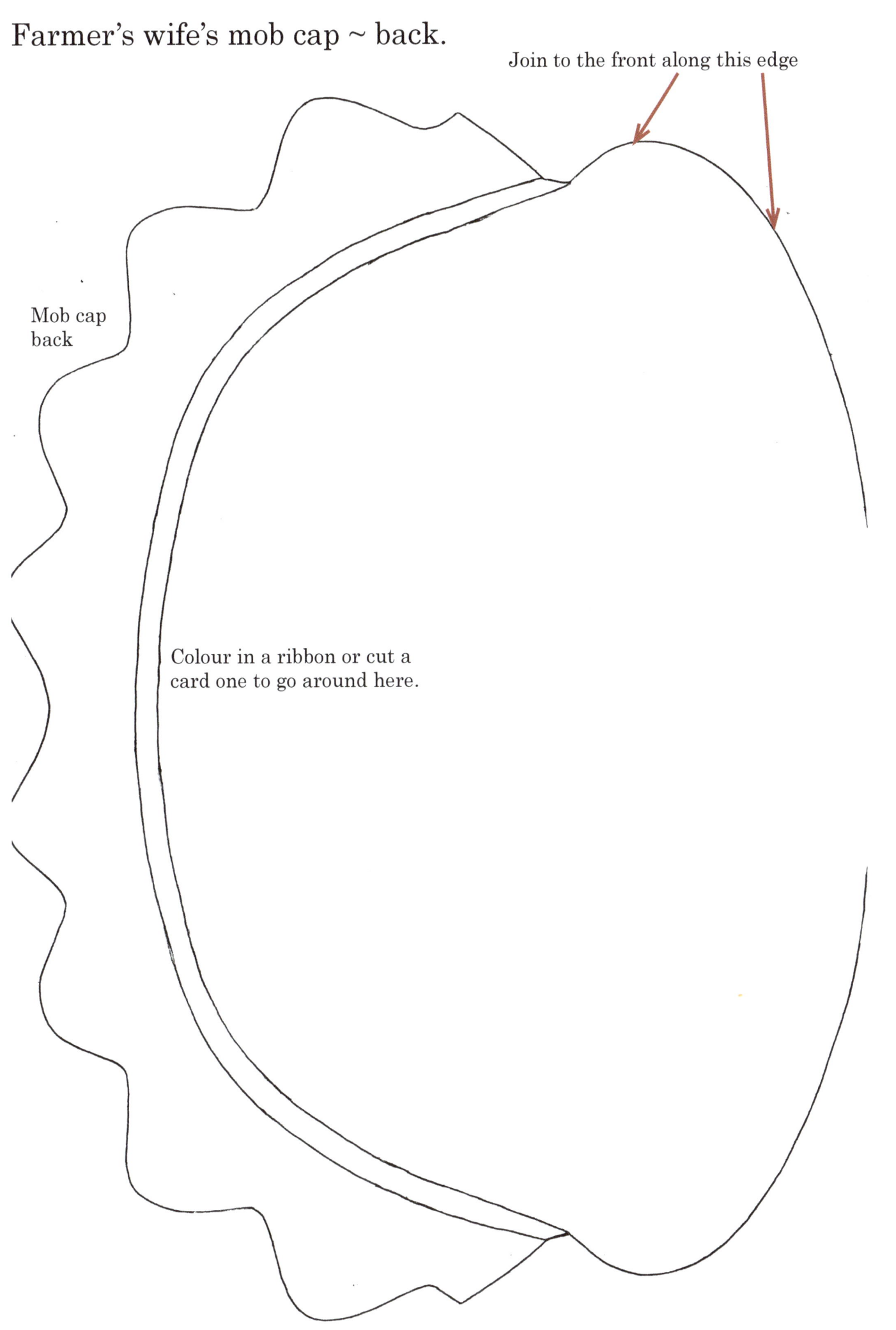

Join to the front along this edge

Mob cap back

Colour in a ribbon or cut a card one to go around here.

Farmer's wife's mob cap front and boy's cap front

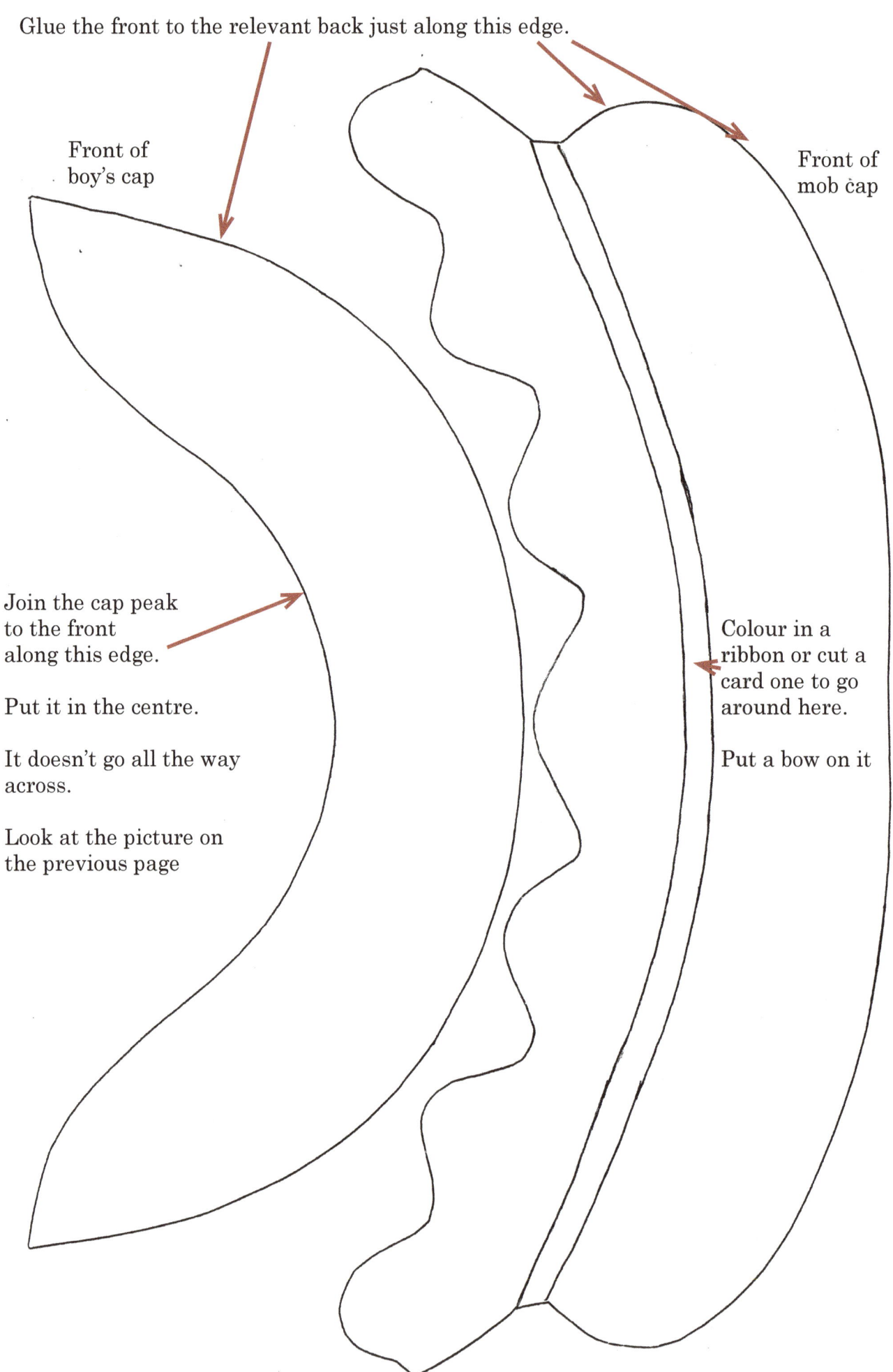

Glue the front to the relevant back just along this edge.

Front of boy's cap

Front of mob cap

Join the cap peak to the front along this edge.

Put it in the centre.

It doesn't go all the way across.

Look at the picture on the previous page

Colour in a ribbon or cut a card one to go around here.

Put a bow on it

Boy's cap templates ~ peak and back

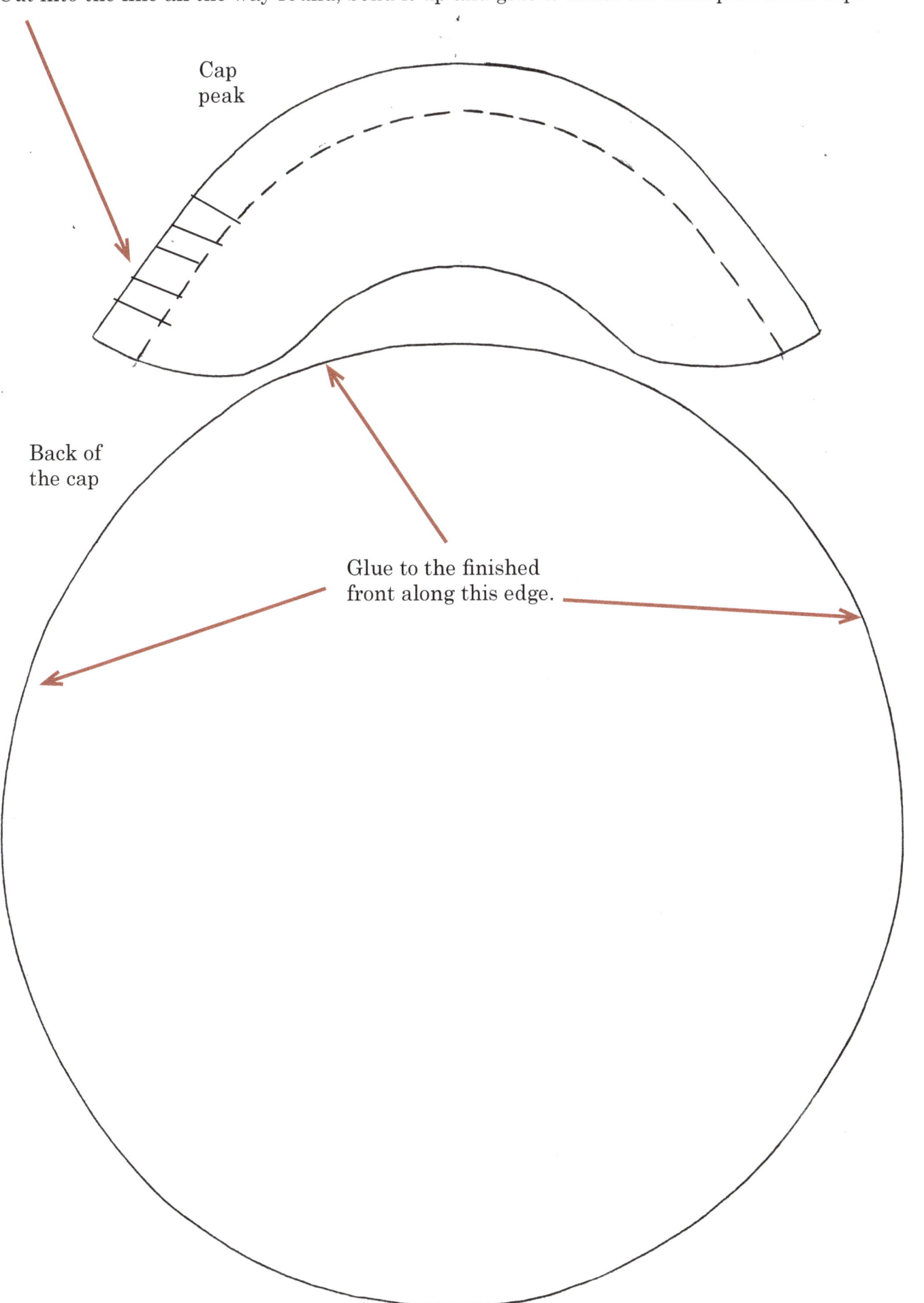

Set materials

Paints

1. Acrylic water-based paints. School issue poster paints are suitable for most large background work and undercoats.

2. Student or artist quality tubes are better for effects, details and brighter areas or objects as they contain more pigment.

3. Acrylic house paint can be used. White to undercoat (gives good coverage, less colour is needed on top and the final colour is brighter) and for mixing to lighten colours.

Note:- For a pale colour start with white and add small amounts of colour until it is right.

Colours needed

Red ~ bright (eg. flag red) ~ cadmium red.
Blue ~ (eg. sky) ~ cobalt.
Yellow ~ (eg. canary) ~ cadmium yellow
Black ~ can be house paint (small pot) or tube, or school poster paint which is much cheaper.
White ~ acrylic house paint is best. Decant some into smaller containers with lids.

Note:- Every colour can be mixed using different amounts of these, eg. green = yellow + blue.

Useful extras ~ Green (light and deep)   Purple
                Brown (burnt sienna)   Orange
                Deep yellow (raw umber or yellow ochre)   Turquoise
                Indigo (very dark blue)

Note:- Meat trays and plastic plates are useful as mixing palettes.
When mixing, start with the main colour then add small amounts of others to brighten and change eg. white to lighten, indigo to darken, black to grey it down.
Mixing too many colours together will result in dirty brownish-grey! Use black sparingly.

Crayons, water based markers, textas and coloured pencils can also be used for smaller areas and outlines but will not show up as well as paint.

Brushes

* Small to medium house painting brushes can be used for larger areas.
* Different sized cheap bristle oil painting brushes from hardware stores or art supply shops.
* Some fine and medium point, soft acrylic watercolour brushes. Cheap ones will do.
  Wash brushes between using different colours or use a different brush for each colour.

Other materials

Containers for clean and dirty water.
Spray bottle of water---to keep paint moist spray mixed paint often and also when finished for the day, then cover it with plastic wrap.

Rags for wiping brushes, hands, spills and mistakes.
Sponges for effects or soaking up excess.

Ruler or straight-edge. A large set-square or the corner of something big and flat eg. A sheet of cardboard/mat board.

Soft (4-6b) pencils for sketching before painting. Charcoal - but dust off before painting.

Set effects

Trees on light-weight cardboard
Paint or wet both sides and dry flat under weights, then draw and paint the trees, etc on.
This stops cardboard from curling. Can always rewet and dry again under weights.
Edges of trees, etc can be wriggly and random! No straight edges.
Yellow to deep/blue green for grass/foliage and bits of brown or grey, purple or deep indigo for shaded areas.

Scenery.
Simplify, alter, improve or change illustrated scenery from books to suit your play.
If Jack and Jill's well is too high up for the puppeteers, drop the hill down but keep the well the same – it must be in the right proportion to the puppets.

Perspective
Paint front objects in strong colours and distant ones paler or slightly greyish, or pale purplish/bluish to give scenery depth.
Front objects are large and to increase distance make things smaller as they get further away.

Some techniques
Make 2D round objects (tree trunks, buckets, etc.) appear real by shading edge with different tones.

For rough surfaces stipple with darker/lighter paint using the end of a stiff brush, crumpled rag, or paper dipped in paint. Useful for trees, bushes, rocks, stonework, etc. Practice!

For wood ~ Apply main colour, then use a large stiff brush with darker or lighter tones to mark wood grain. Don't overdo it!

Note:-
In reality and nature because of varying light nothing is one flat colour all over.
3D objects on stage will create their own light and shade because of their shape.
Drawn and painted 2D objects need shaded and lighter areas to appear natural and 'real'.
It depends on what effect you need.
A row of perfectly flat looking daisies could be very effective in some situations, but to look natural they would have to be shaded and look flexible.
No straight edges in nature so perfection in everything makes it appear stiff and unnatural.

Use children's books with good illustrations for ideas.

Theatre scenery

Theatre scenery is amazing with its exaggerated perspective. Whether simple or very detailed it will have the incredible effect of depth and spaciousness.

Each type of puppet, cardboard rod, glove and marionette has required Colleen's thought and experience in live theatre to work out the right sizing. All the templates have the sizing written on them to give you an idea of size for your creations.

Looking ~ really looking at your scenery size and perspective is worth the effort to get it right. Study the perspective of the things in your visual world and try it in your theatre.

Templates for
tree groups

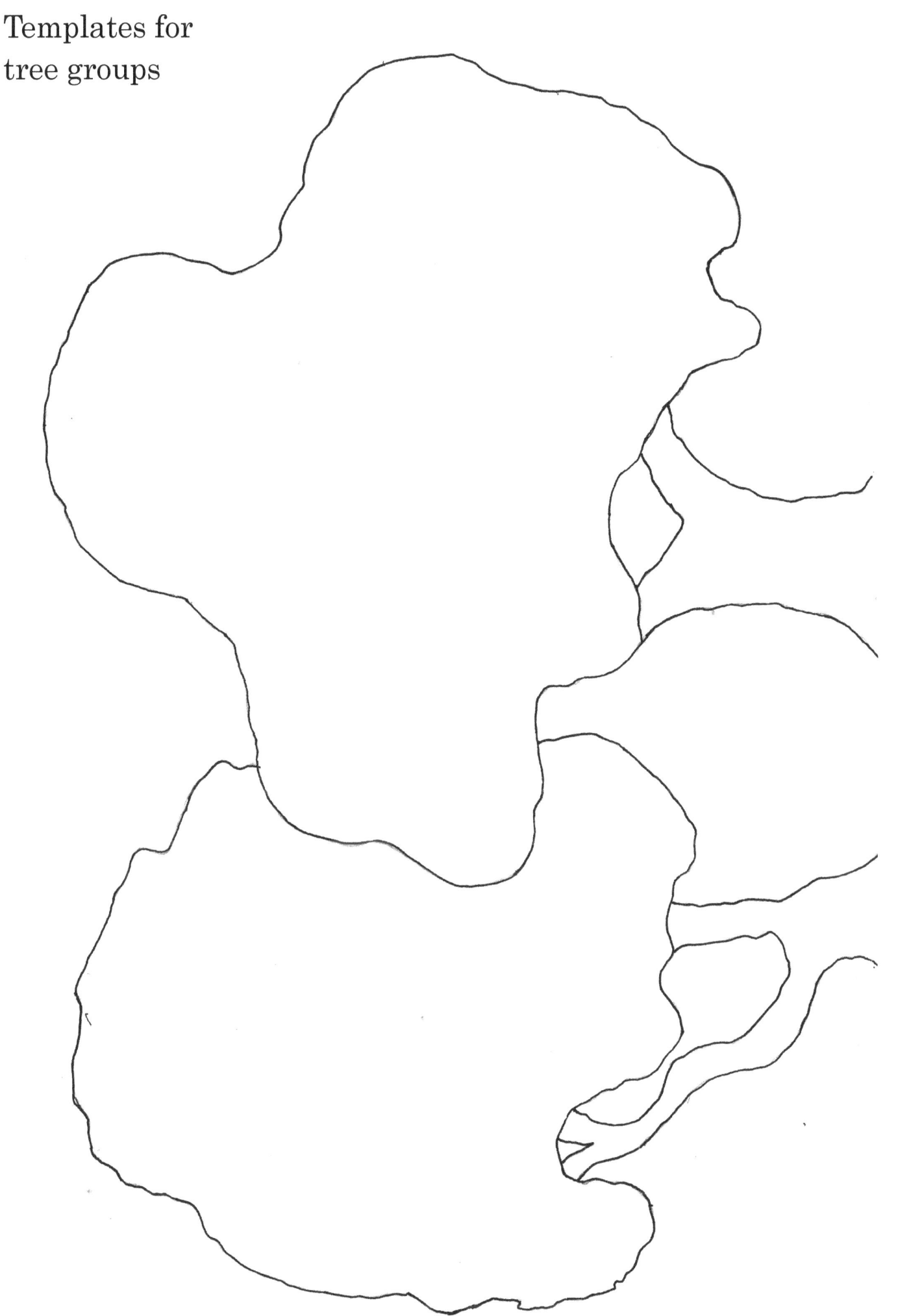

These trees have light tops so stay up without strings going up to the clouds.
Note shading of light and dark to give roundness and reality. 21cm high x 29cm wide.

28cm high
7cm wide

10 cm high

These trees are small to give perspective. They can be taller but must not block the view of your puppets.

Different arrangements.

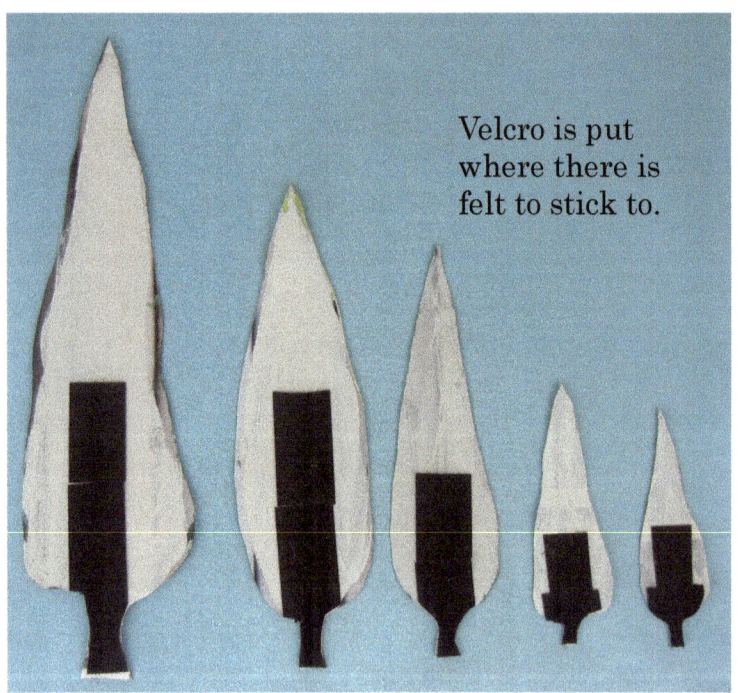

Velcro is put where there is felt to stick to.

These bulkier trees need strings to the clouds. 20cm high x 28cm wide. Templates for these are on the previous page. Put velcro right across. It works better.

Individual trees can be arranged in any order.

All the trees are the same scale to show variety. Be creative and have fun.

These shrubs are 15-18cm W x 9cm H (group), 13cm x 14cm (single).

The bottom group is three pieces of scrap card overlapped and so it appears more 3D than the one above it.

66

30cm wide.

75cm high.

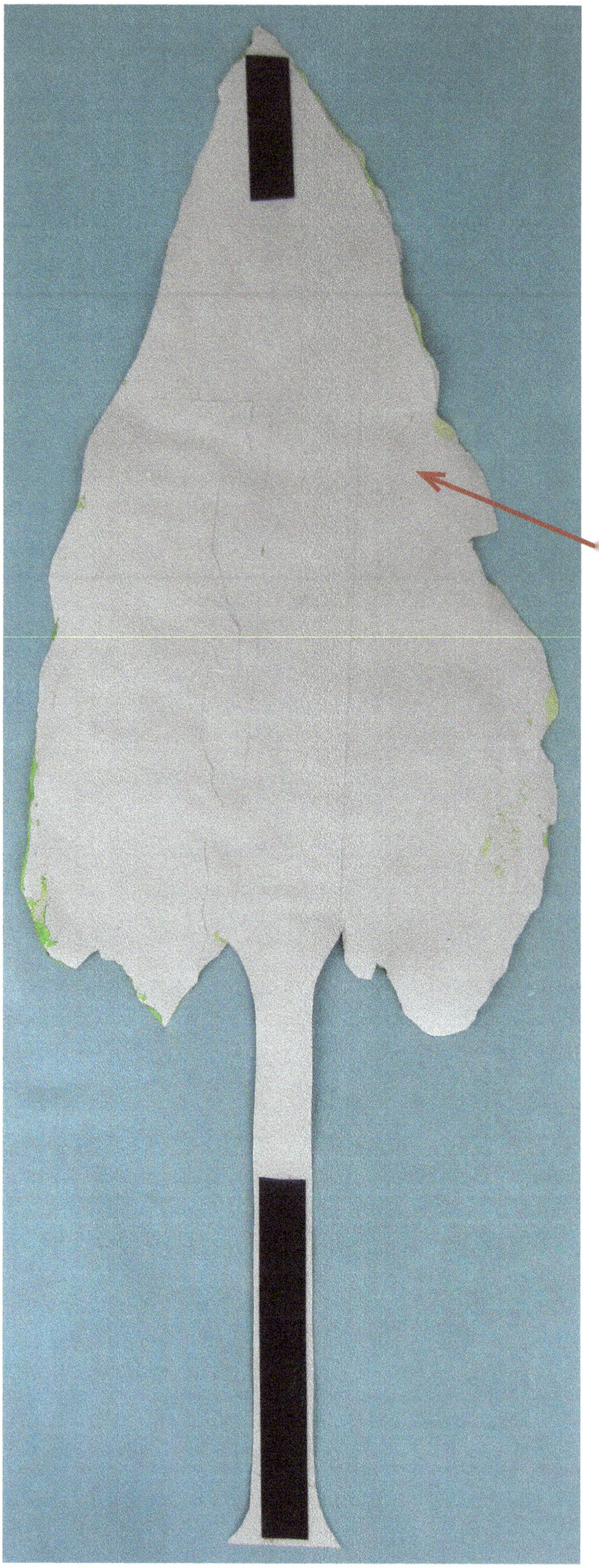

Velcro onto the green felt at the bottom and onto the white felt cloud at the top.
Strengthen the trunk and canopy with a light-weight cardboard.
The shading from light to darker colours from left to right makes the object look round.
Make the light come from one source or side. The shadow will only be on one side.
These trees are still 7 : 1 ratio. Sizes are very important for reality and the 3D effect.
Start with the plain scene. Add one item at a time moving it around, even grouping large and small on the green felt. See the incredible change it can make.

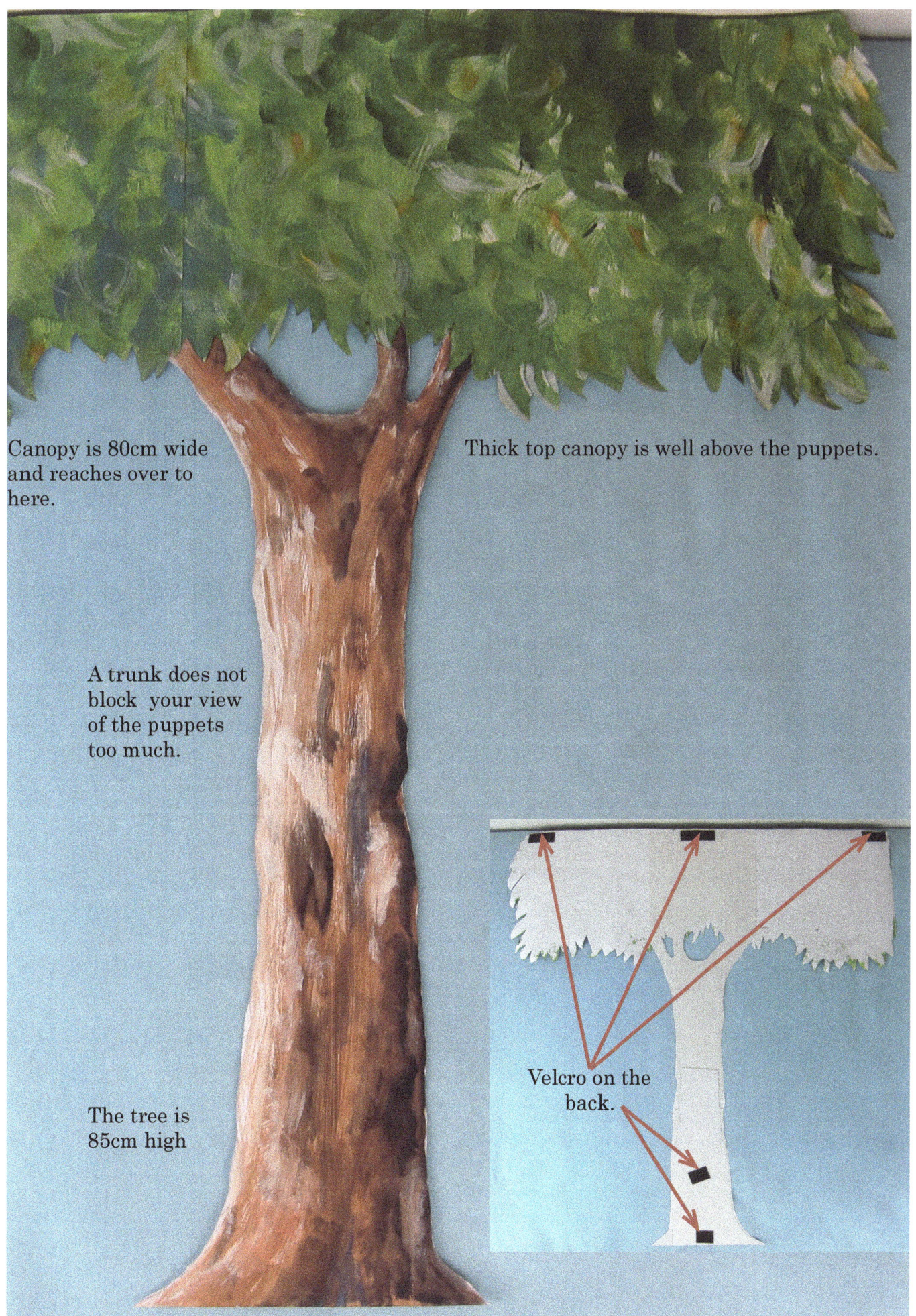

Canopy is 80cm wide and reaches over to here.

Thick top canopy is well above the puppets.

A trunk does not block your view of the puppets too much.

Velcro on the back.

The tree is 85cm high

It is important to realise the large size of this tree. It doesn't fit on the page, it goes onto the next page. Keep the middle band across the backdrop fairly open so you can see your puppets.

Nursery rhyme ~ human

Jack and Jill

Jack and Jill went up the hill
To fetch a pail of water.
Jack fell down and broke his crown
And Jill came tumbling after.

Up Jack got and home did trot
As fast as he could caper.
He went to bed to mend his head
With vinegar and brown paper.

Materials for your puppet ~
Head   2 paper plates, white or coloured paper and cardboard.
       Paper, glue, pens, paint, paint brushes
Body   Two 3 x 50cm long strips of strong cardboard and two 3 x 10cm strips.
       A piece of material about 60 x 60cm.
       2 x 8cm material tape or material to reinforce the centre hole.
       Glue that will stick material to material or cardboard.

Making the puppet. Turn to p 23-28, p 36, p38, and p 39 for the instructions.

Performing the play

With nursery rhymes the skeleton script is already well known.
Take Jack and Jill. Say it and just act it in the proscenium.

As you say it again move across the proscenium and up the hill, pause to get water, tumble down, go home, come in again and go to bed at the side of the stage.
Do it again putting in more action - get the feel of it and hold the puppets up properly.

Now ask a few questions~

Why are they going to get water?

How do they go? Together? Jill going slower? Eagerly? Jack jumping around/racing?

How do they get their water?

How do they tumble down? Actions and noises. Collapse, sit, cry, etc.

How do they go home? Running, walking, complaining, crying? Does Jill help him?
How does he get fixed? By whom? Go to bed? How does it end?

Remember Jill has her part to play all the way through.

So this simple nursery rhyme provides the opportunity to learn to correctly hold up the puppet, act and speak for it, exaggerate (it is drama), keep it simple or really expand it with fun material.

If several groups do this play they can see who makes it the most entertaining and they are able to watch the other performances, gaining more understanding of theatre.

1. The bucket can be lowered down into the well by using an A4 page rolled tightly as an axle.
2. Mount the axle along the back of the well through two right angle card support brackets.
3. Join a card handle on to the end of the axle projecting beyond the proscenium side.
4. Tie and glue a cord around this axle. Join a flat card bucket on the free end of the cord.
5. The cord should wind round on the axle and the bucket go up and down. (Illustration p 71)

Mother

Jill

Velcro on the palm of the hand will hold things.

The hand can be acted by attaching a kebab/chop stick

Jack

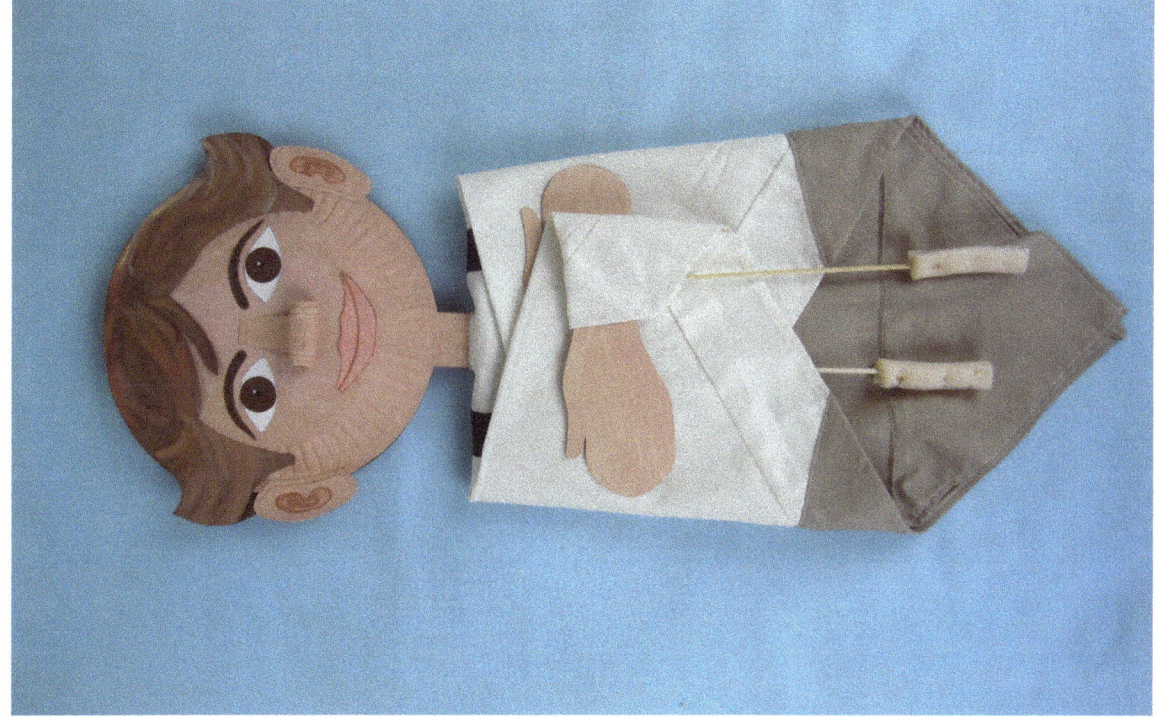

Scenery can go outside the proscenium

Axle replaces this beam

Velcro block 'X' behind here.

Handle on this end

X Velcro block

Card bucket on end of rope

Card right angle

Axle O hole through card

Card rt angle   Handle
axle
post   post

Front

Make a brown cap the shape you want then cover it with strips of brown paper.

Back

Cut some off the base of the hill if too high but keep the well the same size.

Painted front view of the bed with material stapled on. Cut up boxes to make props.

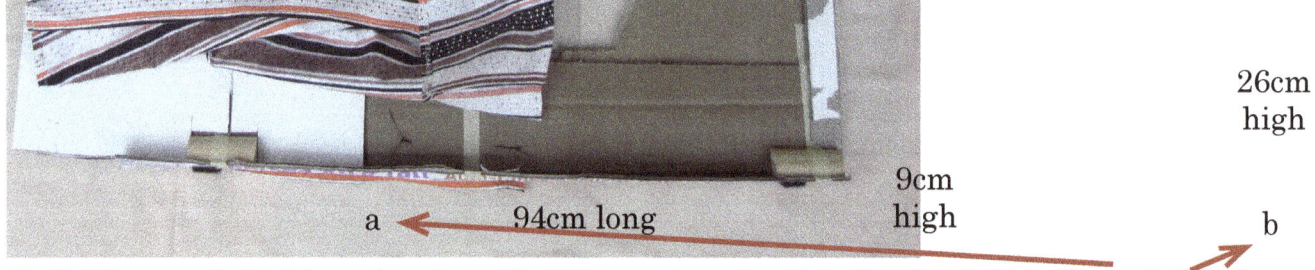

a ← 94cm long   9cm high   26cm high   b

Back view, material hanging down for puppet to get under. 2 velcroed blocks a & b on base.

71

A few white clouds sewn onto the sky can be used for a tall tree on the backdrop.

Green felt sewn onto a blue see-through material. Velcro trees, shrubs, etc onto it.

As I went over London Hill

As I went over London Hill,
London Hill, London Hill,
As I went over London Hill,
So early in the morning.
I shook my head on London Hill. . .
I scratched my head on London Hill...

I waved to you on London Hill. . .
I rubbed my tum on London Hill . . .

This is a song with endless possibilities you can make up your own verses and actions for the puppets to do together.

There's a Hole in my Bucket

1. There's a hole in my bucket, dear Liza, dear Liza,
   There's a hole in my bucket, dear Liza, a hole.
2. Then mend it, dear Georgie, dear Georgie, dear Georgie,
   Then mend it, dear Georgie, dear Georgie, mend it!
3. With what shall I mend it, dear Liza?
4. With a straw, dear Georgie . . . a straw!
5. The straw is too long, dear Liza.
6. Then cut it, dear Georgie . . . cut it!
7. With what shall I cut it, dear Liza?
8. With a knife, dear Georgie . . . a knife!
9. The knife is too blunt, dear Liza.
10. Then sharpen it, dear Georgie . . . sharpen it!
11. With what shall I sharpen it, dear Liza?
12. With a stone, dear Georgie . . . a stone!
13. The stone is too dry, dear Liza.
14. Then wet it, dear Georgie . . . wet it!

Nursery rhyme ~ animal

Three Little Kittens

Three little kittens they lost their mittens,
And they began to cry,
Oh, mother dear, we sadly fear
That we have lost our mittens.
What! LOST YOUR MITTENS, YOU NAUGHTY KITTENS!
Then you shall have no pie.
Mee-ow, mee-ow, mee-ow.
No, you shall have no pie.

The three little kittens they found their mittens,
And they began to cry,
Oh, mother dear, see here, see here,
For we have found our mittens.
Put on your mittens, you silly kittens,
And you shall have some pie.
Purr-r, purr-r, purr-r,
Oh, let us have some pie.

The three little kittens put on their mittens,
And soon ate up the pie.
Oh, mother dear, we greatly fear
That we have soiled our mittens.
What! Soiled your mittens, you naughty kittens!
Then they began to sigh.
Mee-ow, mee-ow, mee-ow.
Then they began to sigh.

The three little kittens they washed their mittens,
And hung them out to dry;
Oh! mother dear, do you not hear
That we have washed our mittens?
What! washed your mittens, then you're good kittens,
But I smell a rat close by.
Mee-ow, mee-ow, mee-ow.
We smell a rat close by.

Some other Nursery Rhymes

THERE WERE THREE JOVIAL WELSHMEN ~
adapted to things the puppeteers know.
THREE BLIND MICE.

MISS POLLY HAD A DOLLY
ANNA ELISE
THE QUEEN OF HEARTS
POLLY PUT THE KETTLE ON

LITTLE BOY BLUE
Little Boy Blue,
Come blow your horn,
The sheep's in the meadow,
The cow's in the corn
But where is the boy
Who looks after the sheep?
He's under a haystack
Fast asleep.
Will you wake him?
No, not I,
For if I do,
He's sure to cry.

Making the puppets

Choose what colour material you want your cat to be so you know if you will be able to paint the head that colour or colours easily.
The piece needs to be 50 to 60cms square.

Turn to p 23 and make a basic plate puppet.

Turn to p 29 and follow the cat puppet instructions through to p 38.

Performing the play

The rhyme is easy, the cast consists of three little kittens and their mother.

Say the rhyme and act what you are saying in the proscenium.

The kittens come on stage to mother, go off searching, come in again to mother, and eat their pie. They look at their dirty mittens, wash them and come to mother again. She smells a rat close by.

Repeat it doing more actions and learning to hold the puppets high and erect. Practise this until it becomes comfortable/natural.

Play around with options.
Who goes off stage? Mother and kittens hunt for the mittens. They all go off stage and the kittens come in searching, find them and cry for mother to come in.

How does each one purr? How does each play around, walk, creep, bounce, etc.?

How do they pretend to put on their mittens?

How do they eat their pie ~ all the same/differently? Noises? Messy?

How do they look at their mittens and sigh? Lick them, try to clean them?

Does Mother leave or do they all go?

Place a tub of water (prop) on stage. The kittens wash and pretend to hang out the mittens. A line could be lifted across the stage with the mittens hanging above the kittens.

Mother comes in and Mee-ows.

She smells a rat close by. How does she act that important bit?

How does it end?

Once again this simple nursery rhyme gives lots of opportunity for the actor to practise holding the puppet correctly, act and speak for it, it's a cat, exaggerate (it is drama), keep it simple or expand it with fun material or minor adventures..

If several groups do this play they can see who makes it the most entertaining. By watching each other's performances they'll gain more understanding of what theatre involves..

Making a rat

Strong thread, drink straw, kebab stick, skewer.
1. Make 2 holes in the straw with a skewer.
2. Cut out shape in card.
3. Cut two short front lines.
4. Fold on the dashed lines.
5. Make 3 small holes at 'O's.
6. Join front together.
7. Push kebab through centre hole. Do step 7 and 8 so rat stays on and in place.

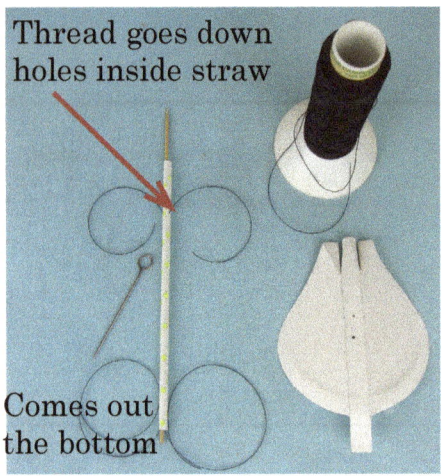

Thread goes down holes inside straw

Comes out the bottom

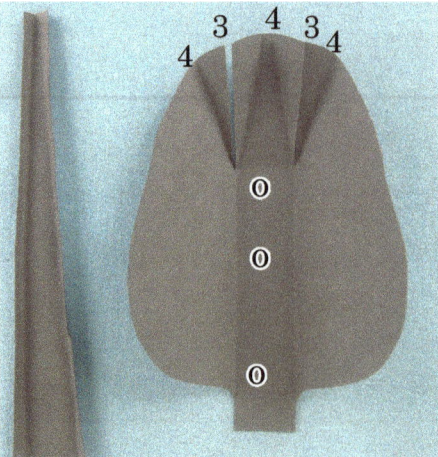

Tape around top. Peg it until dry.

8. Tape or paper round kebab. Put extra glue on tape end.
9. Put tape again under rat with extra glue at the end.
10. Tie knot on threads.
11. Join 'back', a bit at a time.

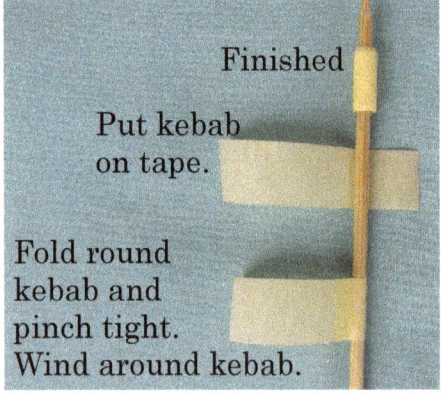

Finished

Put kebab on tape.

Fold round kebab and pinch tight. Wind around kebab.

Leave space for movement.

Peg until dry.
Push threads into rat.

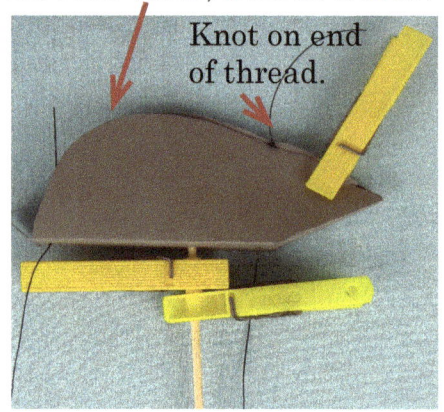

Knot on end of thread.

12. Cut out ears. Paint and glue them on.
13. Draw on eyes and nose.
14. Cut the tail out in paper (card is too hard to roll small). Roll it. Keep rolling it and tightening it until it is thin enough for the tail. Glue it down the join.

15. Make small cuts all round the end, bend out and glue the tail onto the body.

16. Paint when dry.

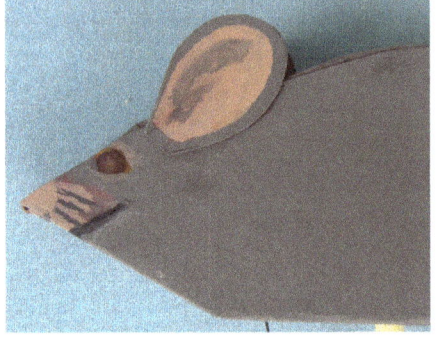

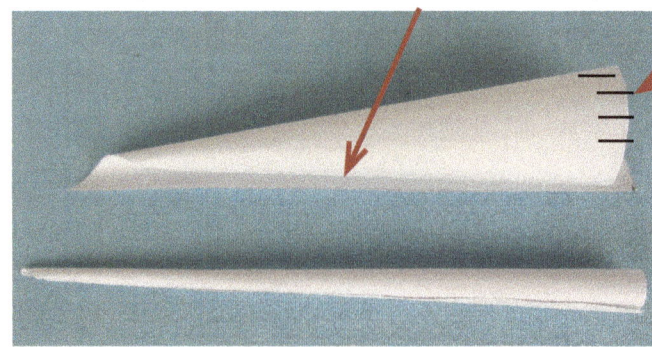

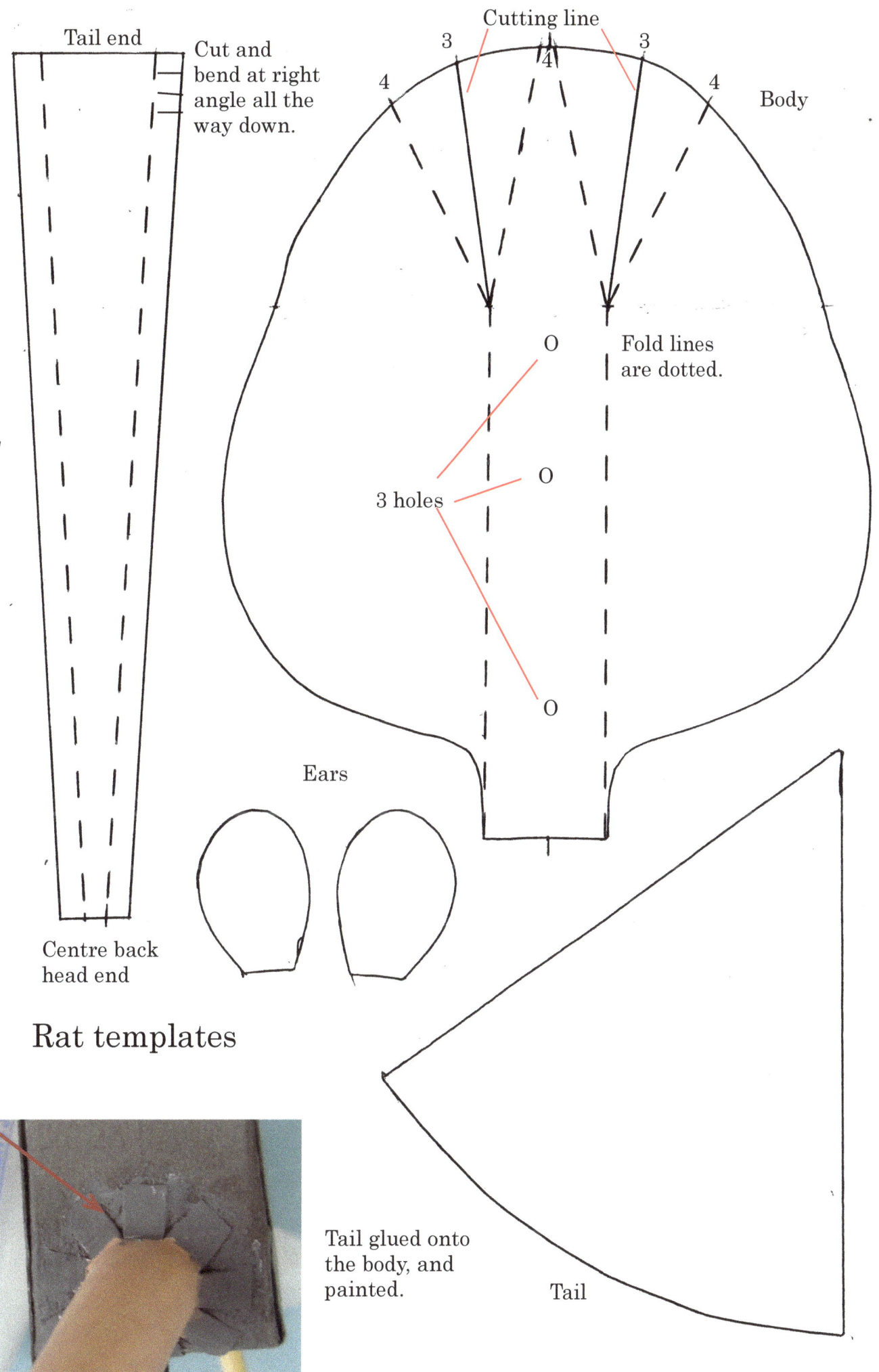

Rat templates

Hang the rocks with thread from a curtain rod so the rat can come in front of them, or mount it like the tub below, with velcroed wood blocks, if the rat is happy to stay behind it.

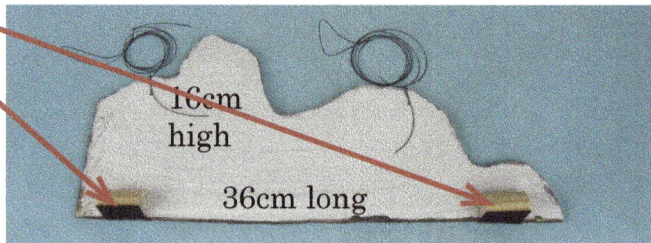

16cm high
36cm long

Handle is cut out, painted and glued on. Tub is shaded at ends to make the it look round.

Small wood block with velcro to hold it in place on the proscenium.

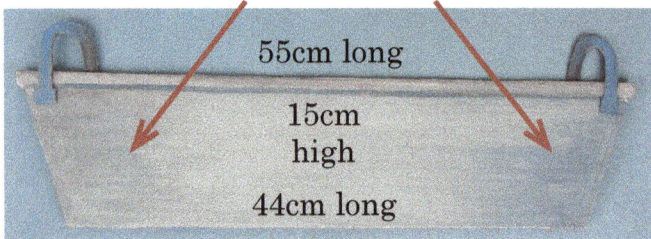

55cm long
15cm high
44cm long

Grass base and clothes line

Glue two 100cm x 2.5cm and two 100cm x 3cm lengths of card together. Then glue them together at right angles with 2 wood blocks behind.

View end on

Wood block

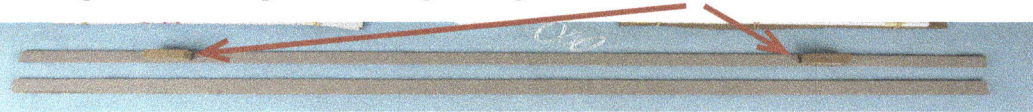

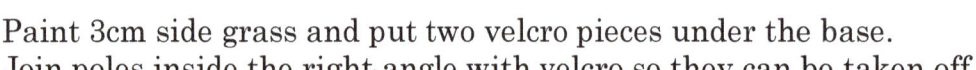

Paint 3cm side grass and put two velcro pieces under the base.
Join poles inside the right angle with velcro so they can be taken off.

23cm high

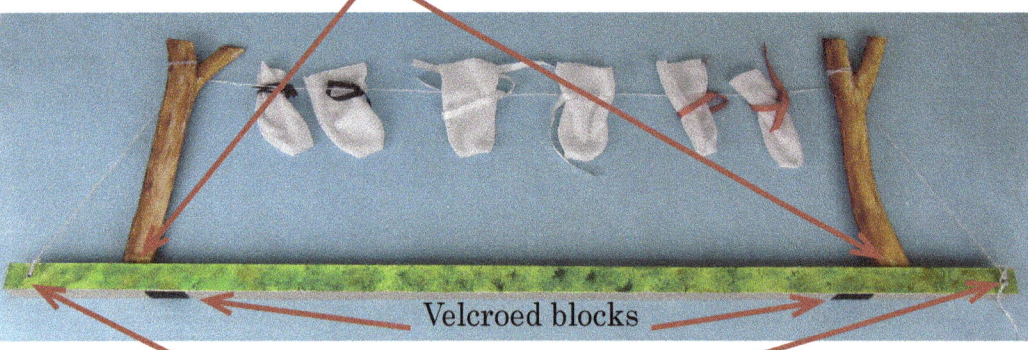

Velcroed blocks

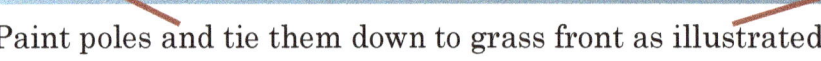

Paint poles and tie them down to grass front as illustrated.

Run string across and hang the mittens or another pair of mittens on it.

Make two clothes line poles with card + a tightly rolled A4 page mounted behind for strength.

The hills must be low enough for the puppeteers to see over them to their puppets acting.

The scenery is up over the curtain rod so I can talk with the puppeteers and they can see themselves in a large mirror in front of the theatre. Children would be standing not sitting.

The scenery is dropped down into place and puppeteers can see their puppets shape through the sky. N.B. The tub is only just big enough.

Clothes line grass base mounted on the proscenium frame with velcro and string attached.

I Love Little Pussy

I love little pussy,
  Her coat is so warm,
And if I don't hurt her
  She'll do me no harm.

So I'll not pull her tail,
  Nor drive her away,
But pussy and I
  Very gently will play.

She shall sit by my side
  And I'll give her some food;
And pussy will love me
  Because I am good.

Wet Washing

The farmer's wife and the three blind mice

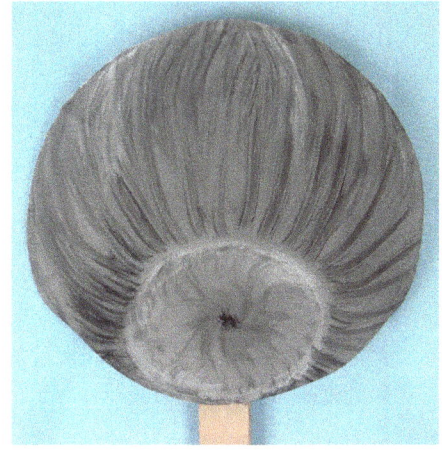

1. Go to p 23 and make a basic plate puppet using a 23cm plate.
2. Follow the instructions to p 27 using these templates or your own to make the head.
3. Go to the body p 36, hand instructions p 38 and hand template p 39.

The eyebrows are placed this way to show surprise and anxiety at seeing the mice.

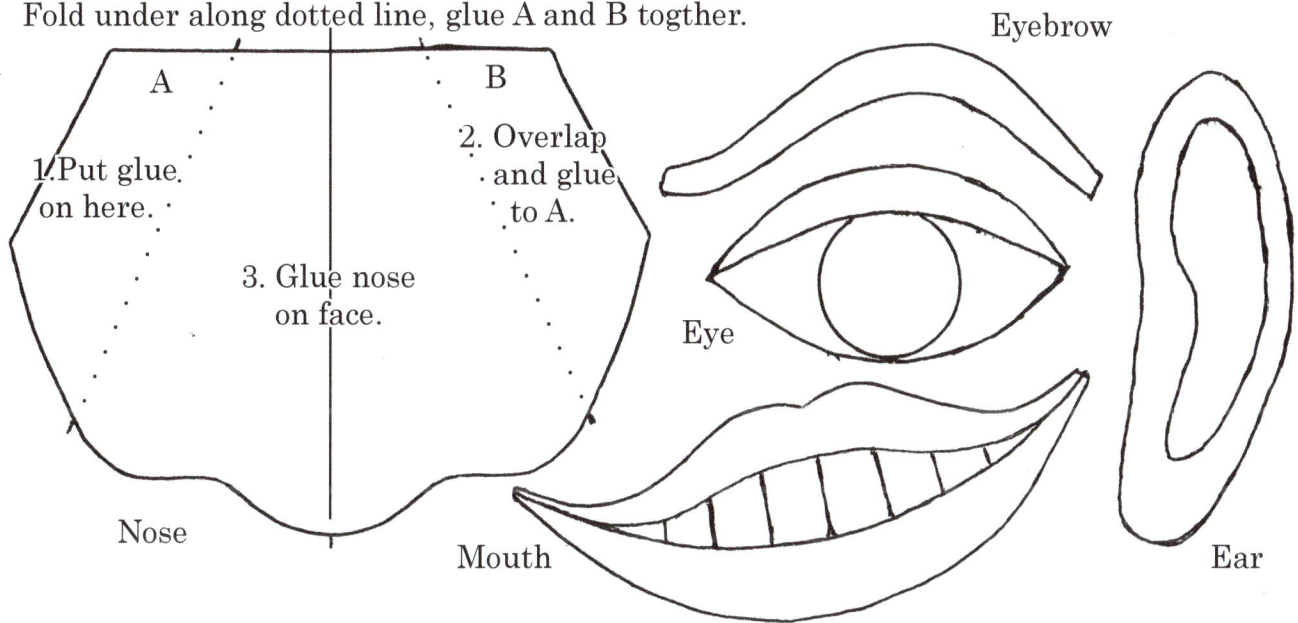

Strong thread, kebab stick, straw, skewer, templates.
1. Put thread through 2 holes made in straw with skewer.
2. Cut out shape in card.
3. Cut two short front lines.
4. Fold on the dashed lines.
5. Make 3 small holes at 'O's.
6. Push kebab through centre hole. Do step 8 and 9 so mouse stays in place.
7. Push thread into mouse. Peg it until dry.

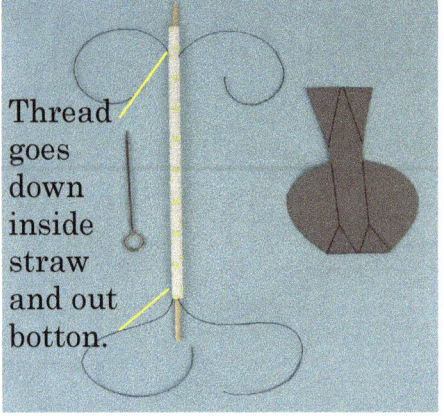

Thread goes down inside straw and out bottom.

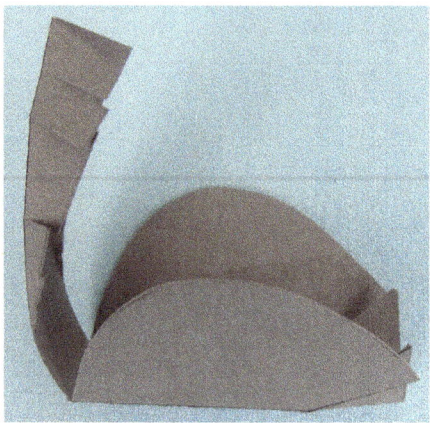

Tie a big knot.

8. Tape or paper round the top of the kebab.
9. Put tape under mouse with extra glue at the tape end. It tucks inside the straw.
10. Join front together.
11. Join back together from the tail, a section at a time.

Finished
Put kebab on tape
Fold round kebab and pinch tight.
Wind around kebab.

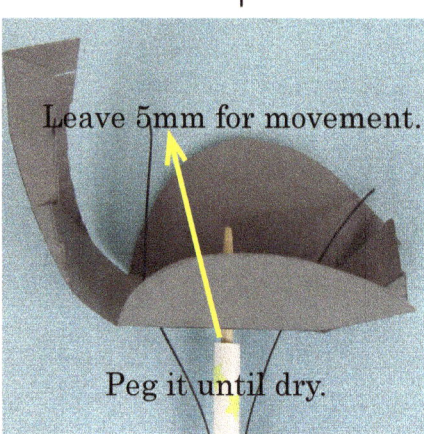

Leave 5mm for movement.
Peg it until dry.

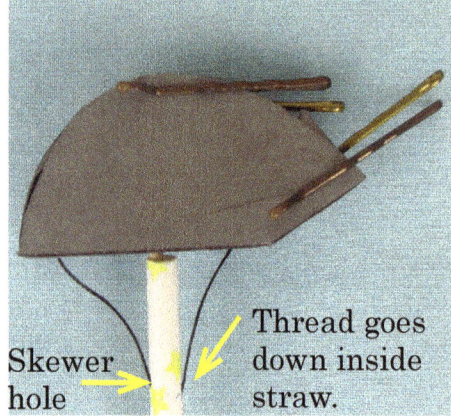

Skewer hole
Thread goes down inside straw.

12. Draw on the eyes and nose, then cut out the ears, colour them in and stick them on.
13. Follow the instructions on the next page to make the tail.

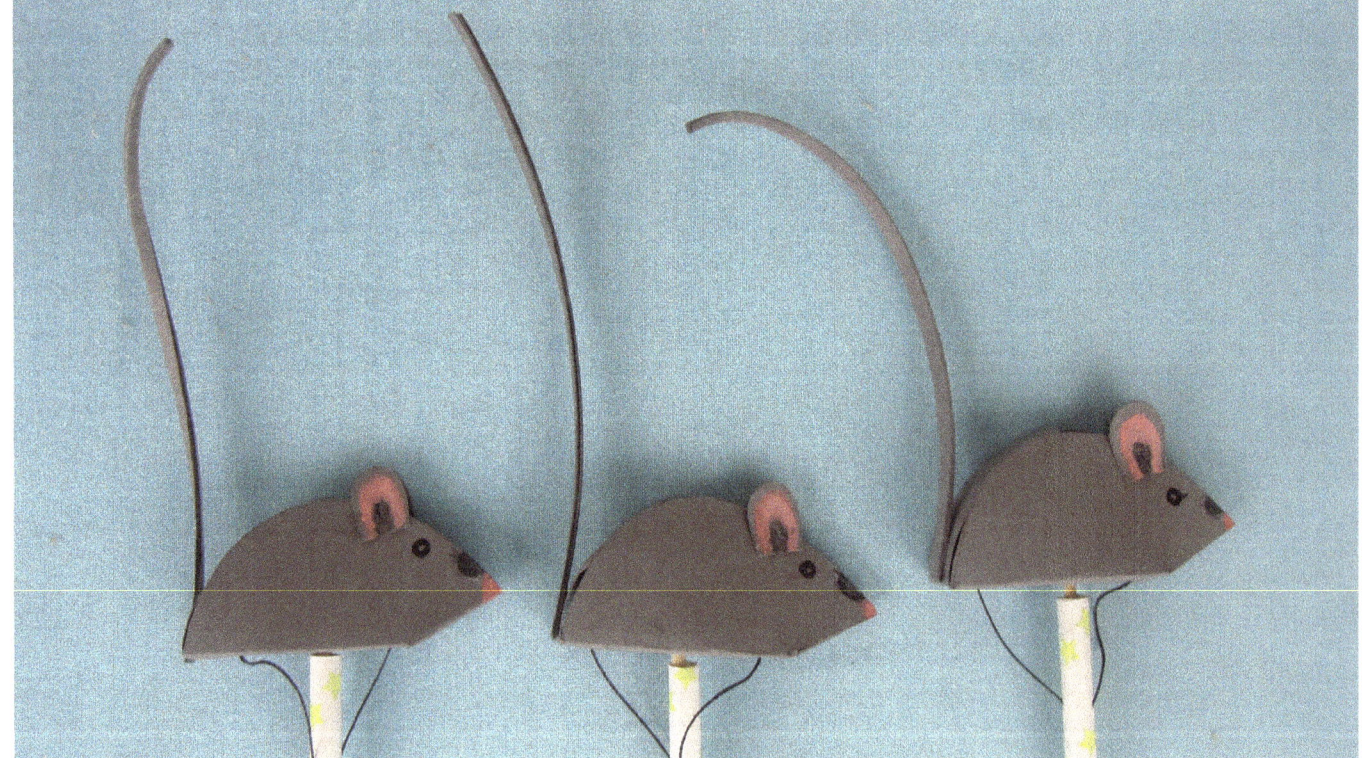

Three Blind Mice

Three blind mice, three blind mice.
See how they run, see how they run!
They all ran after the farmer's wife,
Who cut off their tails with the carving knife.
Did you ever see such a thing in your life,
As three blind mice?

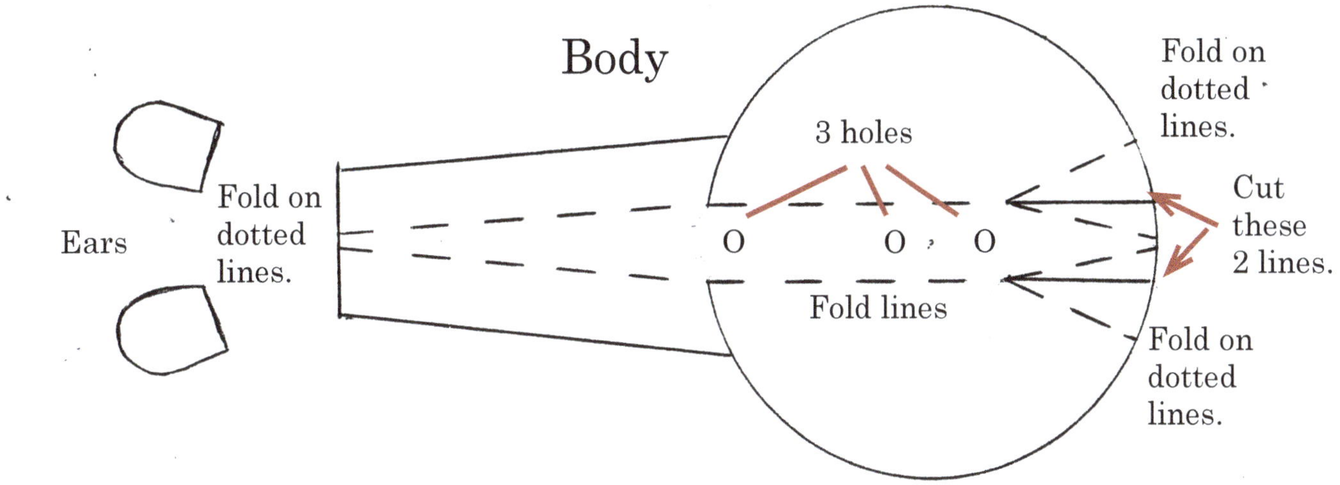

Body

Ears — Fold on dotted lines.

3 holes

Fold lines

Fold on dotted lines.

Cut these 2 lines.

Fold on dotted lines.

Tail

Mark tapered strips with the point at opposite ends.

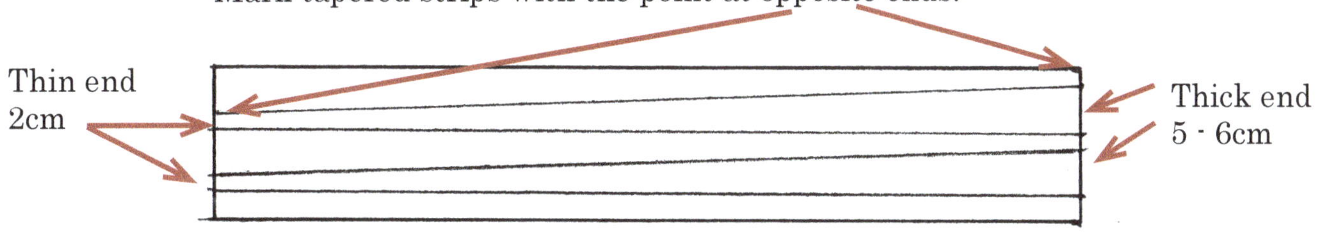

Thin end 2cm

Thick end 5 - 6cm

1. Stick 4 pieces of cardboard together. Allow to dry.
2. Cut out, leaving each strip the way it curls, for style.
3. Glue the thicker end onto the body.

Use the cream back drop from Jack and Jill. Put a table top with short legs on the front proscenium, or a window/piece of kitchen furniture on the backdrop for the scenery.

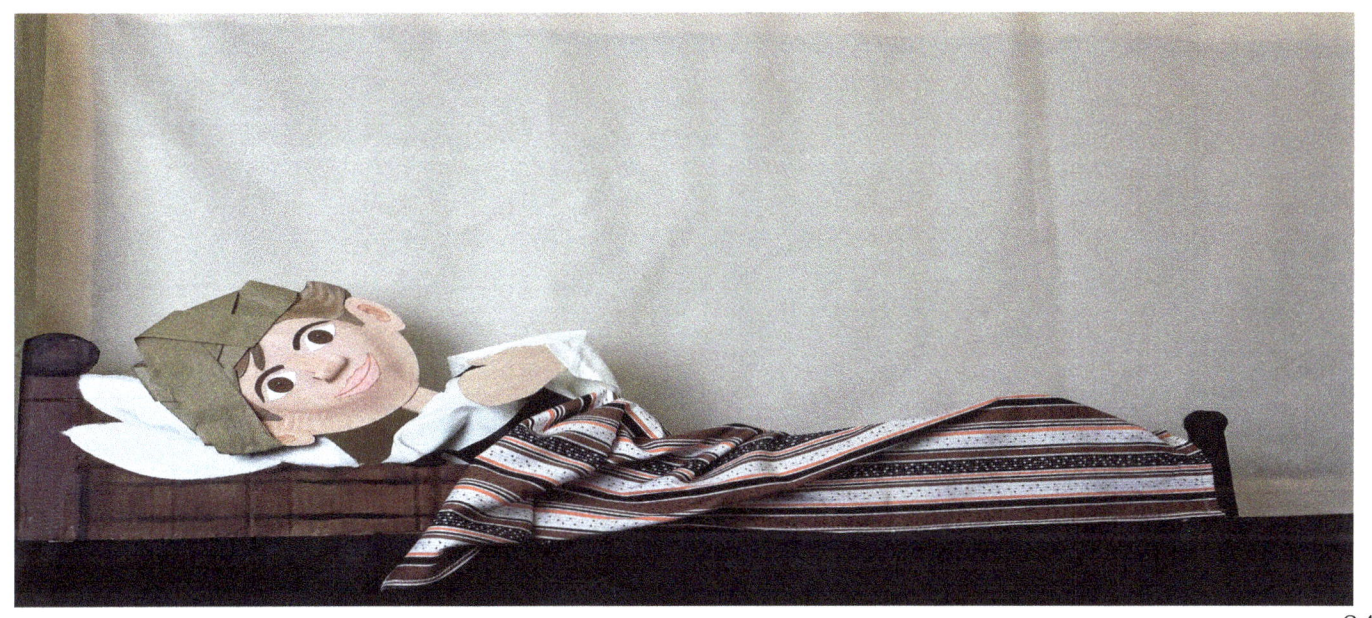

 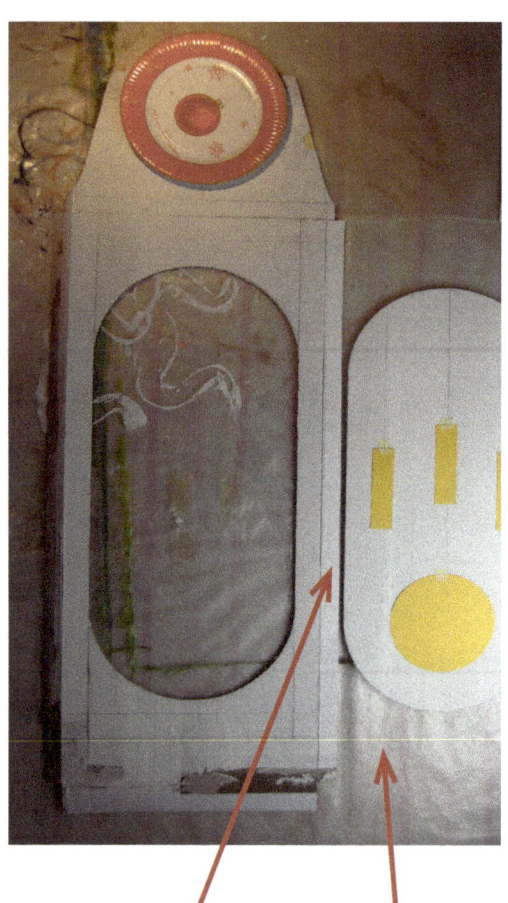 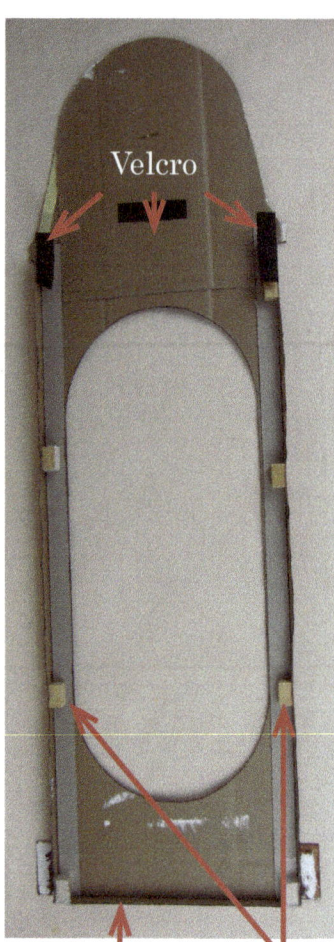

1. Draw the clock on a large piece of card. Face is a paper late.

2. Cut out the glass front. The weights and pendulum are yellow cardboard.

3. Bend and glue sides and bottom to wood blocks.

4. Put cord through a card disc, spread out, glue in place.

6. Cover the tube with gold paper.

8. Glue a small paper plate to card. Trim it.

10. Glue a dowel on the top half.

 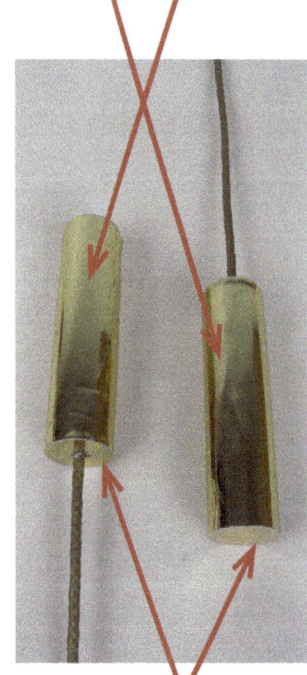  

5. Cut an inner roll. Tape around it will help you cut it square.

7. Cover ends with gold.

9. Glue gold paper onto plate at edge.

Point

11. Glue a kebab on bottom half.

Grandfather clock

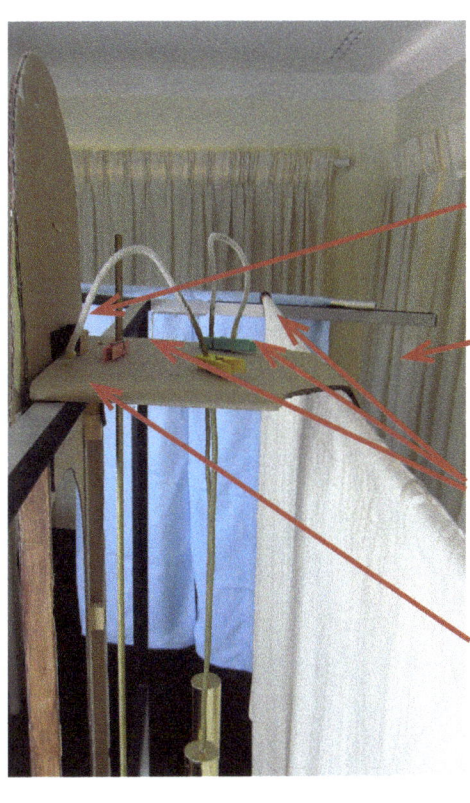

Velcrod block joining to the velcro on the clock.

Cardboard bent over the back curtain rod.

Cords and dowel are held by pegs.

Card sitting on proscenium bar and latched with velcro strip.

This clock face was taken off the webb and printed on shiny photographic paper.

The hands were drawn on transparent plastic, coloured in then cut out and mounted.

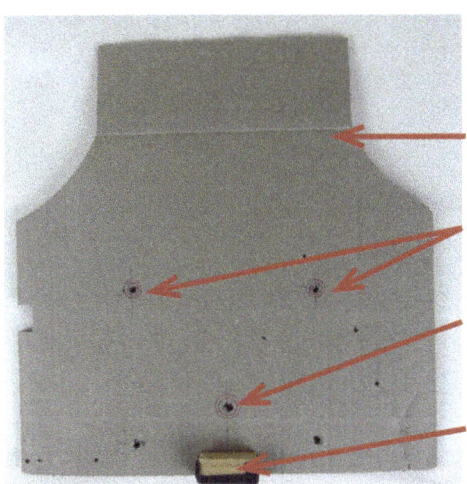

Fold line to bend over rod.

Holes for the weight cords.

Hole for the pendulum dowel.

Glue on a velcrod block to join the clock front to this and keep things in place.

Cardboard resting on proscenium

Velcro strip from clock side onto proscenium bar, see back at no. 3.

Pendulum hole

Cords coming through.

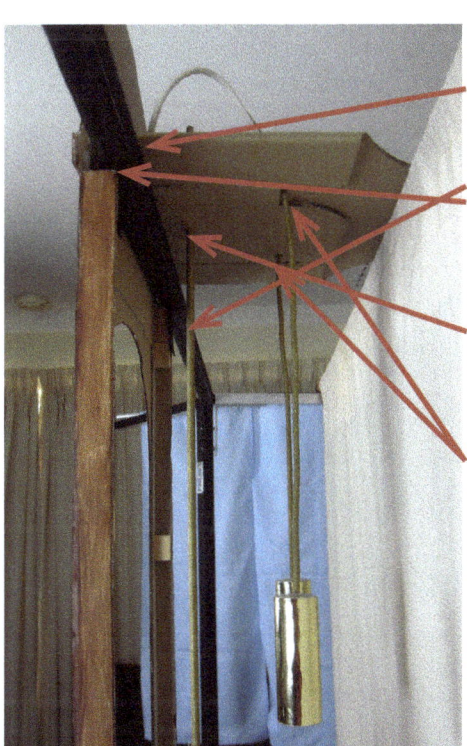

The clock has some velcro on the bottom, the back of the clock and top two sides as seen in the illustration no. 3.

The kebab needs to be long enough to hold and operate it down out of sight.

Henny Penny

NARR   Once upon a time, a fat little hen called Henny Penny was pecking about in the yard when ...whack! Something, maybe it was an acorn, hit her on the head.

H P   Chook-chook-choooook! Oh dear, oh dear! The sky must be falling in. Yes, that's it. The sky is falling in. I must go and tell the king.

NARR   And off she went, trippity-trip, trippity-trip, until she met Cocky Locky, the rooster.

C L   Where are you going?

H P   Don't you know? The sky's falling in! I'm going to tell the king.

C L   Then I'll come with you.

NARR   And off they went, trippity-trip, steppity-step, until they met Ducky Lucky, the big yellow duck.

D L   Where are you going?

ALL   Don't you know? The sky's falling in! We're going to tell the king.

D L   Then I'll come with you

NARR   And off they went, trippity-trip, steppity-step, waddle-wobble, until they met Goosey Poosey, the neat, white goose.

G P   Where are you going?

ALL   Don't you know? The sky's falling in! We're going to tell the king.

G P   Then I'll come with you.

NARR   And off they went, trippity-trip, steppity-step, waddle-wobble, wiggle-waggle, until they met Turkey Lurkey, a busybody of a turkey.

T L   Where are you going?

ALL   Don't you know? The sky's falling in! We're going to tell the king.

T L   Then I'll come with you.

NARR   And off they went, trippity-trip, steppity-step, waddle-wobble, wiggle-waggle, strut-strut-strut, until who should come leaping and loping towards them but Foxy Loxy, the sleekest of foxes.

F L   Hey! Where are you all going?

ALL   Don't you know? The sky's falling in! We're going to tell the king.

F L   Well I never! Just fancy that! If that's so I'd better come with you and show you the shortest way to the palace. Follow me, everyone, if you please.

NARR   And off they went. Trippity-trip, steppity-step, waddle-wobble, wiggle-waggle, strut-strut-strut, straight into a dark hole....the fox's den. Pounce!
Each one was grabbed by Foxy Loxy and gobbled up, except for Henny Penny. She had turned about and bustled off home.

H P   Chook-chook-choooook! I do believe it's time I laid an egg today.

NARR   And so the king never knew that the sky had fallen in.

The end

This is a simple story of one puppet being joined by others on a journey together, going across the stage several times. This one requires more co-operation and skill to work well.

They are all bird characters except for the fox.

It is still best if two groups perform two different versions of the same play. Plenty of extra script can be added in.

A simple scene could be part of the chook house on the front of the proscenium and a back ground of green with a few bushes.
The chook house can be replaced with a bush on the first circuit of the stage to create the illusion of travelling along, the log for the rooster, the pond for the duck, etc.

Build the bird characters with their noises, walk and actions, etc.

There needs to be a bush hiding a big dark hole at the side of the stage on the last trip across.

Most children are right handed so the action is best going from their right to left across the stage.

Plan where each bird will meet Henny Penny. They have to go beside her until they all go around the back of the stage, when they can drop back to the end of the line. Henny Penny drops back at the end, turns around and goes home to lay an egg. She could go right back to the chook house talking about the things she passes on the way and how she needs to get home to lay this egg. She's glad to arrive home and go in to lay her egg.
Act all the sorts of things these birds do, have the audience in stitches with laughter.
All this has to be worked out because the puppeteers themselves have to move easily around each other.

Making the puppet.

1. Decide what character you will be making and choose a 60 x 60cm piece of material for it.

Turn to its page and follow the illustrated instructions on how to make it.

Henny Penny
The instructions are on p 35.

Foxy Loxy
Instructions are on page 33.

Cocky Locky

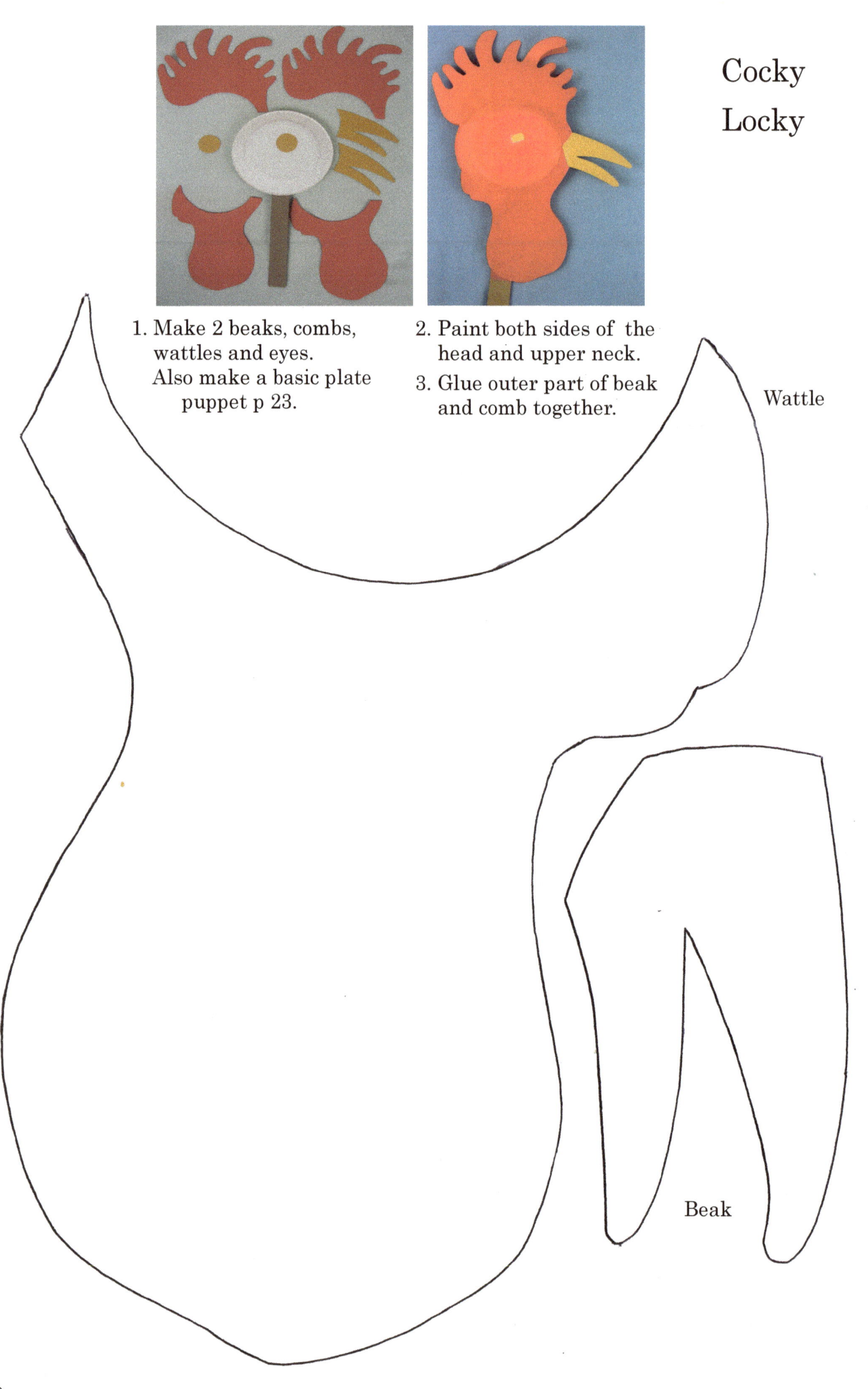

1. Make 2 beaks, combs, wattles and eyes. Also make a basic plate puppet p 23.
2. Paint both sides of the head and upper neck.
3. Glue outer part of beak and comb together.

Wattle

Beak

4. Place open side over plate edge, marking where they go.
5. Glue them on.
6. Glue on wattle and eyes.

Note his colour has been changed because he was too red.
Also his wattle is smaller.

Go to p 46 the for tail instructions and kebab extension p 43.

Eye

Comb

Eye

Eye

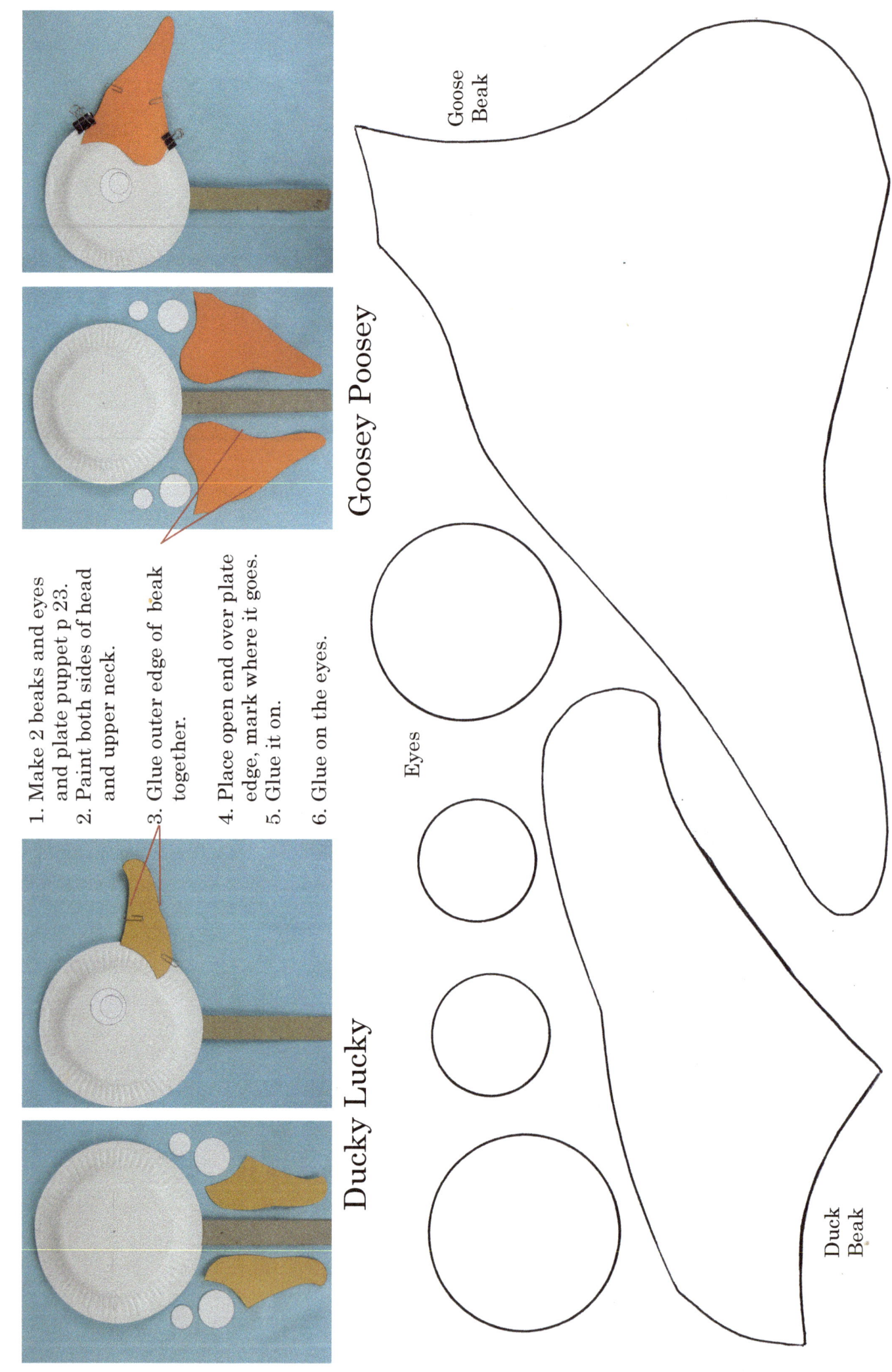

Goosey Poosey

Ducky Lucky

1. Make 2 beaks and eyes and plate puppet p 23.
2. Paint both sides of head and upper neck.
3. Glue outer edge of beak together.
4. Place open end over plate edge, mark where it goes.
5. Glue it on.
6. Glue on the eyes.

Goose Beak

Eyes

Duck Beak

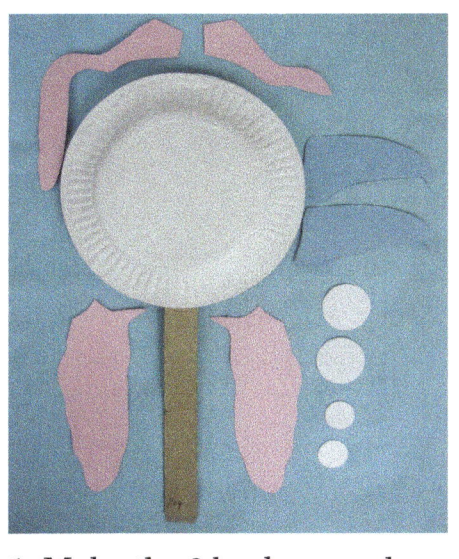 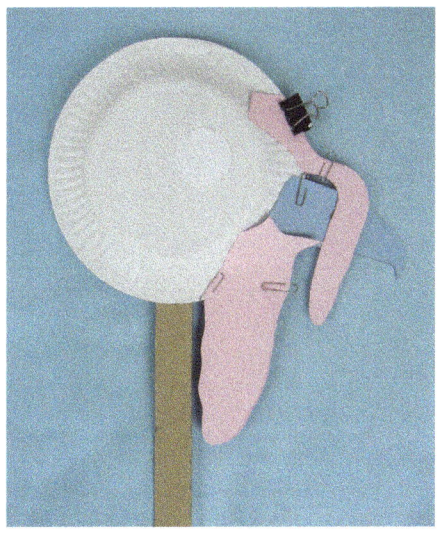 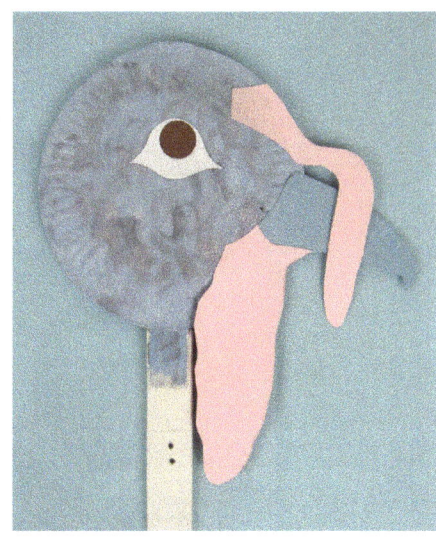

1. Make the 2 beaks, snoods, wattle pieces and eyes. Also a basic plate puppet p 23.

2. Paint both sides of the head and upper neck.

3. Glue outer edge of beak together.

4. Place it over plate edge, mark position.

5. Glue it on.

6. Glue the eyes in place.

7. Glue snood and wattles on.

Turkey Lurkey

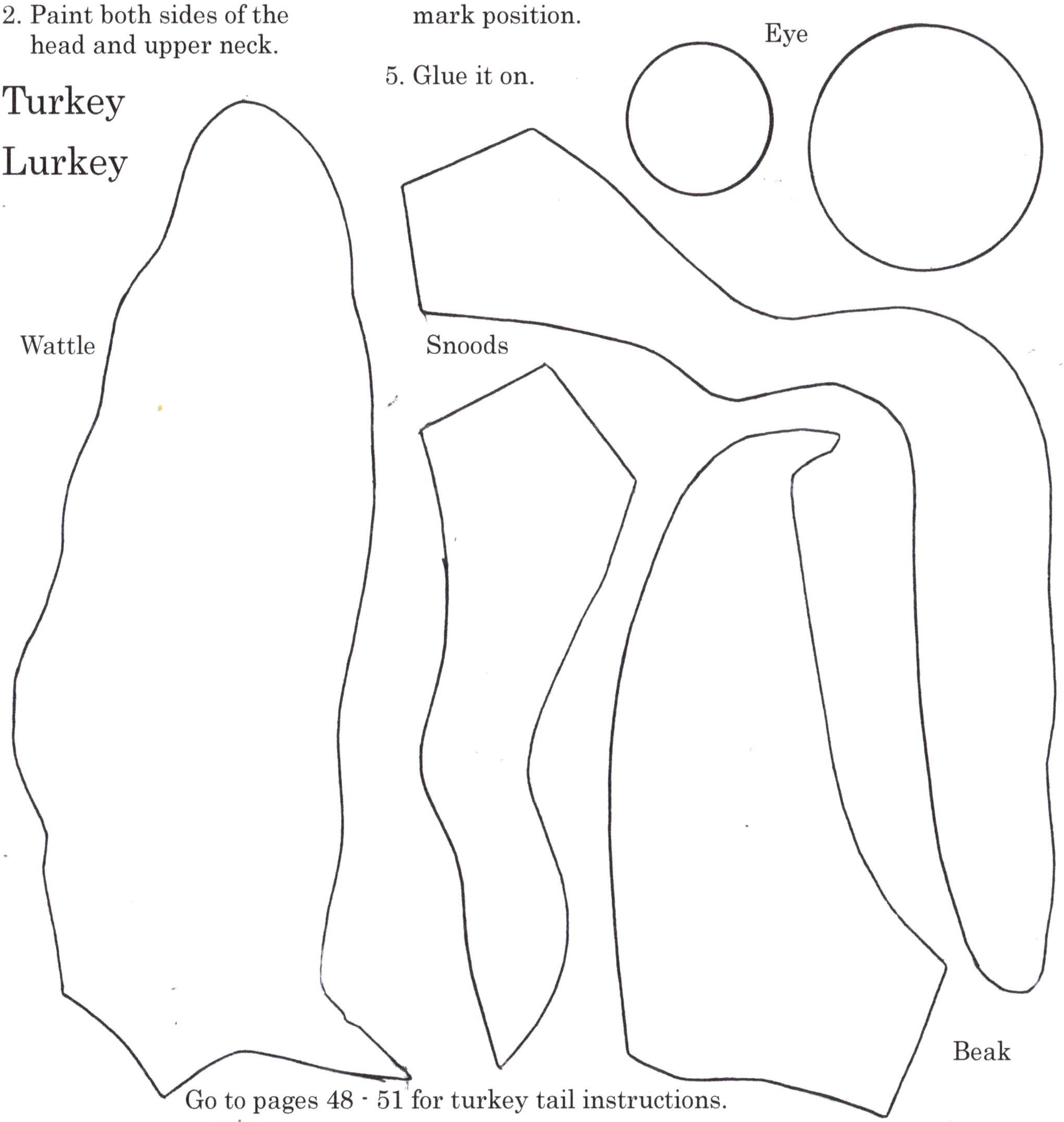

Wattle

Snoods

Eye

Beak

Go to pages 48 - 51 for turkey tail instructions.

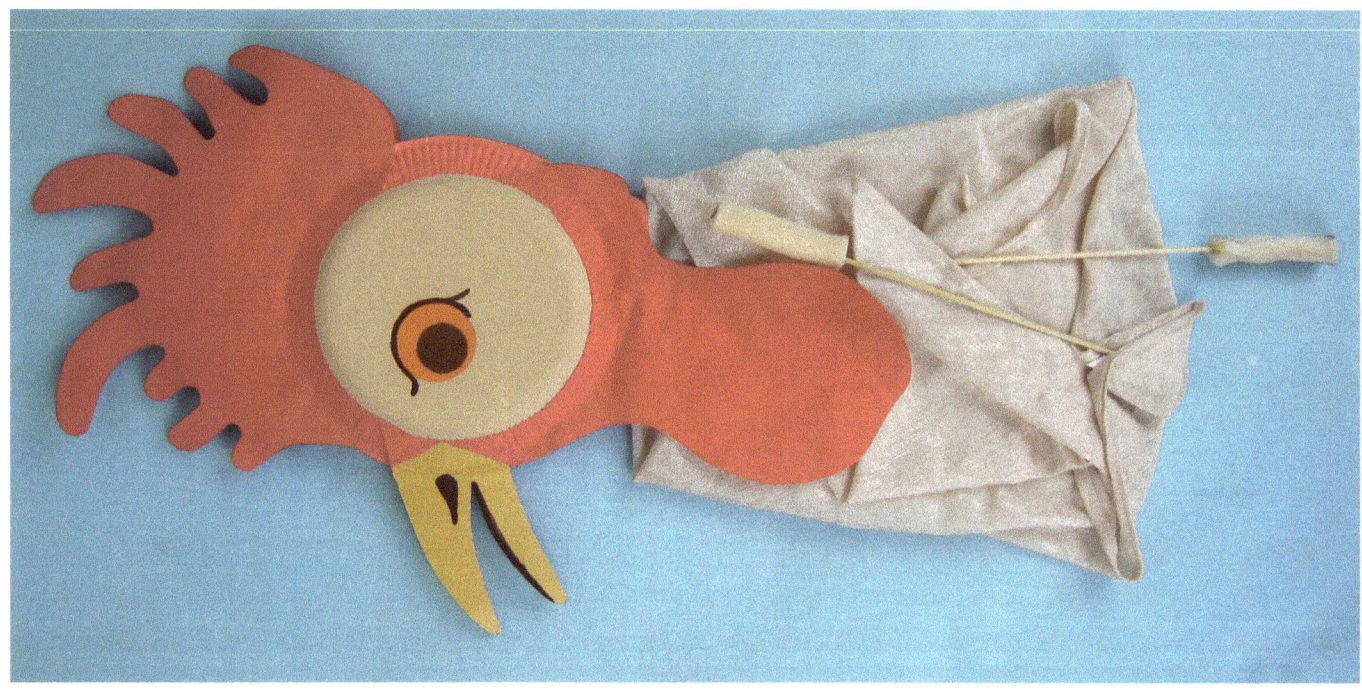

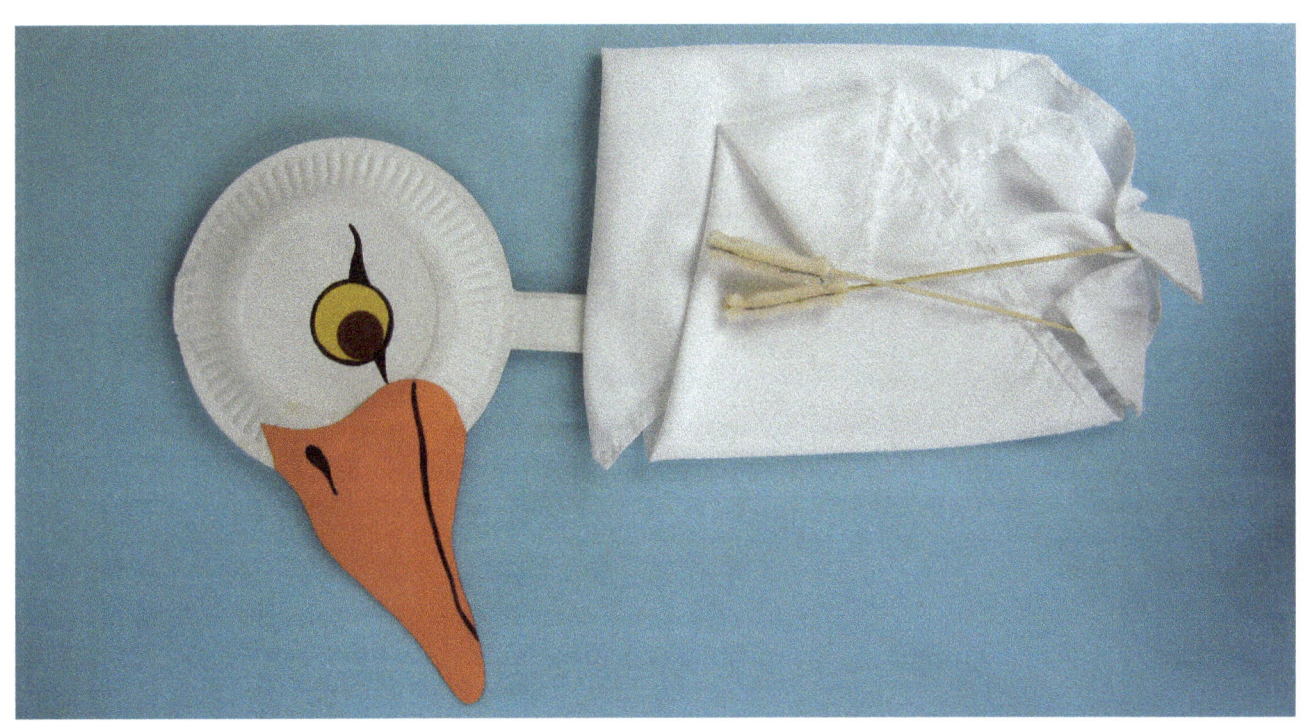

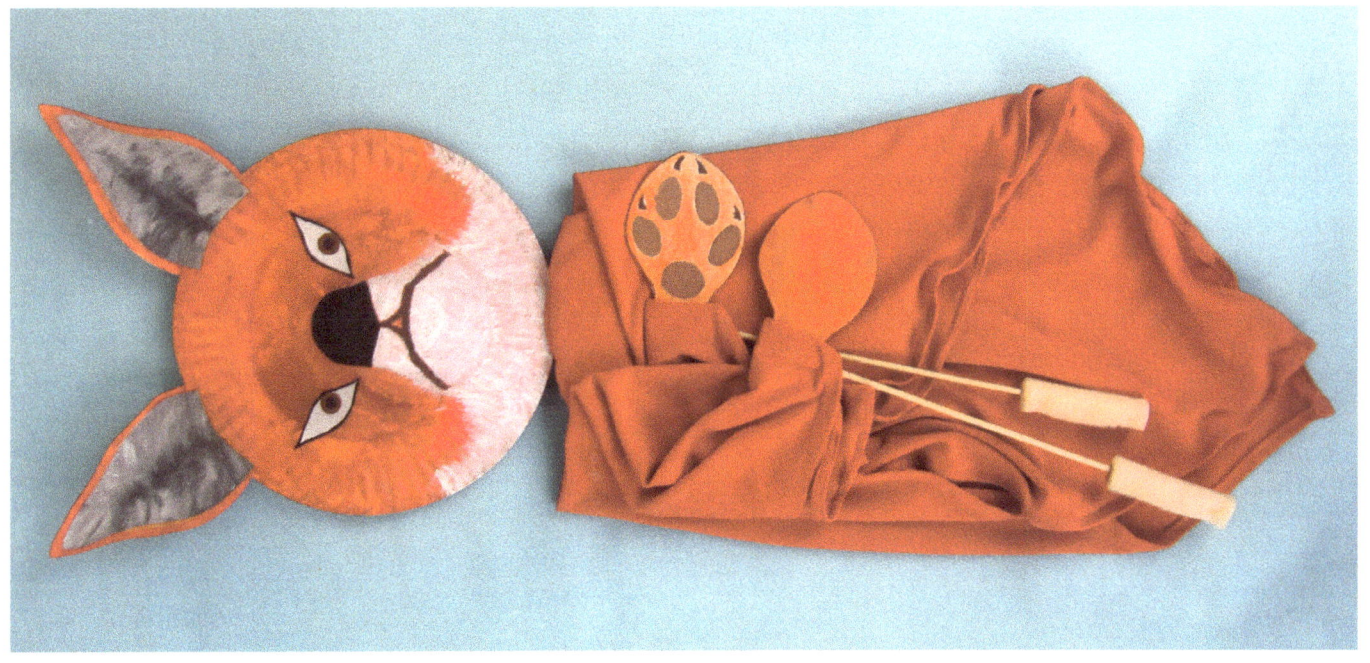

Pond

Water with just the tops of the reeds showing because you are not at ground level. While Henny Penny is going around the back put the pond in. The duck can waddle on and get into it, swim around and dive, shake her tail, preen, etc. She can quack and talk too.

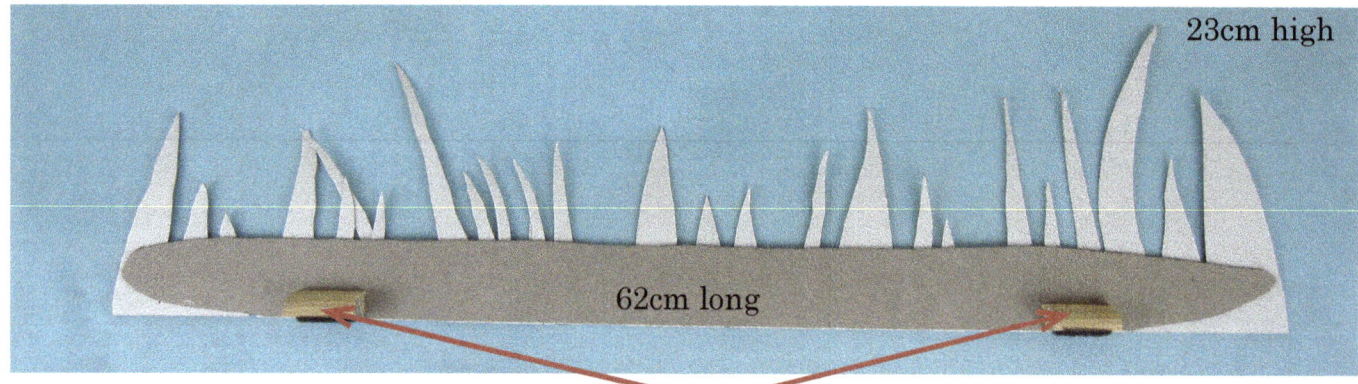

23cm high

62cm long

The back of the reeds with 2 small wood blocks with a piece of loop velcro glued on.

These trees were used on one of the scenes. Medium to tall ones would also suit well.

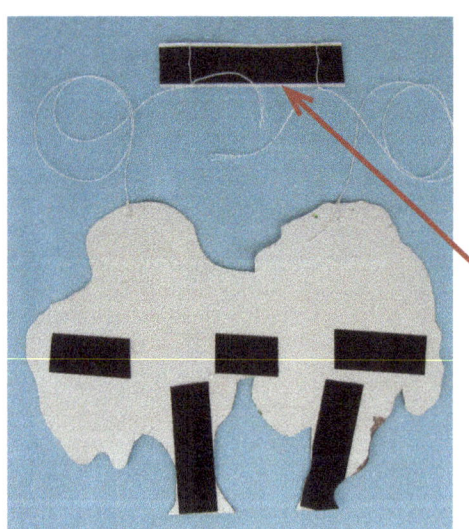

These trees need strings up to the clouds to hold them upright because they are higher on the felt so tend to fall forward.

Black stick-on velcro hook with the white paper still on (same colour as the cloud) ~

or use white sew-on hook.

84cm high

23cm wide

Chook house

It is flat cardboard with a velcroed block on its base and left side.

73cm high

Strings

40cm wide

26cm wide

59cm wide

Fox hole

It hangs from a curtain rod, placed between the theatre front and the back drop, so the puppets go in front of it and are thrown down the hole by the fox.

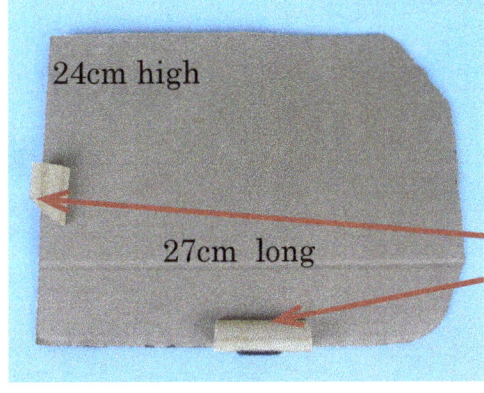

24cm high

27cm long

The log must be large because the rooster is large.

Back of log with a velcroed block on the bottom and side edge.

The rhyme ~ 'My Black Hen' can be used with Henny Penny who goes back home to lay an egg and thereby escapes from the fox!

The birds could sing the first part of 'Follow the Yellow Brick Road' from the Wizard of Oz, as they go off stage around the back and the scene changes.

My Black Hen
Higgledy, piggledy, my black hen,
She lays eggs for gentlemen;
Gentlemen come every day
To see what my black hen doth lay.
Sometimes nine and sometimes ten,
She lays eggs for gentlemen.

Chook eats outside her house, puts her wing to her head when hit, can circle, sit down, talk to herself, get up and go. Add in more and she can repeat a different one of these actions each time she meets a new animal.

The rooster could give a few good crows from up on the log as Henny Penny crosses the stage, and then jump down. Hold him high to allow for the illusion of his body being under him.

Duck can preen, etc., dive, her tail can be sticking up when they come along. Then she pops up like a duck does. She comes out of the pond and walks off slightly in front of Henny Penny.

Small trees on the back ground with duck, rooster and Henny Penny meeting goose.

Green grass background with goose, duck, rooster and Henny Penny meeting turkey.

The fox throws each one down the hole but Henny Penny turns and leaves to go home because it is time to lay an egg. What are they doing that they don't notice what is happening?

Tails ~ another addition to these puppets that opens up more opportunities for fun.

With these wings and tails the birds can do all the actions you have seen birds do, or that you can imagine, so enjoy acting them. Make their calls and sounds, etc.

Cocky Locky can cock-a-doodle-doo, fly and be a very proud, strutting bird.
Turkey Lurkey has quite a tail and gobbles noisily.

Exaggerate these animals' quaint ways. Go round the back of the theatre and make each meeting interesting and fun.

You can play or sing 'Follow The Yellow Brick Road' as you go around the back.

Ducky Lucky has a pond (it can be bigger) and she just has to come along and hop into it, swim around and be diving when Henny Penny arrives.

She can shake herself when she gets out and waddle after Cocky Locky.

Foxy Loxy is very cunning and he talks them into following him right into his hole so he must talk a lot as they go along and they can answer him.

The Little Red Hen

NARR	Once upon a time on a fine spring day, the Little Red Hen found an ear of wheat.
LRH	Cluck, cluck, cluck! I will plant it. (Pause) Who will help me plant the wheat?
DUCK	Not I.
CAT	Not I.
DOG	Not I.
PIG	Not I.
LRH	Then I will plant it myself. (She plants it)
NARR	And she did. Very soon it began to grow. It grew tall and strong. It flowered. The flower changed into an ear of wheat that ripened ready for harvesting.
LRH	Who will help me cut the wheat?
DUCK	Not I.
CAT	Not I.
DOG	Not I.
PIG	Not I.
LRH	Then I shall cut it myself.
NARR	And she did. Now it had to be threshed to separate each little seed from its husk.
LRH	Who will help me thresh the wheat?
DUCK	Not I.
CAT	Not I.
DOG	Not I.
PIG	Not I.
LRH	Then I shall thresh it myself.
NARR	And she did. The wheat was then ready to be taken to the mill where it would be ground into flour.
LRH	Who will help me carry the wheat?
DUCK	Not I.
CAT	Not I.
DOG	Not I.
PIG	Not I.
LRH	Then I shall carry it myself.
NARR	And she did. The miller ground the wheat into flour and the Little Red Hen carried it home in a sack.
LRH	Who will help me make the flour into dough for the bread?
DUCK	Not I.
CAT	Not I.
DOG	Not I.
PIG	Not I.
LRH	Then I shall make it myself.
NARR	And she did. She mixed dough in a bowl with yeast, sugar and water then set it to rise. Soon the bread was ready to go into the oven to bake.

LRH	Who will help me bake the bread?
DUCK	Not I.
CAT	Not I.
DOG	Not I.
PIG	Not I.
LRH	Then I will bake it myself.
NARR	And she did. Before long the smell of newly baked bread drifted from the kitchen. The duck smelt it. The cat smelt it. the dog smelt it. the pig smelt it.
DUCK	Quack, quack.
NARR	The cat smelt it.
CAT	Meow.
NARR	The dog smelt it.
DOG	Woof, woof.
NARR	The pig smelt it.
PIG	Oink, oink.
LRH	Who will help me eat this bread?
DUCK	I will.
CAT	I will.
DOG	I will.
PIG	I will.
LRH	No, you won't. You wouldn't help me to plant, cut, carry, mill or bake the bread so I will eat it myself.
NARR	And she did, but first she called her chickens:
LRH	Chook-chook-chooook!
CHICKS	Peep-peep-peep!
NARR	And the little Red Hen shared the bread with them.

A longer script and more puppets

A simple story with puppets entering and exiting in all different ways throughout the play.
In this story there are very different animal characters to make and act - great fun.
I still suggest that two groups perform two varied versions of the same play.

The scene could be a farm yard with part of a tree on one side and a barn on the other side.
The group can be towards the tree side so they can act under it.

The Little Red Hen is able to come in and go off on the tree side to plant, inspect and harvest. The animals move off or stand in the side wing. She can go off the barn side and some can follow her out that way or come in before her and join the others then she comes in. Vary it!

Each time she disappears off stage the animals need to do some behaviour typical to them, staying on stage or running off barking, curling up to sleep by the tree, oinking, waddling and quacking, etc. (There are a lot of animal things they can do and comments they can make) to show time is passing. Also make their "no" sound different every time..

They can slowly come over to the barn as bread is cooking and this time they have plenty to say and act excitedly (dog can wag tail, pig can squeal and wiggle tail, etc.)
She can come out and, to emphasise her "no," go back in.
How does it end? You decide! Make it good!

1. Make 2 beaks, combs, wattles, eyes and a basic plate puppet p 23.
2. Paint both sides of the head and upper neck.
3. Glue outer edge of beak and comb together.
4. Place open side over plate edge, mark where they go.
5. Glue them on.
6. Glue on wattle and eyes.
7. Make the body p 37.
8. Do the wings p 43.

Little Red Hen

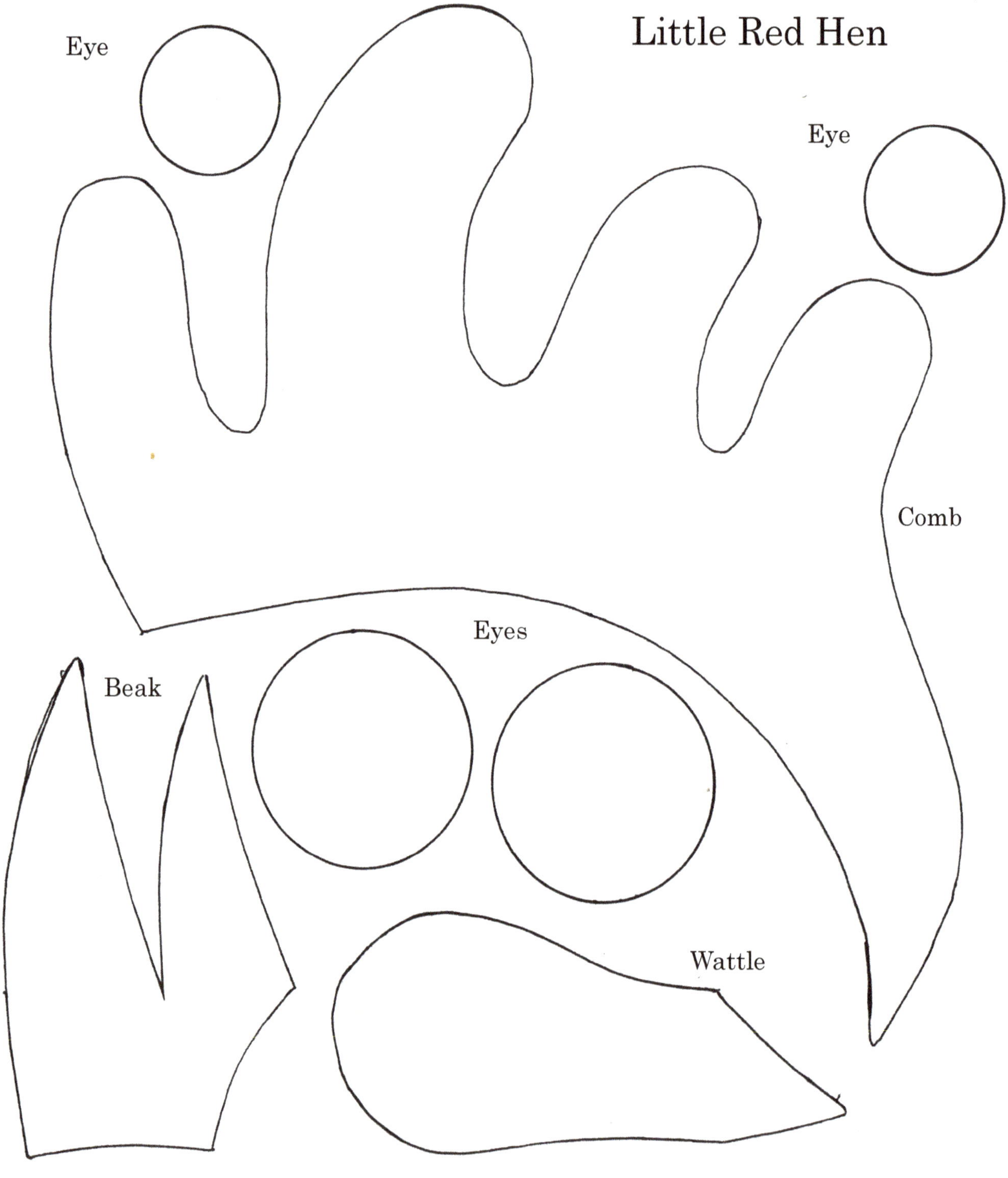

Eye

Eye

Comb

Beak

Eyes

Wattle

103

Chickens

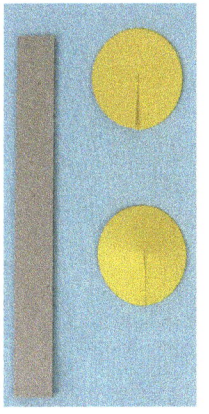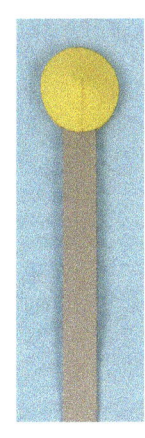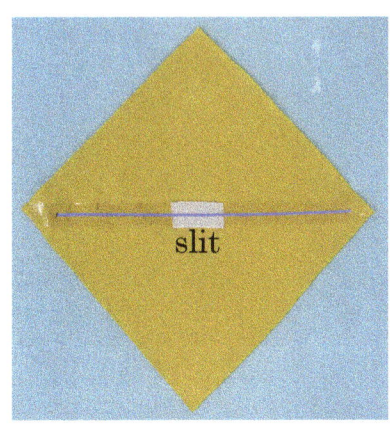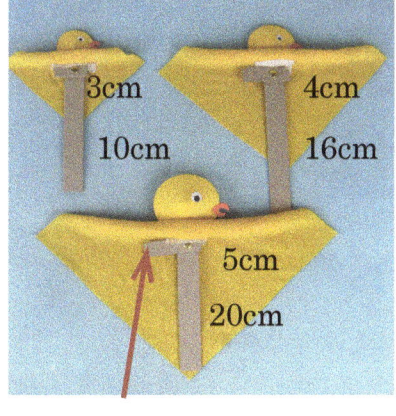

1. Cut a 30cm x 2cm cardboard strip.
2. Cut out two 5-7cm circles and make a cut into the centre of each.
3. Glue them into a very slight cone and then onto either side of the card strip.
4. Cut square of yellow material.
5. Reinforce the middle and cut the slit for the cardboard strip.
6. Put the body on and hold it there with a 3/4/5cm strip.
7. Glue on eyes and a beak.

The chickens can be slightly different sizes or all the same.

The small one here is cute but a bit too small.

Duck

1. Choose the 60 x 60cm piece of material for the puppet body.
2. Make a basic small plate puppet as shown on p 23.

3. Paint both sides of the head and upper neck.
3. Make the head with 2 beaks and eyes the same as the Hen on the previous page but without the combs and wattles.

4. Turn to p 37 and make the body.
6. Then do the wings p 43.

Cat

1. Choose the 60 x 60cm piece of material for the puppet.

2. Make a basic plate puppet as shown on p 23.
3. Turn to p 29 'making a cat puppet' and follow the instructions through to p 38.

Dog

1. Choose the 60 x 60cm piece of material for the puppet body.
2. Make a basic small plate puppet as shown on p 23.
3. Select a shape for the snout. This one is a 1/2 cup measure as illustrated.
4. Go to 'Animal head' p 33 and follow points 4 to 8 for the snout.
5. Continue with all the appropriate points from p 33 through to p 38 to complete the puppet.

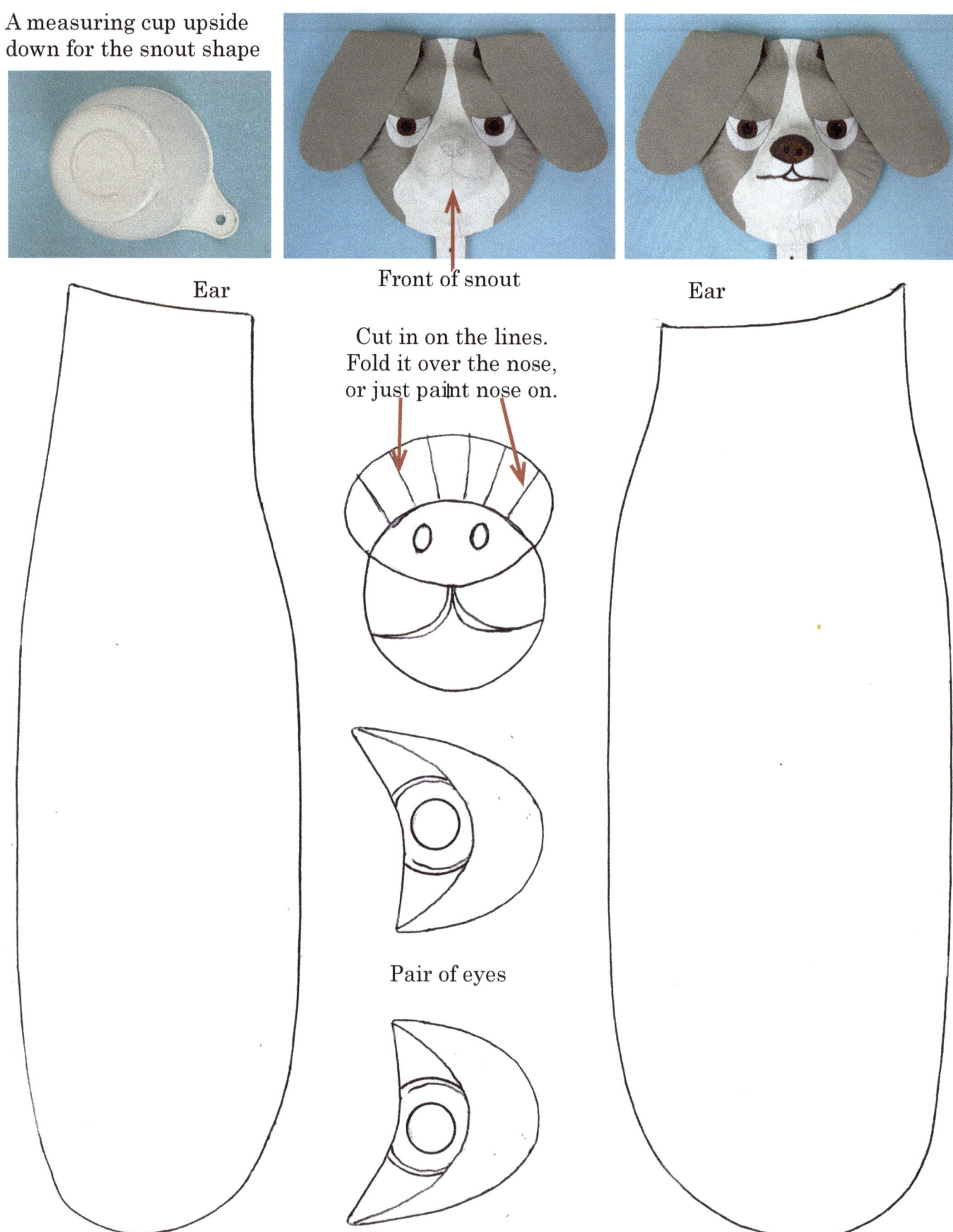

A measuring cup upside down for the snout shape

Ear

Front of snout

Ear

Cut in on the lines. Fold it over the nose, or just paint nose on.

Pair of eyes

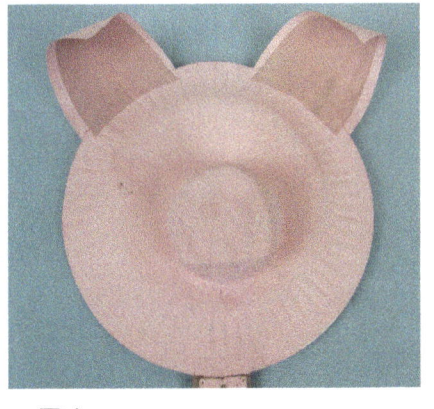  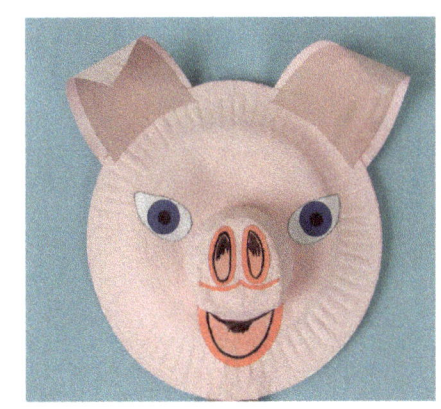

Pig

1. Choose the 60 x 60cm piece of material for the puppet body.

2. Make a basic small plate puppet as shown on p 23.

3. Select a shape for the snout.

4. Go to 'Animal head' p 33 step 4 (cover it with plastic⋯) and continue to 8 for the snout.

5. Then continue on p34 through to the completed puppet.

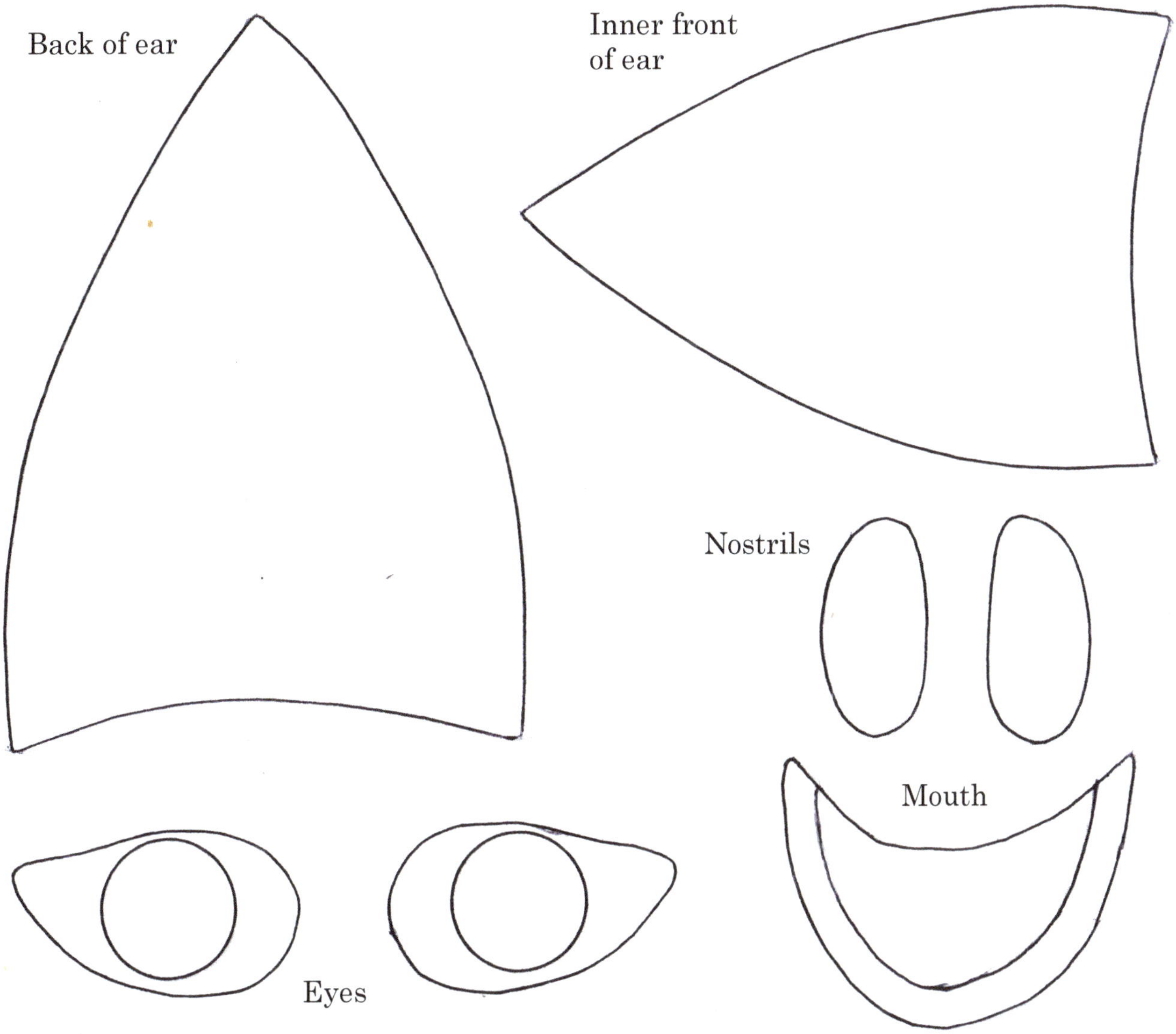

Back of ear

Inner front of ear

Nostrils

Mouth

Eyes

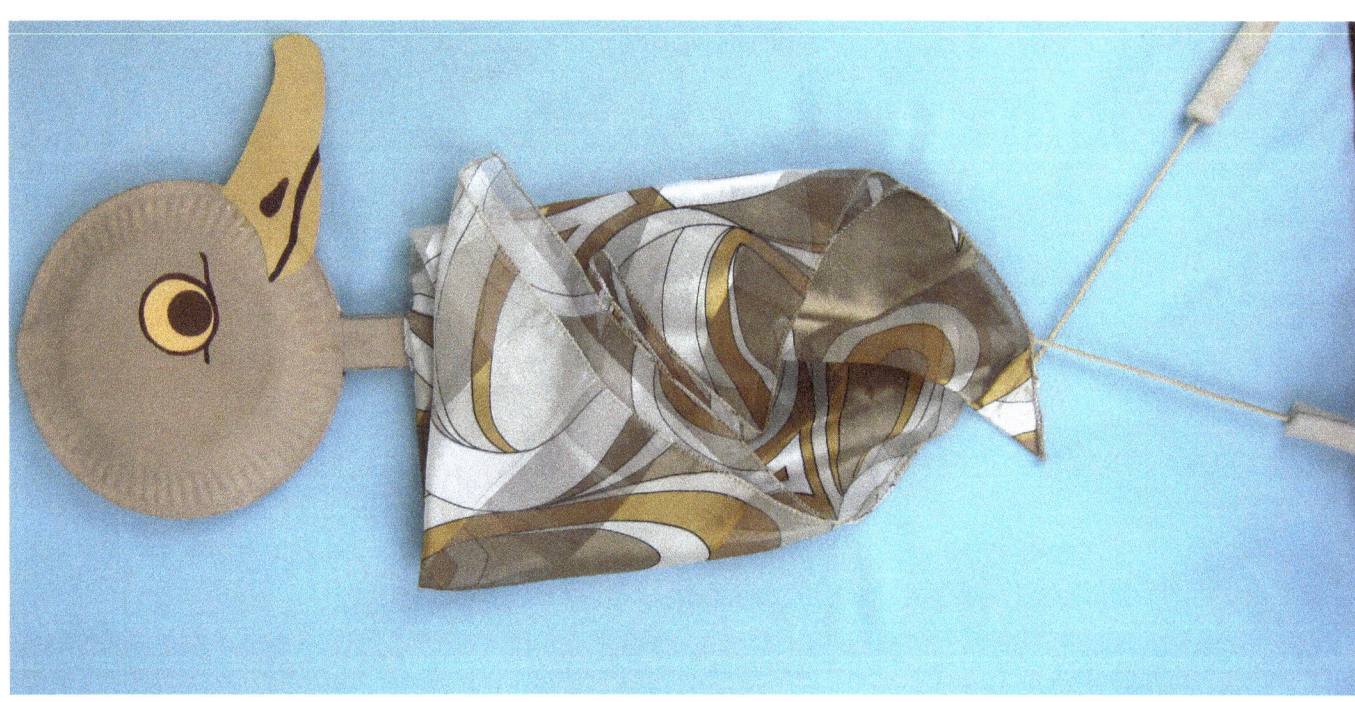

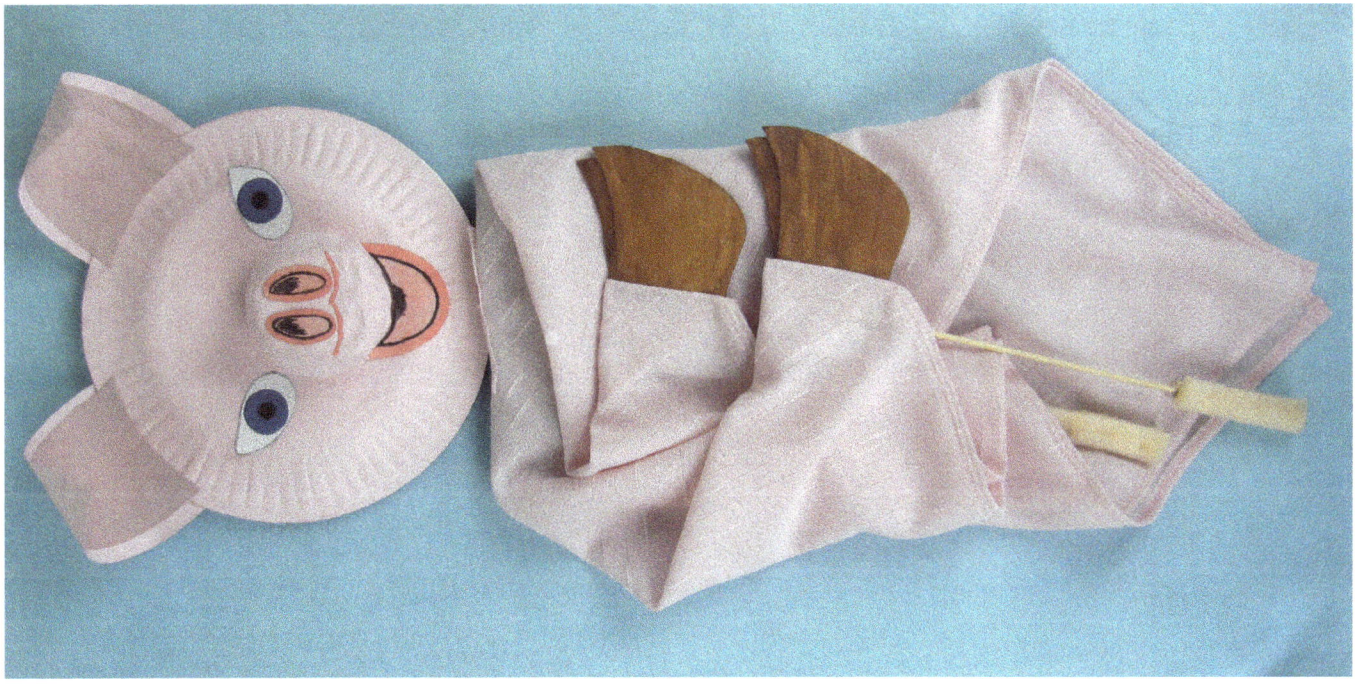

Ears of wheat drawn on cardboard, coloured, cut out and tied together. Two is enough to carry. 25cm long.

25cm long

9cm high

17.5cm long

Loaf drawn and painted on cream cardboard then cut out.

18 x 10cm

Small piece of folded material sown together, written on, a fluffy light filling and then a tie to carry it by.

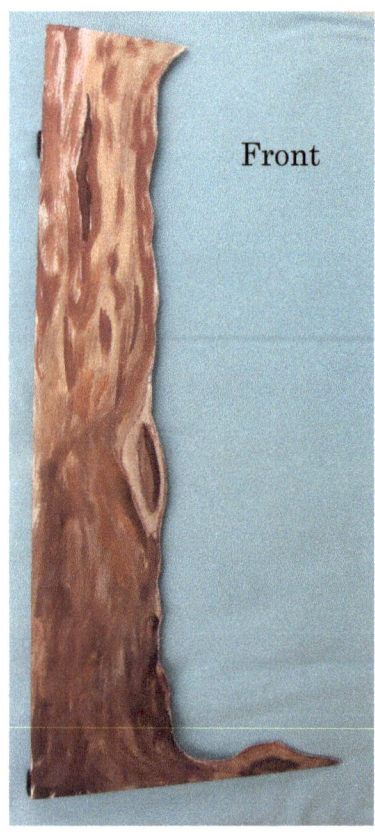
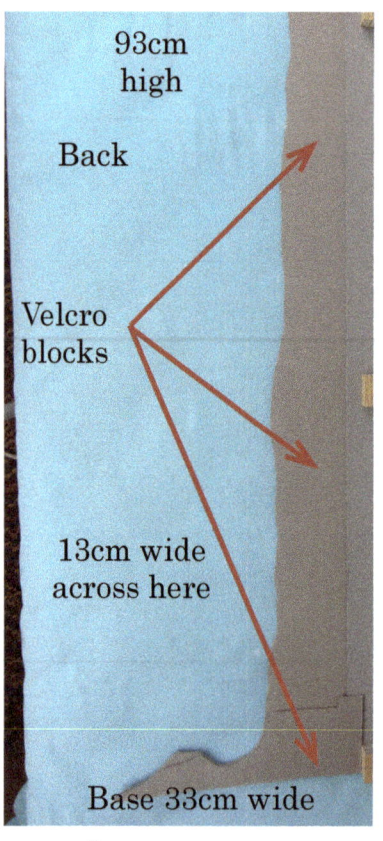
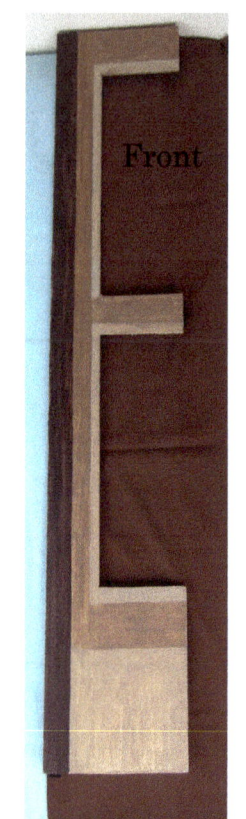
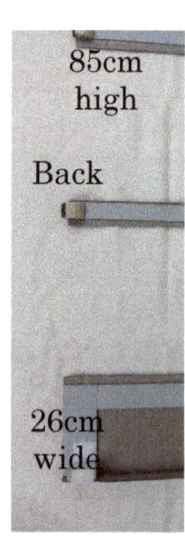

Part of a tree trunk

The barn window

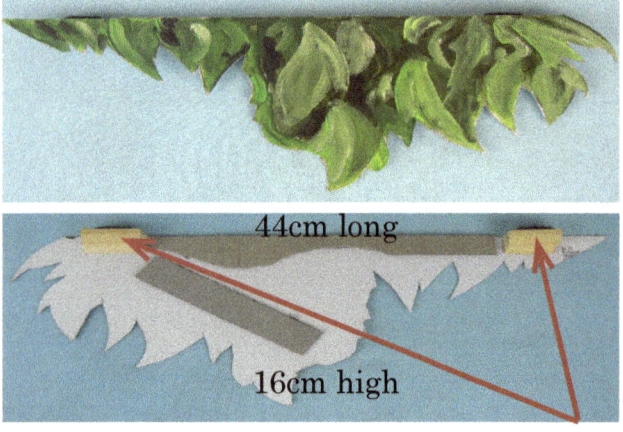
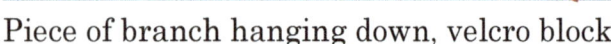
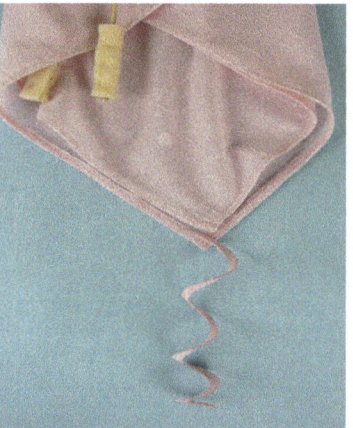

Piece of branch hanging down, velcro block   Pig tail   Duck tail

We forgot to hang the strip of brown material behind the barn. LRH is holding the wheat ears.

Here she has come in with the bag of flour. Puppets are in a different order.

This was taken before we had made the big tree behind, see how the tree adds to the scene.

The Little Red Hen and the grains of wheat

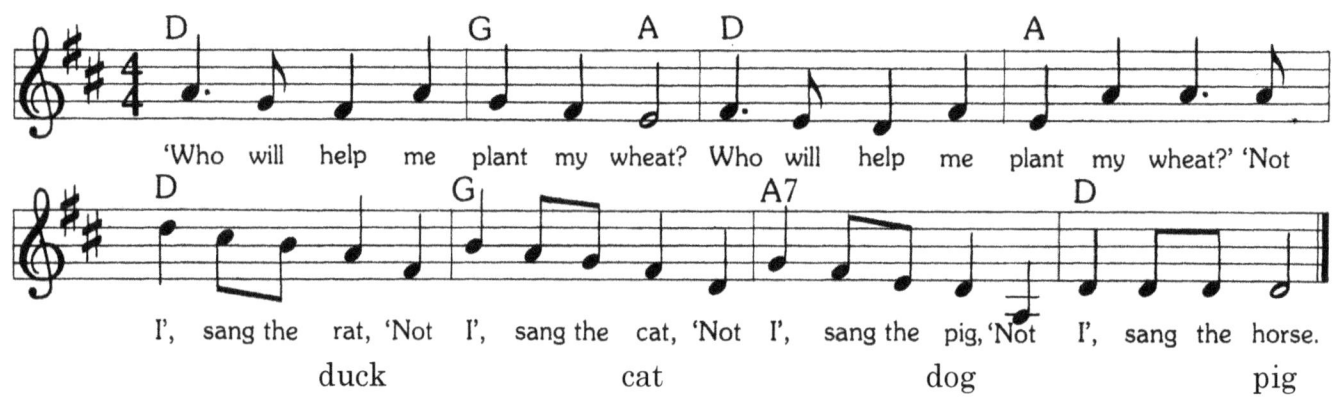

Pat - a - cake

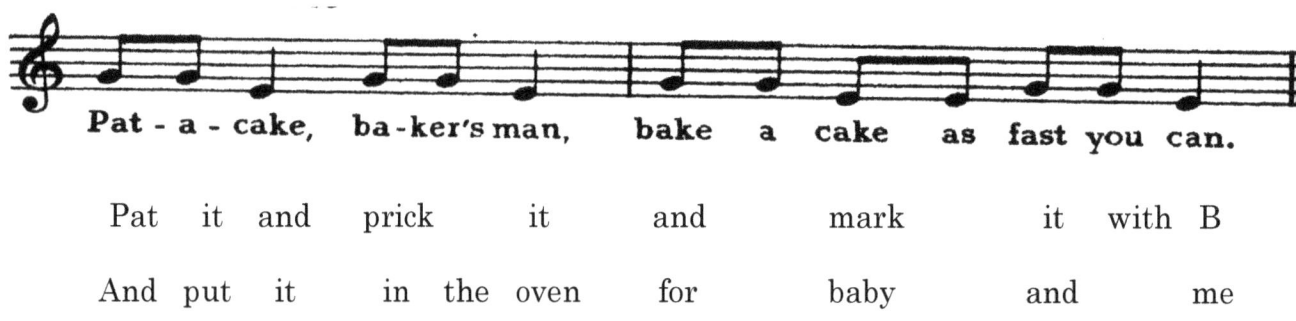

Five Little Chicks

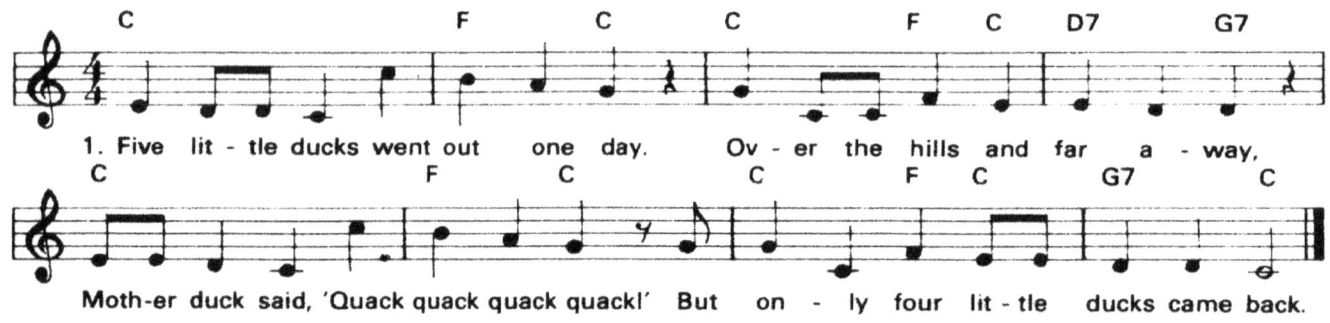

Change this song to 5 little chicks went out one day.

Five little chicks went out one day.....
Four little chicks went out one day....
Three little chicks went out one day....
Two little chicks went out one day.....

One little chick went out one day,
Over the hills and far away,
Mother chook said, cluck, cluck, cluck, cluck!
And none of those little chicks came back.

Old mother chook went out one day,
Over the hills and far away,
Mother chook said, cluck, cluck, cluck, cluck!
And all of the five little chicks came back.

Eat Brown Bread

Cows in the Clover

Narrator Once upon a time a farmer said to his boy.

Farmer Whatever happens, the cows must not get in to the clover paddock. It's nearly ready to be cut.

NARR Then he put on his hat and drove off to town. He couldn't have gone far when the boy noticed that the cows were in the paddock.

Boy Hey, hey! Get out of there! (He shouts as he runs to the paddock. He yells, he waves his arms, he chases and chases the cows).

Narr And do they come out? No! They kick up their heels and run to the other side of the paddock.

Cows Moo!

Boy (Sitting down by the gate, he cries) Boo hoo!

Horse (Coming on stage) What's wrong?

Boy The cows are in the clover and I can't get them out.

Horse Stop crying. I'll get them out. (Trots into the paddock) Neigh, neigh! (He stamps his feet, he paws at the air, he chases the cows.)

Narrator And do they come out? No! They kick up their heels and run to the other side of the paddock.

Cows Moo!

Horse (Sits down next to the boy.)

Boy Boo hoo!

Horse Neigh, neigh!

Cat (Coming on stage) What's wrong?

B, H The cows are in the clover and we can't get them out.

Cat Stop crying. I'll get them out. (She pads into the clover paddock) Meeow, meeow! (she arches her back, she shows her claws, she hisses and spits and scratches the cows.)

Narrator And do they come out? No! They kick up their heels and run to the other side of the paddock.

Cows Moo!

Cat (Sits next to the boy and the horse)

Boy Boo hoo!

Horse	Neigh, neigh!
Cat	Meeow, meeow!
Dog	(Coming on stage) What's wrong?
B, H, C	The cows are in the clover paddock and we can't get them out.
Dog	(Bounding into the paddock) Woof, woof! (He nips at their heels, rushes at their heads, he dances round the cows, round and round.)
Narrator	And do they come out? No! They kick up their heels and run to the other side of the paddock.
Cows	Moo!
Dog	(Sits down beside the boy and the horse and the cat and they cry)
Boy	Boo hoo!
Horse	Neigh, neigh!
Cat	Meeow, meeow!
Dog	Woof, woof!
Rooster	(Coming on stage) What's wrong?
B, H, C, D.	The cows are in the paddock and we can't get them out.
Rooster	Stop crying. I'll get them out. (He struts into the clover paddock.) E-eer, e-eer, e-eer. (He stretches his neck, flaps his wings, he flies and flies at the cows.)
Narrator	And do they come out? No! They kick up their heels and run to the other side of the paddock.
Cows	Moo!
Rooster	(Sits down next to the boy and the horse, the cat and the dog, and they cry.)
Boy	Boo hoo!
Horse	Neigh, neigh!
Cat	Meeow, meeow!
Dog	Woof, woof!
Rooster	E-eer, e-eer, e-eer!
Bee	(Flying by) Stop crying, I'll get the cows out.
B, H, C. D,R	You can't do that! You're too small! The cows are too big! Don't go into the clover paddock.

Narrator	The bee had already gone. She flew to the nearest cow and landed lightly on her ear. Next thing the cow ran out through the gate . The little bee flew on to the next cow. She landed on her ear. And that cow, too, ran out through the gate while the little bee flew to another cow who didn't wait for the bee to land on her ear. Out through the gate she went and the rest of the cows followed her.
Boy	How did you get the cows to come out of the clover paddock?
Bee	I buzzed in each cows ear.
Boy	What did you buzz?
Bee	I said, that if you don't get out of the clover then I shall have to sting you. That's all I said.
All	Oh, we think you are very clever!
Narrator	By the time the farmer came home there was nothing to show that the cows had been in the clover paddock. The clover, which had been flattened each time the cows kicked up their heels, had straightened up again. The farmer was able to make hay the next day.

The End

More complicated action

There are human, animal and bird characters. The bee should be tiny and on a kebab stick.
In this story puppets come on and off the stage freely, interacting then joining the group.

This story definitely requires more co-operation and skill for it to work well.
I still suggest that two groups perform two different versions of the same play.

A simple scene can be a piece of farm fence hanging from a scenery rod.
Back drop is a paddock with a tapered end to give perspective.
A very small fence or bush line can be added on the top edge of the paddock.

Most children are right handed so the action is best going from right to left across the stage.

The group of cows can move on and off on the right of the stage behind the fence.
Animals slowly gather at one side and the cows on the other.

The cows rush off stage each time chased by the animal who then returns to the group.
The next animal is able to come along in front of the fence.

After their discussion they bunch back to let that new animal into the paddock.
The cows have drifted back into the paddock. The animal acts around them then chases them.

Don't rush the story. Make the animals actions and noises very dramatic and funny.
Putting the animals under a big tree balances and adds interest to the scene.

All the actions have to be worked out because the puppeteers themselves have to move easily around each other. It's ok for puppeteers' hands to show when jumping up, etc. at cows.

Farmer

  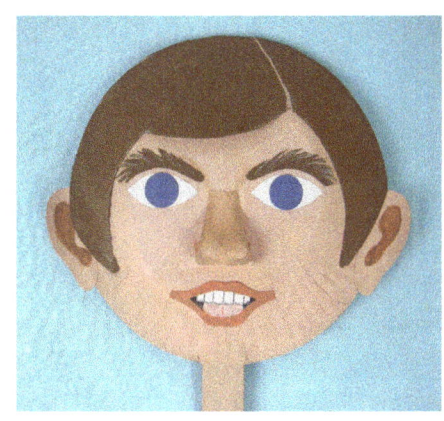

1. Go to p 23 and make a basic plate puppet using a 23cm plate.

2. Follow the instructions on p 25 and p 26 using these templates, or your own, to make the head.

3. Continue on to the body p 36 and hand instructions p 38.

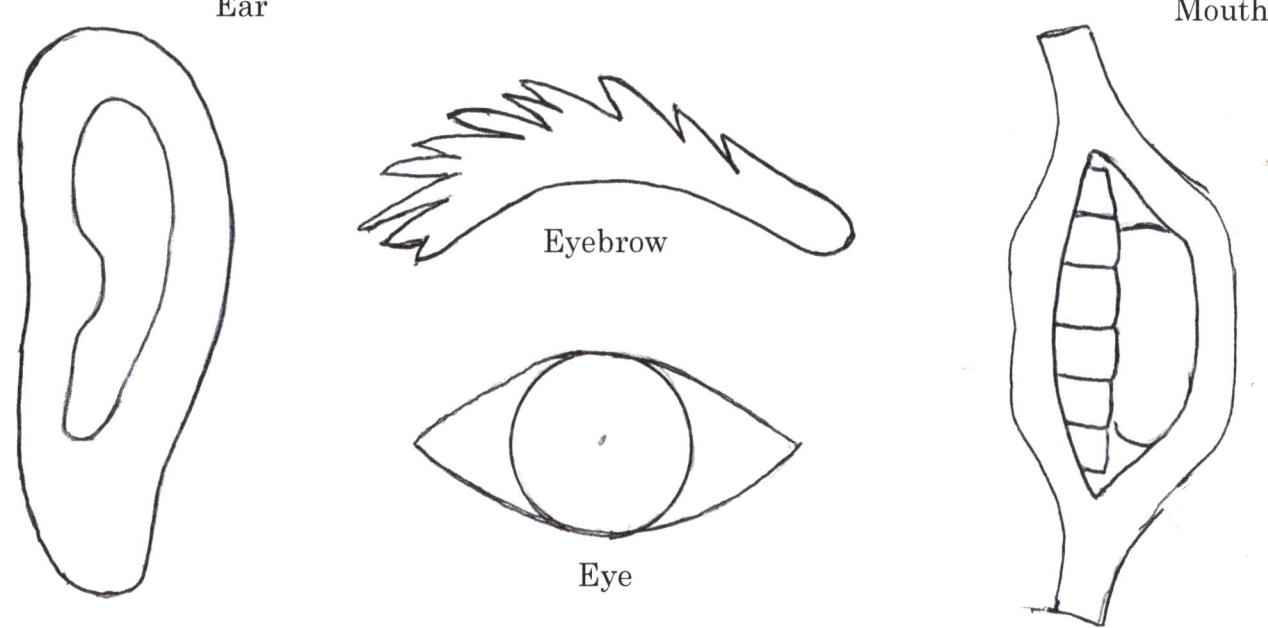

Ear

Eyebrow

Eye

Mouth

Boy

Using an 18cm plate make a basic puppet p 23 and continue to p 25.
Body p 36 and hands p 38.
His hair was shortened and some was trimmed off his ears to bring them in closer to the body, because on a plate they stuck out too much.

Cow

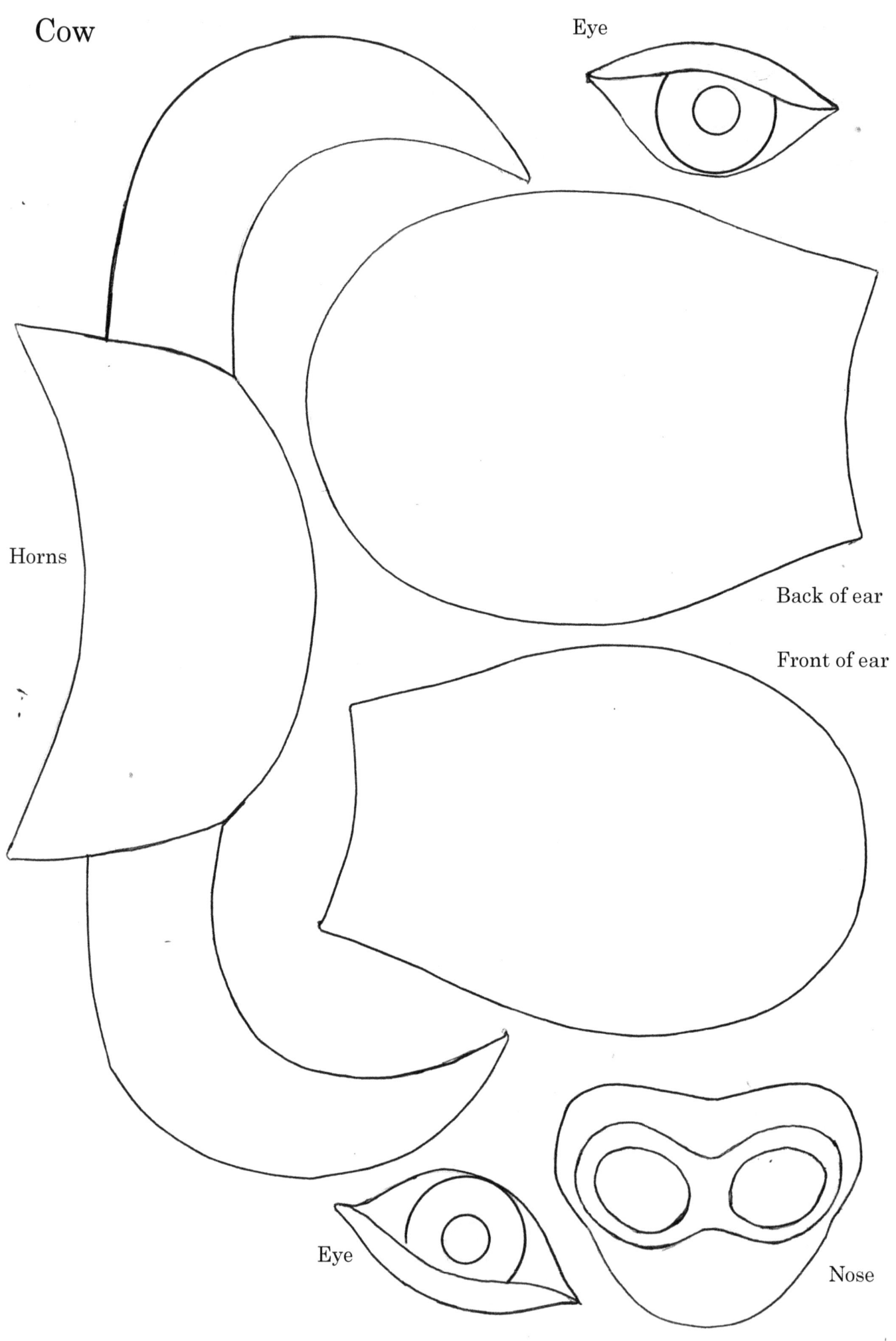

117

Cow

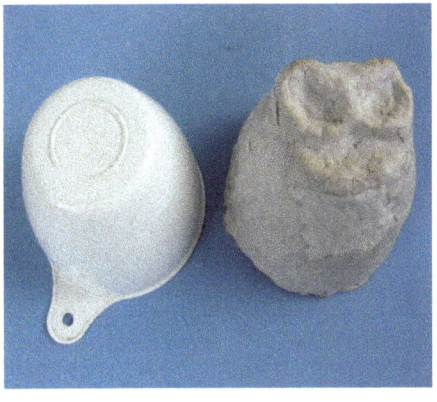
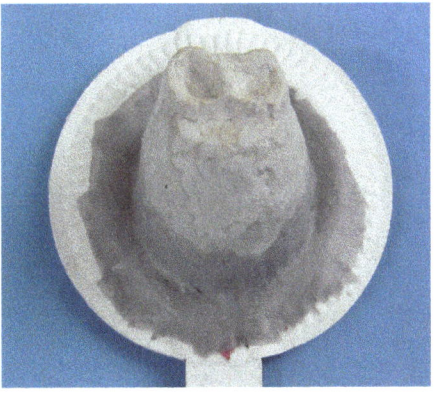

1. Choose a 60 x 60cm piece of material for the body.
2. Make a basic small plate puppet as shown on p 23.
3. Select a shape for the snout, this is a half cup measure.

4. Go to 'Animal head' p 33 and follow points 4 to 8 for the snout.

5. Continue to p 34 and p 36 - 38 to complete the puppet.

Horse

One cup inside another for extra length. Both have a slice removed.

Templates glued on. (above) Side view showing mane. Painting and trims finished.

1. Choose a 60 x 60cm piece of material for the body.
2. Make a basic small plate puppet as shown on p 23.

4. Go to 'Animal head' p 33 and follow points 4 to 8 for the snout.

5. Continue to p 34 and p 36 - 38 to complete the puppet.

White snout template.

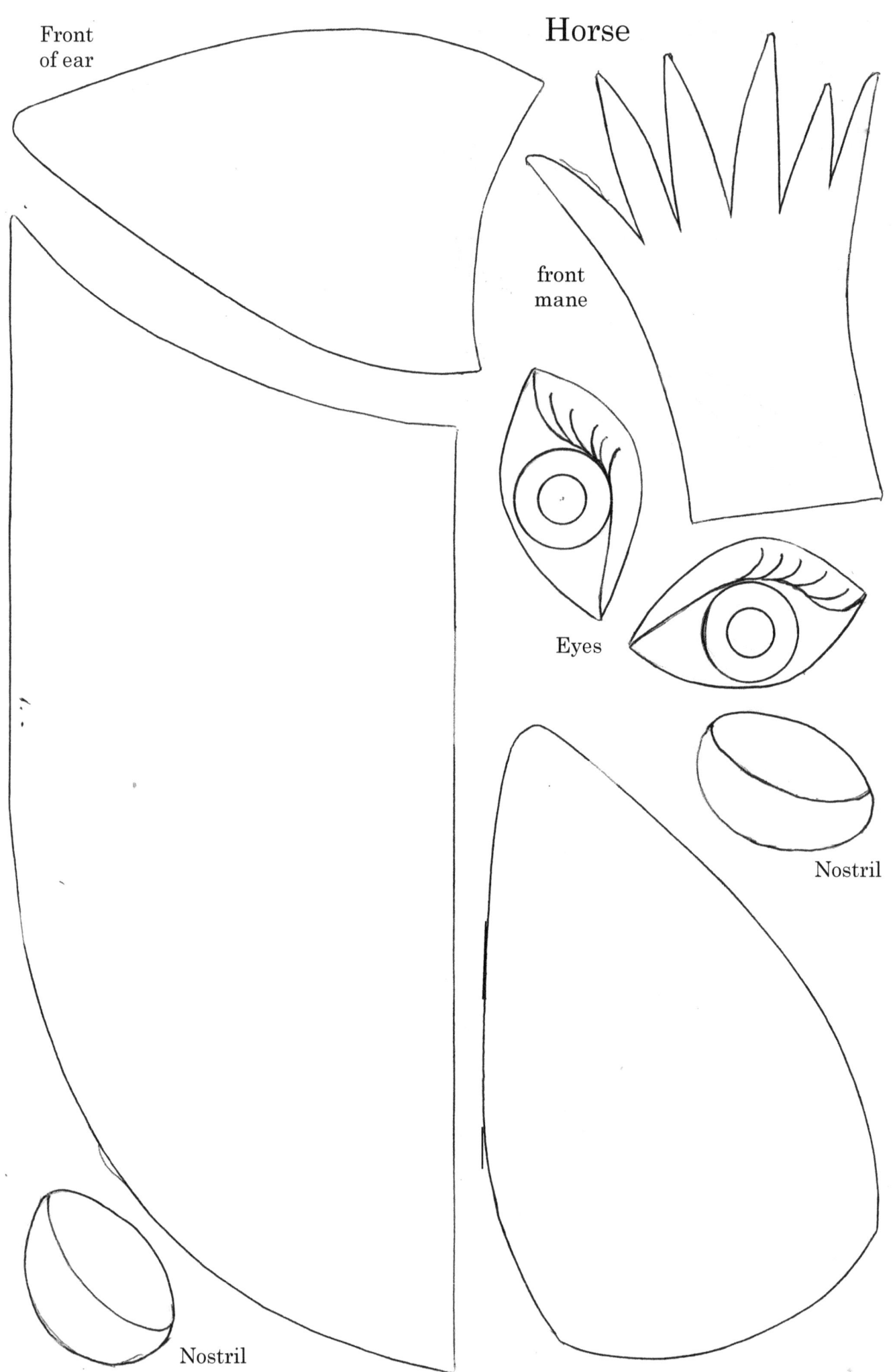

Cat

1. Choose the 60 x 60cm piece of material for the puppet.

2. Make a basic plate puppet from p 23.

3. Turn to p 29 'Cat head instructions' and follow the instructions through to p 32, p 36-38, and templates p 40.

Dog

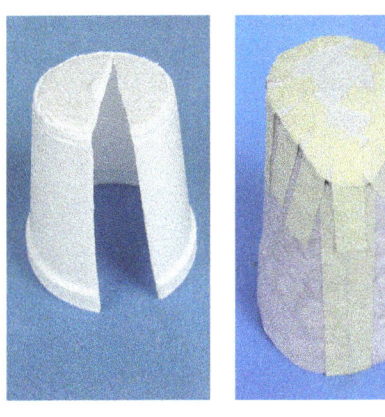  

1. Choose a 60 x 60cm piece of material for the body.
2. Make a basic small plate puppet as shown on p 23.

3. Get a paper cup (this can be shortened) or a shape for the dog's snout.

4. Turn to p 33 'Animal head.' Start at point 4 and follow through to p 38.

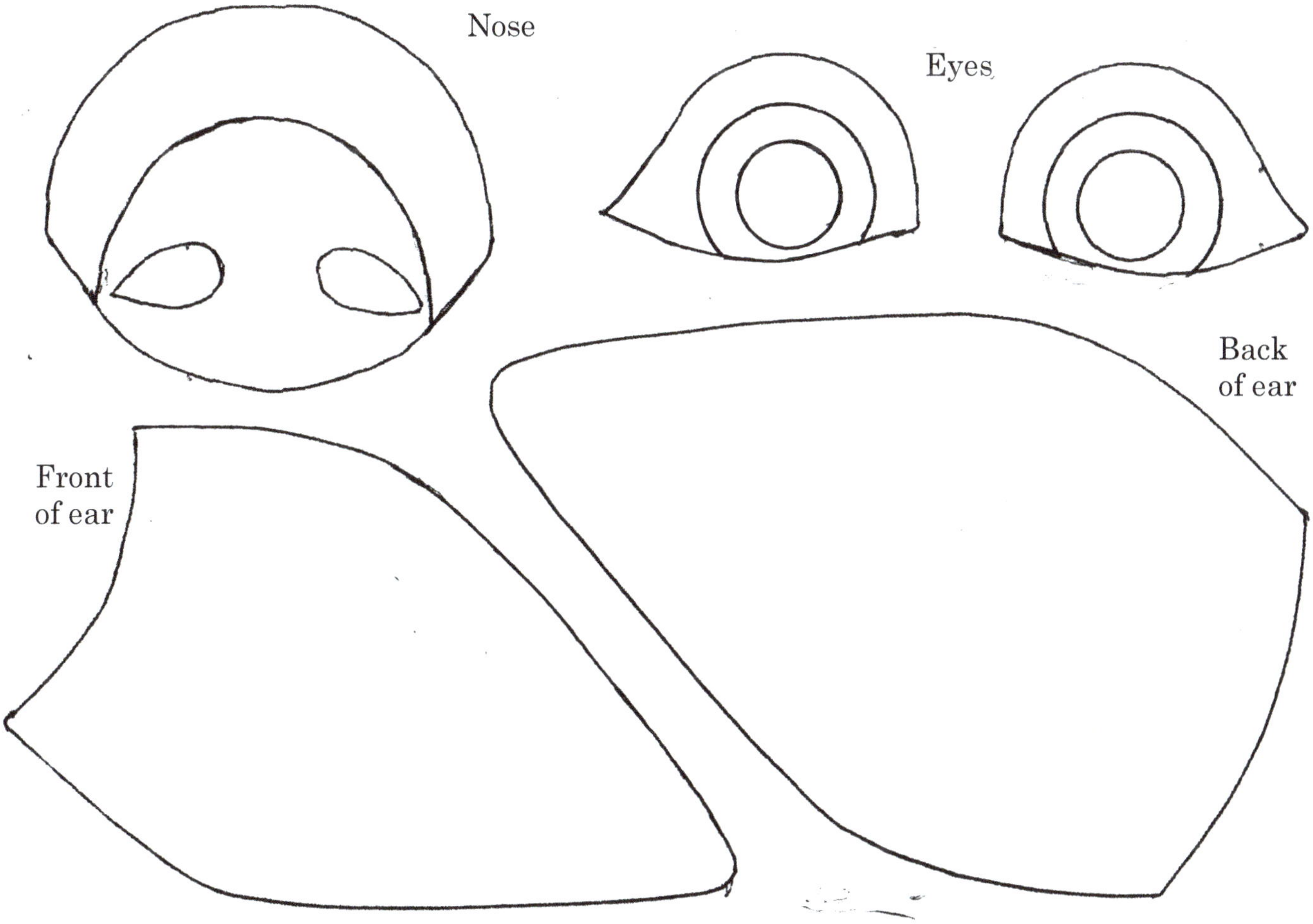

Nose

Eyes

Back of ear

Front of ear

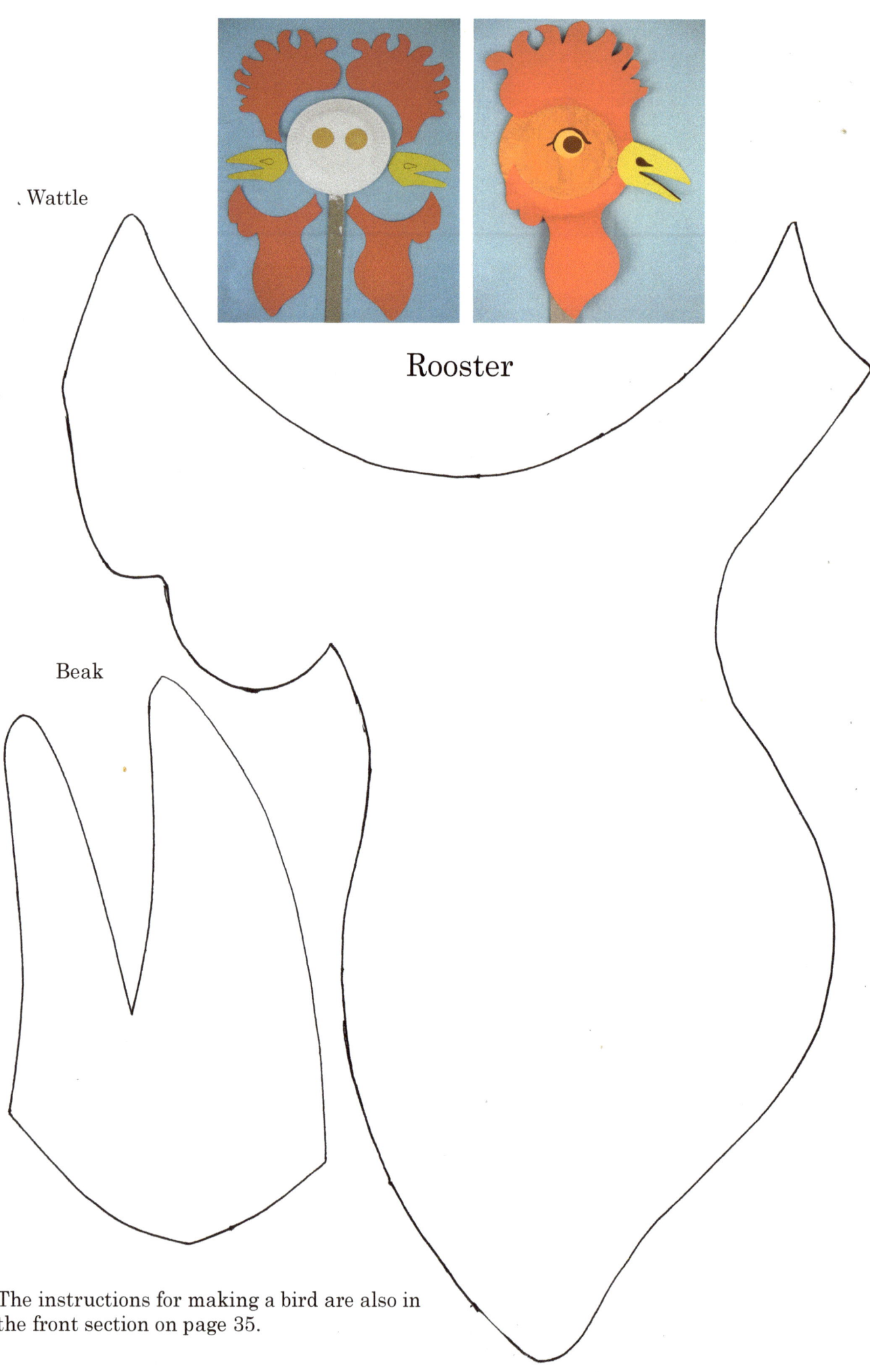

Wattle

Beak

Rooster

The instructions for making a bird are also in the front section on page 35.

1. Choose body material and make a basic plate puppet.
2. Make 2 beaks, combs, wattles and eyes.
3. Paint both sides of the head and upper neck. Glue outer edge of beak and comb together.
5. Put open side over the plate edge and mark the spot.
6. Glue on the wattle and eyes.
7. Go to p 37 and make the body.
8. Add any details.

Rooster

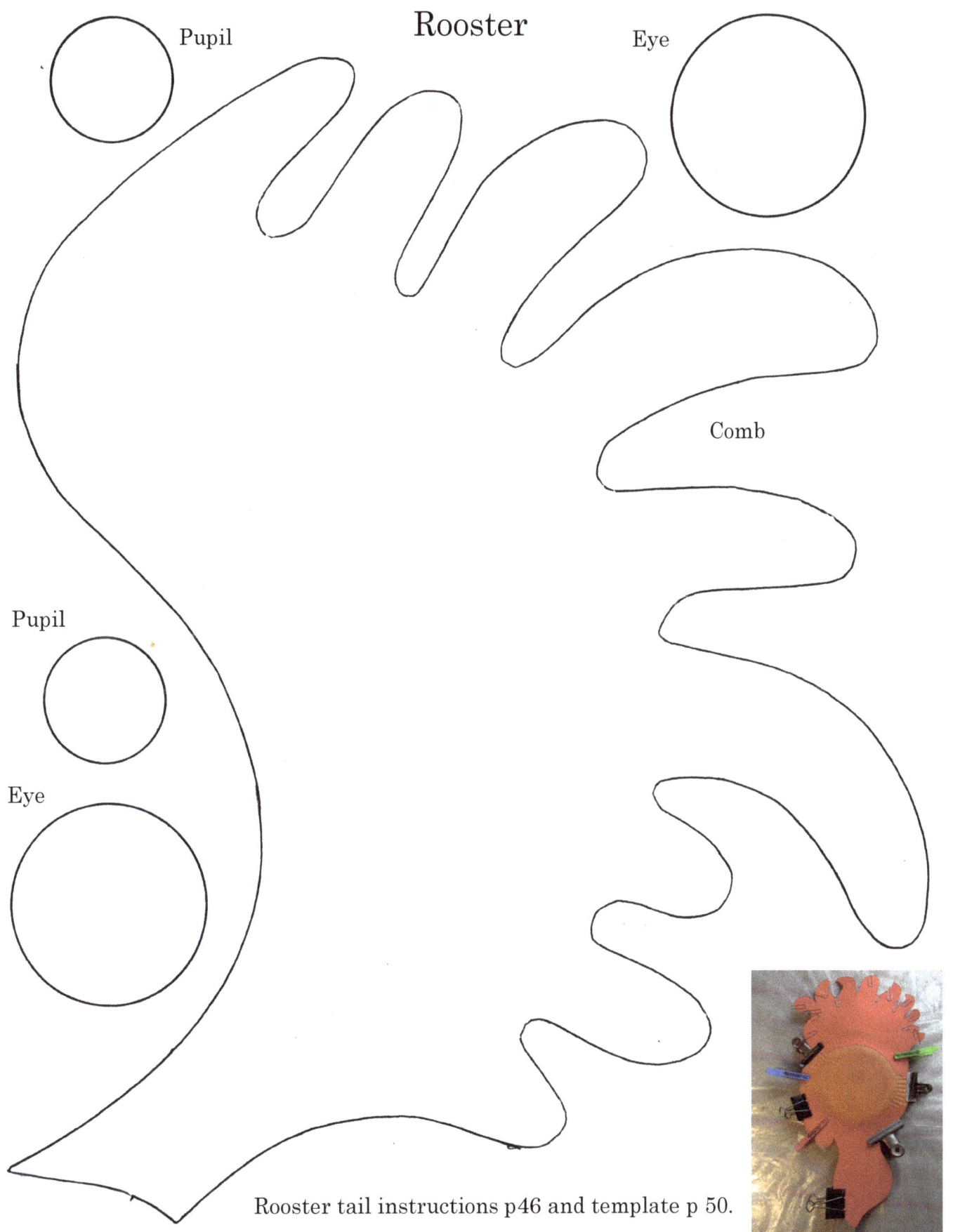

Rooster tail instructions p46 and template p 50.

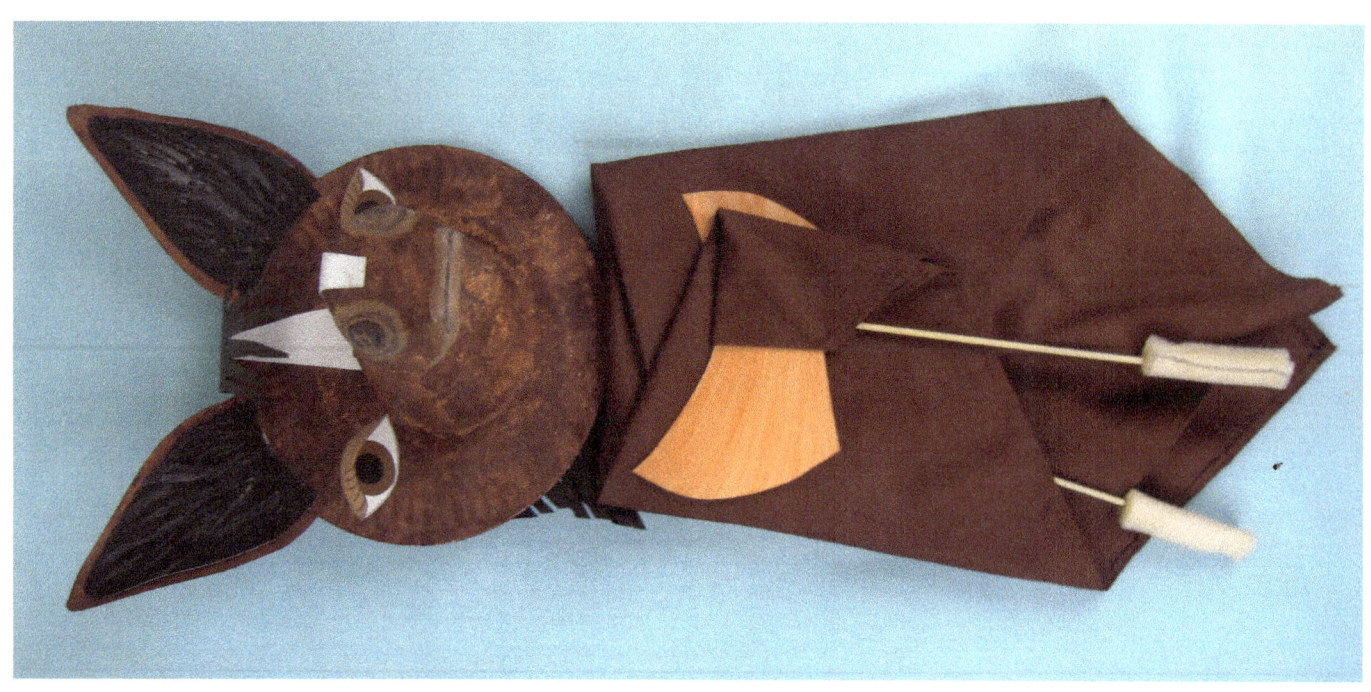
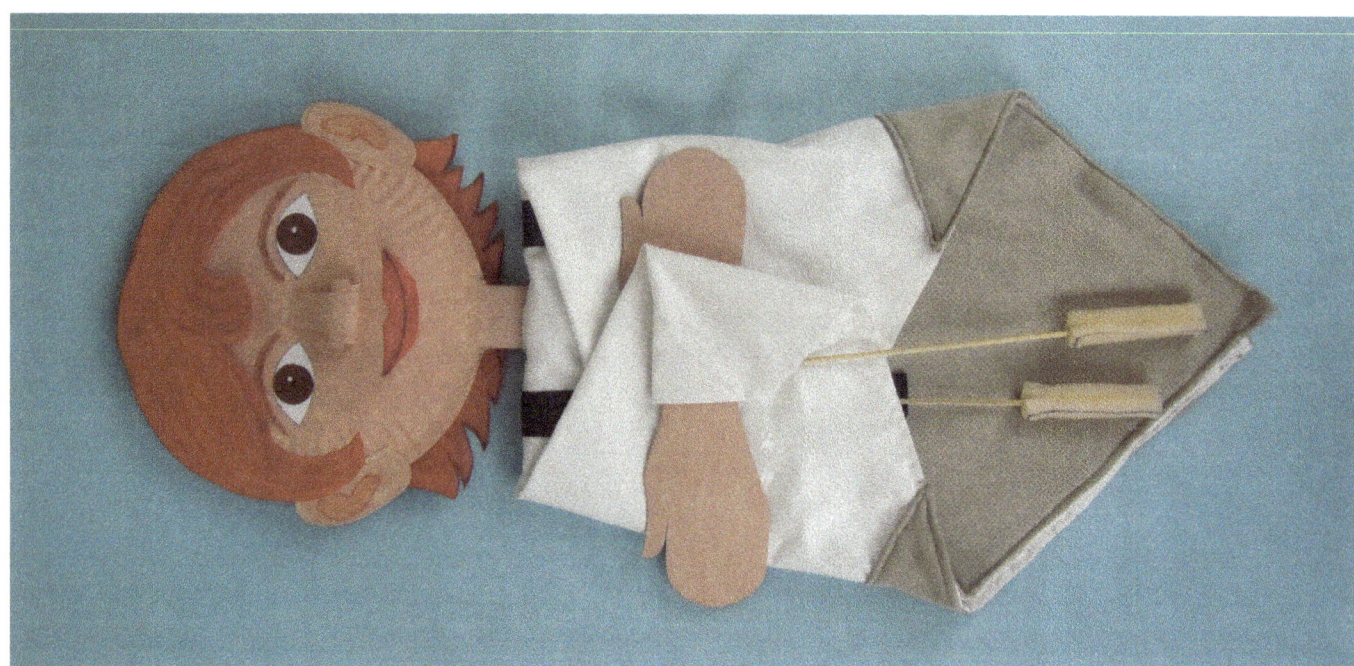
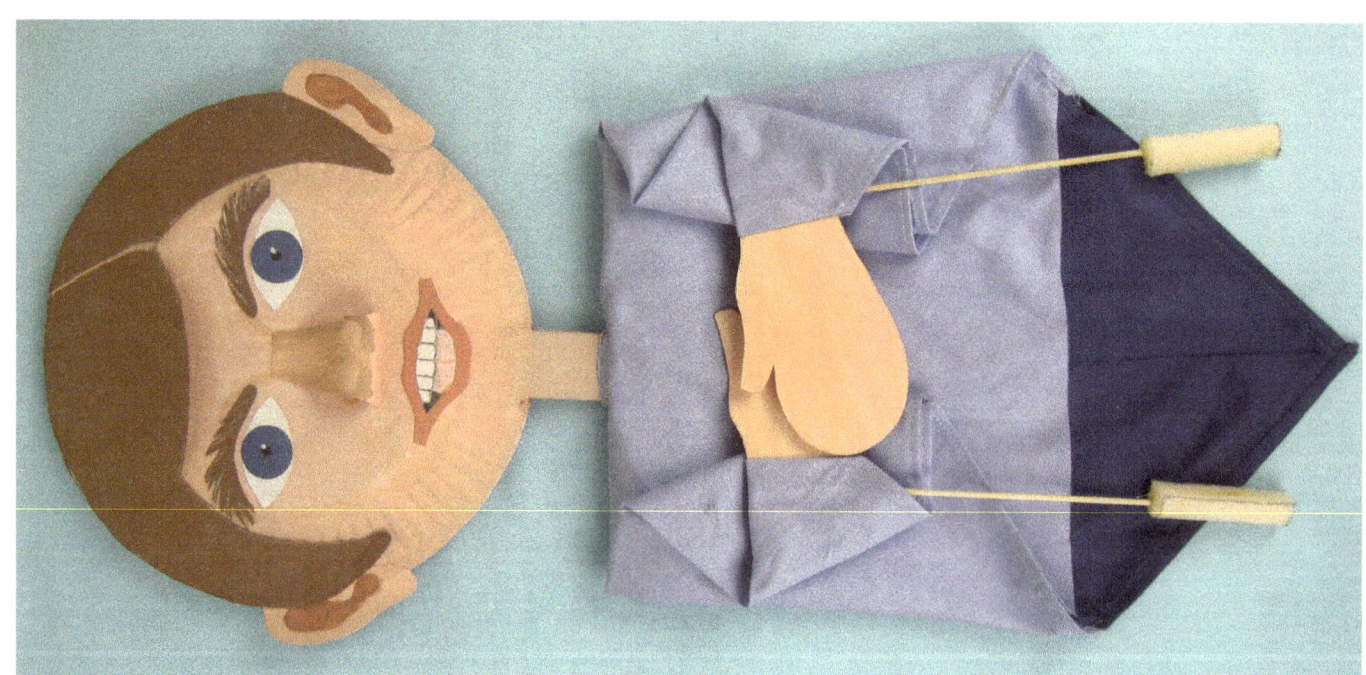

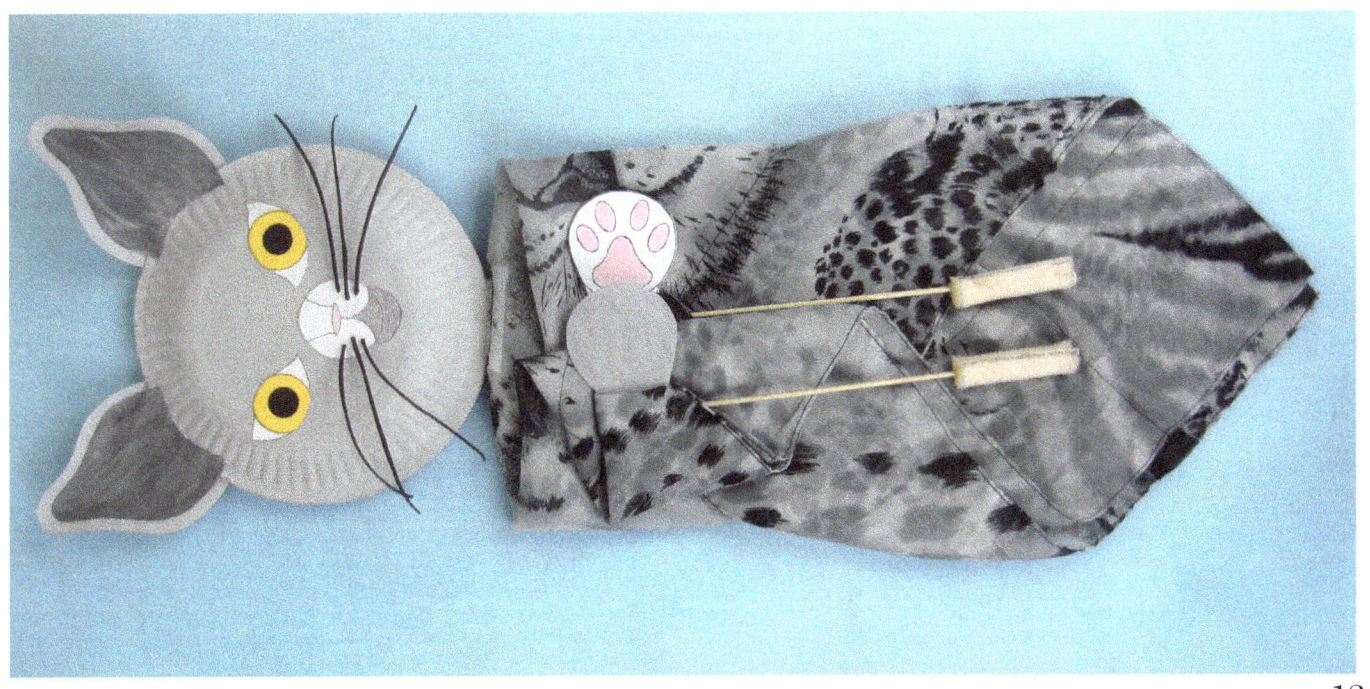

Bumble Bee

Instructions for this tree are on p 68.

80cm wide

85cm high

The templates below are the right size. Colour them in, cut them out and glue them onto cardboard, one on each side. Then glue the bee onto 2 kebab sticks joined together for more length. See p 43.

The big tree adds depth to the scene. They sit under the tree. The cows are in the paddock.

Fence

Fence post and rail painted with shadow to make it look 3D.
The fence hangs from a curtain rod on black thread enabling the cows to go around it and the others can come along in front of it.

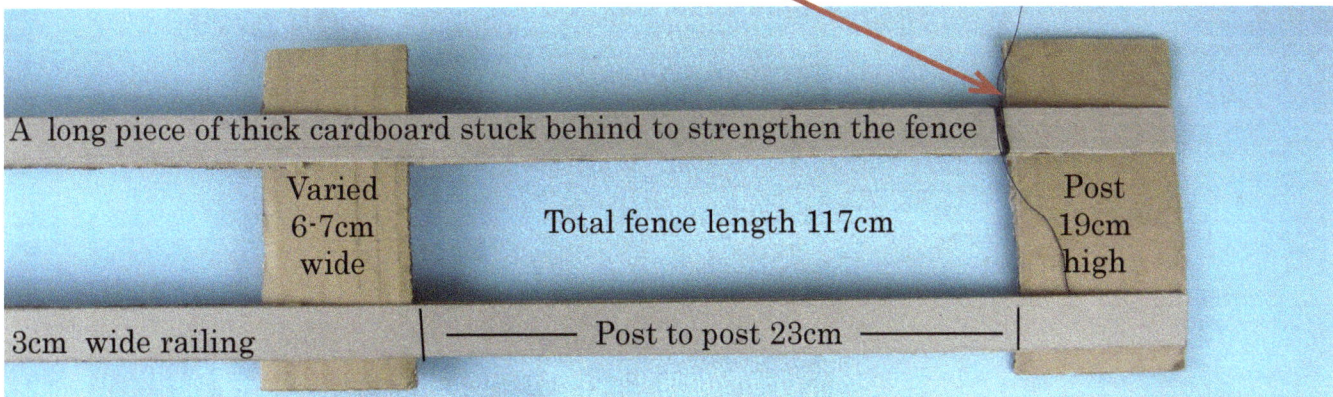

Paddock

The felt is placed in the right position for those sitting in the centre of the audience.

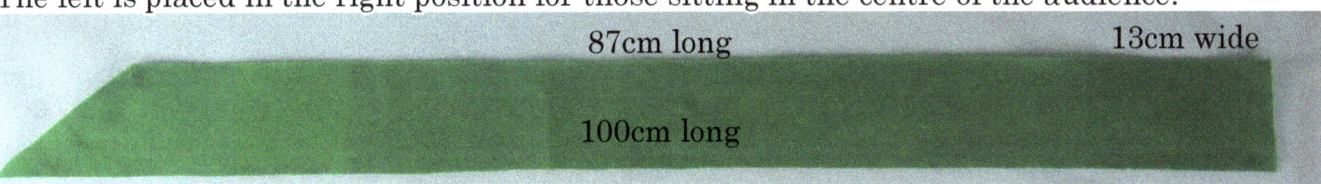

A piece of felt the length of the fence, end sloped for perspective, with velcro stuck on the back.

As illustrated on the previous page the fence hangs and only the top half of it is visible.

Each time the cows rush off stage and out of the visible paddock, vary their return, ie. in a different order, alone, in pairs, together, not all of them, moo, etc.

Two hoofs can be put on the back point of body material and kicked up as they run off stage. The dog can bark and try to round them up or nip their heels.

Extend the kebab sticks on the horse and it can neigh and rear up at the cows.
Give the rooster longer kebabs and it can really use its wings around the cows.
Extend the cats' kebabs and it can jump on the cow, meowing and scratching.

Each one goes right across the stage chasing the cows off, then turning around and coming back. (How do they return, displaying what sort of mood, body language, sound, etc?)
The puppets can shuffle around under the tree, even disappearing off-stage and making room for the the next one to come in at the front.
They all end up back on the stage to watch and cry. Have fun and make this dramatic.
Put in lots of animal actions and sounds, even talking over each other at times.
This is not a passive story. The little bee triumphs where the big noisy ones don't succeed.
Be game. Extend the kebabs so you can stretch out the hands, paws and hoofs for expression.

The farmer (who would benefit with a longer body). The boy covering his eye as he cries. The arms on these puppets can be used to dramatise what the puppet is saying or doing.

The tree makes the scene more 3D, the strings on the fence can be faintly seen.
In this photo the puppets are held up in good view. It doesn't matter if hands show.

The bee is small but very visible. Be game and have a small puppet mixed in sometimes.

What Do You Suppose

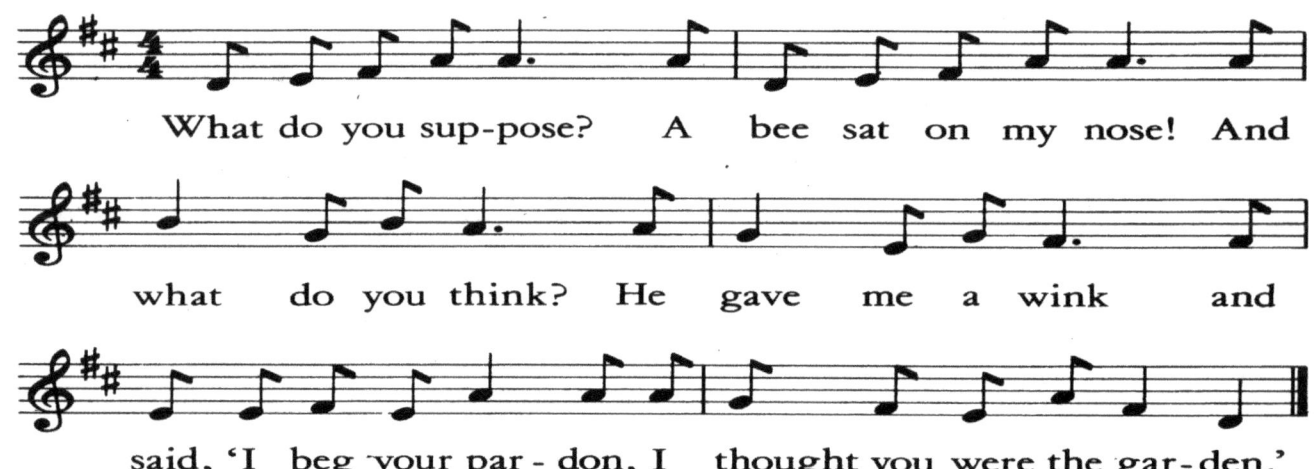

Let your thumb and pointing finger be a bee. Land it on your nose. Then let it fly away.

Here is the Beehive

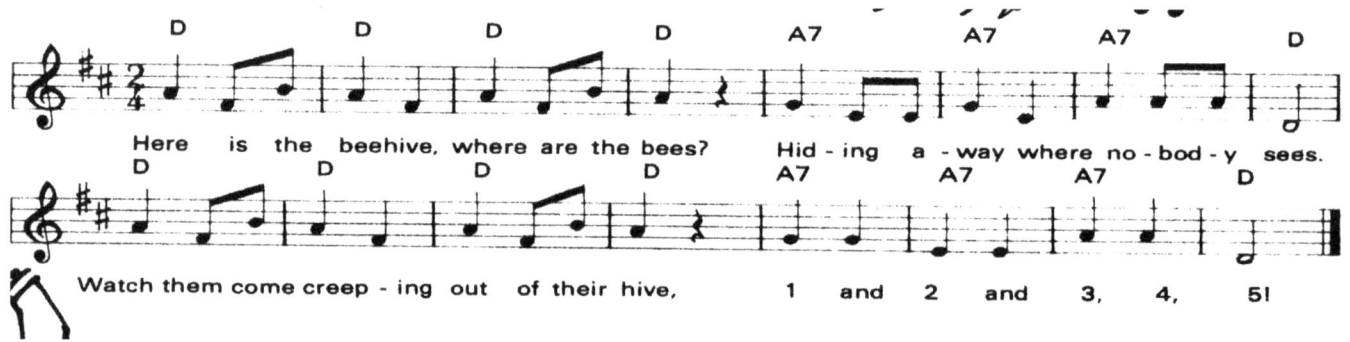

I Went to Visit a Farm

The Flight of the Bumble Bee music by Rimsky Korsakov.

The King Singers do a fabulous performance of it on Youtube.

Acting your puppet

Practise acting your puppet in front of a mirror, holding it up high, even if your hand is seen.

Lengthen the arm kebabs with another kebab for bigger gestures and more expression.

Experiment. Use the hand to touch, scratch or brush head, place in front of eyes or mouth, to wave or beckon, etc. Remember that humans use their hands all the time.

Use the bird's wings, the animal's paws, hoofs, etc, in as many ways as you can think of for expression.

The tail of a bird or animal highlights their body language. Watch a dog's tail wagging in circles or carried alert and, of course, the cat with its tail straight up.

Acting your puppet will make you watch the creatures around you and you will be amazed at what you see. So have fun exaggerating but don't do the action too often or it becomes boring.

A very important rule ~

No acting on stage until scripts are known!!!

It is impossible to hold a script and act a puppet. You need to concentrate on the puppet.

It is fun to video rehearsals for the children to watch and make adjustments.

It's drama!

Speech needs to be loud and clear. It's an excuse to exaggerate actions and expressions.

Microphones are useless because they will pick up all the scene changes and movement.

Choreograph everything

You need to work out how puppeteers will enter, exit, cross, etc.
Group actions can be great fun but need to be done in unison for real impact.
Doing things together boosts acting, confidence and fun.
Always do group actions at a pace everyone can manage.

Practise all curtain openings and closings if you choose to use curtains.

Music that suits each play has been included for more puppetry imagination and skills.

Performances can be done by, and for, any group with these expressive puppets.

It is interesting to have a review session after performances have finished .

There are so many simple additions that make these puppets outstanding. Go for it!

A glove puppetry manual available for this theatre is being revised.

This manual has introduced simple basic puppetry ~

1. The use of nursery rhymes as skeletons for simple stories.

2. Simple stories teach us how to move our puppet and our body right across the stage.

3. Group actions with constant interruptions from a single puppet are more challenging.

4. Actions can take place in a cluster or with others using the whole stage.
5. Complex movements around a centre prop with the fun of doing quick and slow entrances and exits.

Your characters can be used (as they are, with minor trims or alterations) in many other children's nursery ryhmes/stories.

My Grandfather's Clock

MY GRANDFATHER'S CLOCK.

Arranged by **AUBREY KENNETT.**

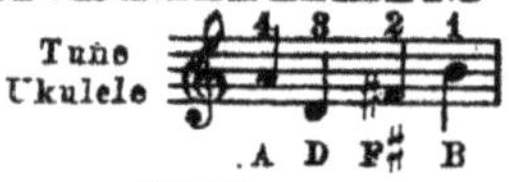

Composed by **HENRY C. WORK.**

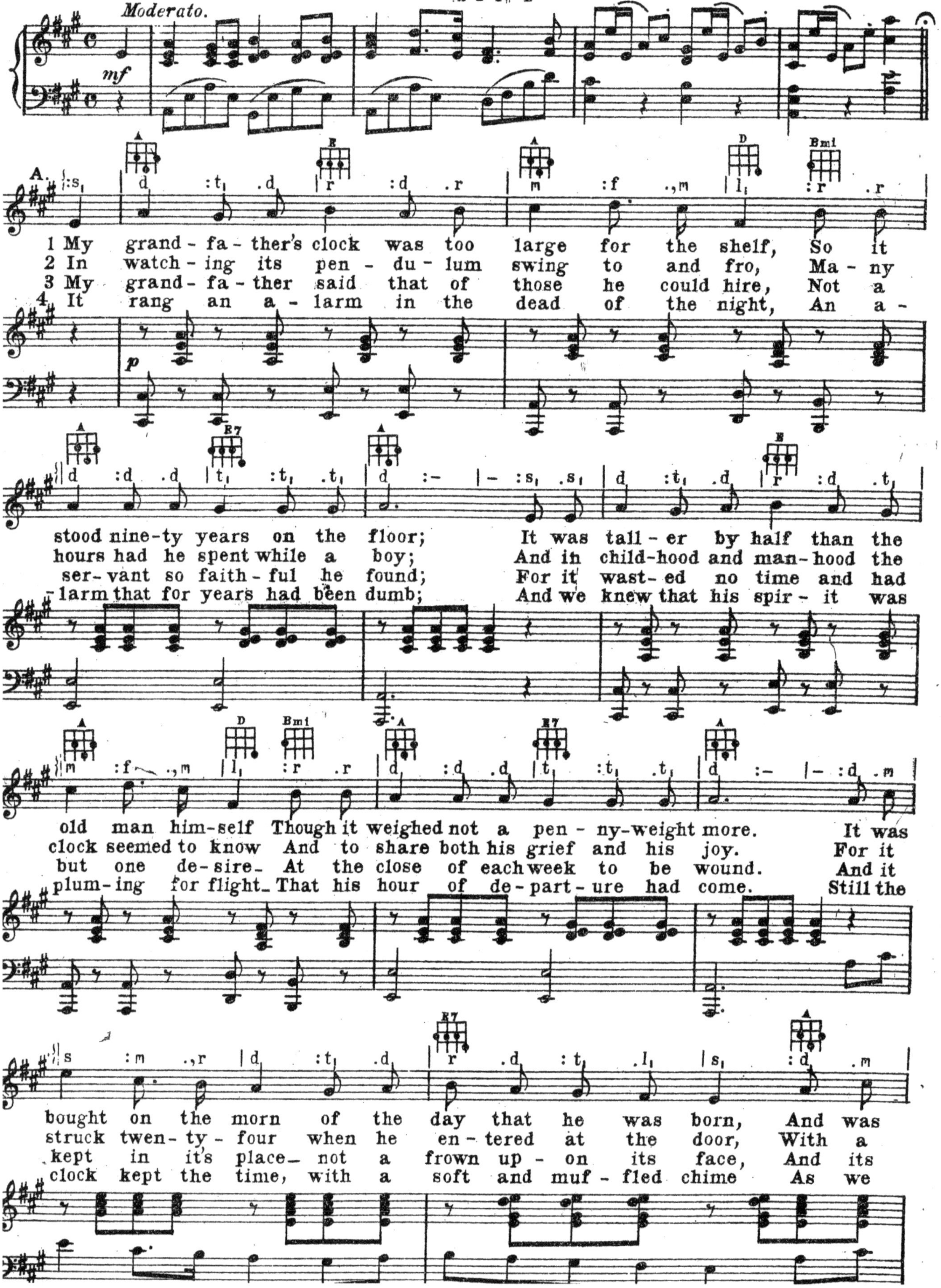

1. My grand-fa-ther's clock was too large for the shelf, So it stood nine-ty years on the floor; It was tall-er by half than the old man him-self Though it weighed not a pen-ny-weight more. It was bought on the morn of the day that he was born, And was

2. In watch-ing its pen-du-lum swing to and fro, Ma-ny hours had he spent while a boy; And in child-hood and man-hood the clock seemed to know And to share both his grief and his joy. For it struck twen-ty-four when he en-tered at the door, With a

3. My grand-fa-ther said that of those he could hire, Not a ser-vant so faith-ful he found; For it wast-ed no time and had but one de-sire— At the close of each week to be wound. And it kept in it's place— not a frown up-on its face, And its

4. It rang an a-larm in the dead of the night, An a-larm that for years had been dumb; And we knew that his spir-it was plum-ing for flight— That his hour of de-part-ure had come. Still the clock kept the time, with a soft and muf-fled chime As we

Our time with these puppets is done
But there are gloves waiting in the wings
We hope you will join us for more fun
And see what you can do with those things ~-

The End

Appendix

Cost of puppet theatre materials for Introducing and Glove puppetry theatre. Australia

Capral Qubelok

4 x 6.5m lengths	$16.00	=	$64.00
8 x rt<	$1.50	=	$12.00
4 x 'T' connectors	$1.50	=	$6.00
4 x 3 Way connectors	$1.50	=	$6.00
8 x end stoppers	80c	=	$6.40
	Total	=	$94.40

Bunnings

4 x 10cm right-angle brackets

4 x small right-angle brackets

6 x 85cm hinges

5mm x 6.5mm blind rivets

18 x 5mm x 38mm nuts and bolts

Small self-tapping screws

Spotlight

4m black block-out material (buy on special) or other material.

Velcro $18.00 for 20m roll = $40 or $60 (Tapes on line)

If curtains included

2 x 5cm x 5cm rt< brackets for the curtain rod

Curtain material, gather tape, hooks and rod or track.

Scenery rack

2 x 6.5m lengths Qubelok	$16.00	= $32	
8 x 3Ways @ $2.00 each		= $16.00	
	Total	= $48.00	

These are rounded prices I paid in 2020

If no money available, borrow some and make a small charge for the performance then pay back the loan. Another valuable experience for the group it boosts confidence and shows there is always a way.

This theatre is also used for shadow puppetry (coming soon). So it has lots of uses for many people and will last for years if looked after.

Have more fun with Gloves

Glove Puppetry

Margaret Arney

Learn more with Marionettes

for more information check out
www.puppetrytheatre.com

Available now

for more information check out
www.puppetrytheatre.com

www.ingramcontent.com/pod-product-compliance
Lightning Source LLC
Chambersburg PA
CBHW042307300426
44110CB00044B/2826

Introducing Puppetry Manual

Have children (or adults) amaze themselves and their audience with a wonderful puppet performance by following this simple, illustrated, step by step puppet manual.

An outstanding resource designed for the graduate or experienced classroom or art specialist teacher working with puppets for the first or the forty-first time.
Sue Dupont - Teacher/educator

www.puppetrytheatre.com

www.ingramcontent.com/pod-product-compliance
Lightning Source LLC
Chambersburg PA
CBHW042307300426
44110CB00044B/2824